Taking Mr. Exxon

The Kidnapping of an
Oil Giant's President

Taking Mr. Exxon

The Kidnapping of an
Oil Giant's President

Philip Jett

Winchester, UK
Washington, USA

JOHN HUNT PUBLISHING

First published by Chronos Books, 2021
Chronos Books is an imprint of John Hunt Publishing Ltd., No. 3 East St., Alresford,
Hampshire SO24 9EE, UK
office@jhpbooks.com
www.johnhuntpublishing.com
www.chronosbooks.com

For distributor details and how to order please visit the 'Ordering' section on our website.

Text copyright: Philip Jett 2020

ISBN: 978 1 78904 573 4
978 1 78904 574 1 (ebook)
Library of Congress Control Number: 2020930625

A CIP catalogue record for this book is available from the British Library.

Design: Stuart Davies

UK: Printed and bound by CPI Group (UK) Ltd, Croydon, CR0 4YY
Printed in North America by CPI GPS partners

We operate a distinctive and ethical publishing philosophy in
all areas of our business, from our global network of authors to
production and worldwide distribution.

Also by the author

The Death of an Heir: Adolph Coors III and the Murder That Rocked an American Brewing Dynasty. St. Martin's Press (Sept. 27, 2017). ISBN-10: 1250111803. ISBN-13: 978-1250111807

For Mom

Acknowledgments

I am exceedingly grateful to my agent, Richard Curtis, of Richard Curtis Associates, Inc., New York, New York, and everyone at John Hunt Publishing Ltd., Alresford, Hampshire, United Kingdom, who gave this book a chance.

During my research, I interviewed several people. I appreciate their time and generosity. They spoke with me and replied to my messages without hesitation. They all are incredible people. It's because everyone was so wonderful and kind to me that it is difficult to name any one person above the others, but there were a few individuals who went above and beyond in my estimation:

Gail Chapman, former FBI Special Agent with the Garret Mountain Resident Agency in Morris County, New Jersey, and former case agent of the Reso case. Gail is a walking encyclopedia when it comes to this case. She gave of her time and knowledge until I'm sure it hurt. Thank you, Gail.

Gary Penrith, former Special Agent-in-Charge of the FBI field office in Newark, and his wife, Lynne. They welcomed me into their home for four hours and were exceedingly gracious. More than that, Gary remained interested and supportive throughout my writing of this book and prodded others to speak with me. It was my honor and privilege to meet and get to know him.

Richard "Rich" Riley, former Chief of Detectives with the Morris County Prosecutor's Office. Rich spoke with me, answered every email, and even gave me a personal tour of all the sites in northcentral New Jersey mentioned in the book. He was so giving of his time. What a great guy.

John Walker, former FBI special agent in charge of the Reso case command post, who welcomed me into his home and reviewed his files with me.

And though I thanked them at the time, I will gladly thank these wonderful people once again:

Michael Chertoff, former U.S. Attorney, U.S. Court of Appeals judge, and U.S. Secretary of Homeland Security.

Thomas "Tom" Cottone, former FBI special agent.

Barbara Cruikshank, former Exxon secretary and personal secretary to Sid Reso.

Sebastian Delia, Union County Jail employee.

Eagle County Colorado Sheriff's Department.

Frank Figliuzzi, former FBI Assistant Director for Counterintelligence; *MSNBC* contributor.

Kent Manahan, former anchor with *NJNews*.

James A. "Jim" Morakis, former Manager of Public Affairs, Exxon Company, International.

W. Michael "Mike" Murphy Jr., former Prosecutor with the Morris County Prosecutor's Office.

Edwin H. "Ed" Petersen, former FBI special agent and former Director of Security for Major League Baseball.

Mark Prach, former Detective Lieutenant with the Morris County Prosecutor's Office.

Sean Price, Membership/Web Coordinator, the Society of Former Special Agents of the FBI, Inc.

Thomas Schmid, Assistant Prosecutor, Morris County Prosecutor's Office.

Vail Police Department.

Leslie Wilson, Federal Bureau of Investigation archives.

Part I

THE TAKING

Chapter 1

At sunrise on the morning of April 29, 1992, Sid Reso stepped into the shower as his wife, Pat, prepared their breakfast. He soon joined her at the table. They sipped coffee and chatted about their upcoming day, what time Sid would be home, and if he wanted anything special for dinner. It was a routine morning in a lifetime of mornings together.

During their thirty-six years of marriage, Sid Reso's career with Exxon had prompted them to move more than twenty times, even living abroad in London and as far away as Sydney, Australia. The two had at last settled down in the United States; there'd be no more relocating outside the country. With their children grown and moved away, they could at last enjoy the many benefits reaped from Sid's hard-earned success — country clubs, golf, dinner in New York City, international travel, grandkids, and each other.

"This is our time," Pat said.

Sid picked up his briefcase and coat, ready to leave for work. He typically left home no later than 7:30 each morning to make the fifteen minute drive to his office in Florham Park, the headquarters of Exxon Company, International ("Exxon International"). As she did most weekday mornings, Pat escorted her husband to the door that led to the garage of their elegant home. "Oh, would you mail this birthday card for me, honey?" she asked. Pat adjusted Sid's suit tie and pocket handkerchief, and smiled at his comfortable face. "I love you."

"Love you, too, sweetheart," Sid said, walking down the steps to the garage. "See you tonight."

The garage door rattled as it rose, and Reso backed his car and turned around to begin his way along the 200-foot drive that emptied onto Jonathan Smith Road. A dozen or more manses set far back with tennis courts and swimming pools lined the manicured cul-de-sac enveloped by dense trees and shrubs that blossomed in the New Jersey spring. The exclusive Washington Valley neighborhood thirty miles west of the Jersey Shore was highly-desired by the wealthy with its new homes on secluded wooded lots, where the chief complaint was that sometimes the mail arrived late.

Being top management at Exxon, Sid Reso had been offered a chauffeur-driven limousine, and he occasionally took advantage of the corporate accoutrement when traveling to the airport or a meeting in Manhattan. Most often, he opted to rebuff the polished and plush limousine to drive his own automobile, a car that appeared more suited for those cleaning the mansions than living in them—a four-year old, white Volkswagen Quantum Syncro GL5 station wagon with blue upholstered interior and a five-speed manual transmission. Though Reso had achieved immense success, he'd also succeeded at remaining a modest man. "To keep my feet on the ground," he once remarked with a laugh, "Pat makes me put out the garbage and wash dishes every night."

Like most workdays, Reso steered the station wagon along the driveway and pushed his favorite classical music cassette into the player. As he gazed through the windshield at the lovely morning, he may have considered his day's schedule or perhaps recalled the pleasure of his most recent golf outing. "He told me he was hoping to play again this weekend, but was worried it might rain," said Charles "Charlie" Roxburgh, a vice president at Exxon International, and a twenty-five-year friend with whom Reso had played golf the weekend before.

Reso spotted the newspaper on the drive as he approached the street. He stopped his station wagon near the curb. That morning, the rolled-up paper lay on the passenger side forcing him to exit the car. Stepping out to the sound of birds chirping at the Jersey dawn, Reso shut the door and left the engine running. He walked around the front of his car, bent over, and picked up the newspaper, a morning ritual he'd performed countless times. He rose and began to turn when —

A white commercial van with darkened windows materialized from nowhere, just a blur really. A large bearded man leapt out wearing a brown ski mask, long dark coat, jeans, and hiking boots. He rushed toward Reso yelling and pointing a large pistol. Stunned, Reso spun around in an attempt to jump back in his car.

"Freeze!" the man yelled. His hand clamped down on Reso's collar and yanked him from behind. "Get in the van!"

"What's going on?" Reso asked, stumbling backward as his abductor jerked him toward the van's side doors. "What's —"

"Just get in the damn van!"

The abductor shoved the five-foot seven, 170-pound executive headfirst inside and jumped in behind him, slamming the van's side door shut; a surprisingly easy feat considering Reso carried a reputation as physically tough, though he'd been weakened by a heart attack three years earlier.

The female driver stomped the accelerator and sped away, leaving Reso's station wagon idling at the end of his driveway. The thrust flung both men against one side of the van and onto the floor.

"Slow down!" the burly man yelled, not wanting to draw the neighbors' attention.

Sid Reso struggled to rise, but his body struck the floor again as the large man pounced and cuffed Reso's right hand, a hand that still clutched the morning newspaper. As the kidnapper attempted to cuff the left hand, Reso spotted a wooden box lying beside him that crowded the rear cargo floor. Its roughhewn construction stippled with nickel-sized holes drilled around its edges conjured a haunting image for the Exxon executive. His enfeebled heart pounded with fear as the box's hinged, open lid bared a constricted interior that waited like a sarcophagus to inter him.

"Get in the box," the man yelled as he tried to cuff Reso's wrist.

Reso jerked his hand away and seized his abductor's arms. They scuffled and then—a gunshot. The explosive blast of the .45-caliber pistol reverberated inside the metal cargo area, piercing the occupants' ears. The consequent smell of scorched gunpowder instantly consumed the van. Reso's blood spattered a side wall, the floor, and the abductor's dark coat and jeans. The bullet lodged in the box's wooden frame. Just like that, a kidnapping had become a shooting, possibly more.

The big man shoved Sid Reso, dazed and clutching his arm, into the homemade coffin. The female kidnapper heard the thud of Reso's body, followed by the sound of groaning. The Exxon president lay motionless. The sizzling hot bullet had entered above his left wrist, traveled up his forearm, and splintered bone as it exploded out above the elbow.

"Did you shoot 'im?" she asked with a north Jersey accent. The masked woman had been nervous and scared. Now she could hardly breathe. Confused over the gunshot, she slowed the van.

"Keep driving!"

The woman wanted to scream back at him, though she did as she was told. Bursting with angry fear, her designer wool gloves gripped the steering wheel so forcefully she must have believed her knuckles would soon squeeze through the hard-plastic. She sucked in a deep breath and reminded herself to observe all traffic signs and use directional signals so not to draw attention, all the while failing to consider the peculiarity of wearing a wool ski mask and sunglasses over her face on the tepid April morning. But just in case there was trouble, she had placed a .357-magnum revolver inside a sports bag that crowded the floorboard beneath her legs.

As she drove out of the subdivision, her partner leaned over the wooden box and attempted to stretch duct tape over Sid

Reso's mouth, but Reso squirmed and tried to rise. The masked abductor pinned Reso down and pointed the large pistol barrel into his face.

The driver then heard duct tape screech from its roll once again as the male kidnapper stretched tape over Reso's eyes. He attempted to stretch a second strip when—

"Dammit!" the kidnapper shouted. The man's glove-covered fingers fumbled with the roll. The tape had stuck to itself and twisted. Worse, sweat streaked into his eyes from the saturated mask, making it difficult to see. He removed his sunglasses and rubbed his forearm across his sweat-filled brow causing the mask's eye holes to become misaligned. "Shit!" The big man gripped the mask as if to rip it off his head, but gathered himself and straightened the eye holes to finish taping. Next, he kneeled and fed ropes crosswise through eyehooks near the bottom of the box, forming a lattice-style restraint that trussed each of Reso's legs, similar to that described in *Gulliver's Travels*.

The large man felt exhausted even though it had been little more than three minutes since he'd leapt from the van to snatch his prisoner. He hadn't expected a struggle. He was surprised he'd become so muddled and had made such a big mistake—shooting his hostage. Even so, he wasn't calling it off. With the binding complete, the five-foot ten-inch, 200-pound kidnapper slammed the lid shut and snapped the three locks on the box's latches.

Moments earlier, Sid Reso had been a man who wielded the utmost power in the world's oil industry. Now he found himself bound like a mummy inside a dark wooden tomb as his kidnappers secreted him to an undisclosed location. Clouded by shock and excruciating pain, his gifted mind must have been racing, searching for the most plausible sequence of his fate, though most likely he was unable to think at all.

The large man crawled from the cargo area into the cab and flopped in the passenger seat, pulling the shoulder harness across his body until it clicked. He peeled the ski mask off his face and his female counterpart did the same, tossing her mussed bleached-blond hair over her collar.

"Is everything all right?" she whispered.

"Just drive!"

* * *

As neighbors watched out their windows that Wednesday morning, April 29, the tranquil scene of blooming azaleas, forsythia, and dogwoods along Jonathan Smith Road had erupted into dysphoria. Men in dark jackets and all form of vehicles, some bearing official insignias and many unmarked, clogged the typically quiet cul-de-sac. A few shouted out orders inside the search perimeter while still others shouted back, "Got it!" "Yessir!" or "Okay!" More sedans and SUVs pulled up and parked. The sounds of car doors slamming and overlapping conversations echoed up the street and into the woods; all creating a spectacle and a cacophony that frightened those watching from their homes.

Though it may have appeared chaotic, it wasn't. Members of the Morris County Prosecutor's Office, Morris County Sheriff's Office, New Jersey State Patrol, and the Morris Township and Morristown police departments carried out their particular responsibilities with sober faces as if choreographed beforehand. Each agency and department was trained and experienced and knew its duties and carried them out with coordination and precision.

A command post was quickly being assembled inside the Reso house where state and local authorities directed the search and coordinated the questioning of anyone who might have seen or heard anything. They telephoned hospitals and doctors, though neither Sid Reso nor anyone matching his description had been admitted. And most importantly, there'd been no John

Doe arriving at the morgue that morning.

"Go ahead and process the exterior of the car," directed an undersheriff from the Morris County Sheriff's Office, who was overseeing the forensics and evidence gathering by the crime scene unit.

Wearing surgical gloves and holding a brush laced with black fingerprint powder, a seasoned deputy with the aid of a young assistant examined the surface along the driver's door. The older deputy twirled the brush on the side of the white station wagon while the younger one removed latent fingerprints with clear adhesive tape. Stepping around him, another deputy snapped photographs of the vehicle from top to bottom and end to end. All were careful not to enter the vehicle or touch anything inside. A tow truck would soon arrive to transport the car to the sheriff's department where it would be impounded and examined without risk of contamination.

But the car had already been contaminated. Upon receiving a call from Sid Reso's secretary informing her that a neighbor had seen her husband's car in the driveway, Pat Reso had hurried up the driveway to investigate. She'd opened the driver's side door that was ajar, turned off the engine, and removed the key from the ignition. She then opened the rear door and saw her husband's tweed briefcase, khaki overcoat, scarf, and black umbrella on the backseat. Her fingerprints would be taken in order to eliminate any prints of hers from the others removed from the doors and door handles.

As the two deputies continued dusting the car, another examined and dusted the white mailbox for fingerprints. Though nothing was found inside, the mailbox stood only feet from Sid Reso's station wagon and might have been touched by a trespasser. When finished, the mailbox and wooden post would be removed and loaded onto an awaiting tow truck that would transport it along with Reso's car to the sheriff's department.

Deputies, detectives, and officers fanned out from the

abandoned car onto the street, the lawn, and into the adjoining woods. The Reso property consisted of more than four heavily-wooded acres, so dense that only a portion of the house could be seen from the street. The same was true of all the neighborhood houses, though spring had not yet fully cloaked the woods with emerald leaves. The houses sat so far apart that only six homes stood along the same section of street as the Reso house. Deer grazed on lawns and occasionally loped across the streets. It seemed as if a forest had engulfed a handful of grand residences, giving the appearance to any visitor driving down the street that they had entered a nature preserve rather than a New Jersey suburban community.

The trees and thick underbrush made the search that day considerably more difficult. To help cover the rugged territory, a canine unit arrived with a German shepherd that could track missing persons by detecting smells on the ground and in the air. The dog could also locate dead bodies. Despite its grim training, the German shepherd had been named, "Buffy." Led by her handler, New Jersey State Trooper Steve Makuka, the well-trained German shepherd quickly discovered that there wasn't a scent of Sid Reso beyond the drive and the car, indicating he most likely had not ventured beyond his own driveway. Still, the entire area had to be searched.

Two white over gray New Jersey Bell vans marked with blue bell logos soon arrived. Workers wearing hardhats and tool belts swarmed the front lawn, burying new telephone lines to the Reso home from a green metal box hidden in shrubs near the curb. Their supervisor in a white shirt and tie stood nearby and conferred with Morris County detectives about the installation of trap and trace equipment and new phone and fax lines for the command post being set up inside the home. The workers also assisted with the installation of recording devices on telephones in a small study and home office down the hall.

It wasn't long before a Morris County Park Police truck

towing a trailer pulled up and unloaded two horses onto the already busy street. Uniformed rangers mounted the horses and entered the thick woods surrounding the Reso home, leaning from their saddles in search of footprints, snapped twigs, broken branches, blood, and fresh earth. To gain a closer look, an officer occasionally dismounted to examine anything that appeared out of place. Shouts for photographs to be taken could be heard through the budding trees, and measurements were made here and there, though when later processed, all revealed nothing.

Residents along the street, having left coffee and breakfast at their tables to venture outside, witnessed the coordinated effort as they stood on their drives in house coats and suits with open hands shielding their eyes from the low morning sun. It was a beautiful April morning, with dew covering the trimmed lawns and birds singing in the tall trees. The sights and sounds clashed that morning, however, as it appeared to many that their street had been stricken by a natural disaster, though most suspected it had been an unnatural one. Neighbors spoke among themselves and quickly determined it was neither a fire nor a medical emergency, nor a burglary or domestic dispute. Whatever it was, it was extremely serious. But the mystery lasted only minutes as those standing outside their homes or gazing through their windows soon received visits from detectives slowly approaching from the street.

"Excuse me. I'm Detective Sergeant George Nunn with the Morris Township police."

After explaining that Sid Reso had been reported missing and his car abandoned at the end of his driveway, detectives questioned each person at every house along Jonathan Smith Road and eventually along nearby streets and even adjoining subdivisions: *Did you see or hear anything unusual this morning? Did you notice any service vehicles on the street, like telephone or cable companies, painters, plumbers, that sort of thing? Anyone walking or riding a bike that you thought looked out of place? Anyone carrying a package?* . . .

"No," was the collective answer.

With the tension and frustration building, some detectives lit cigarettes and enjoyed a brief nicotine respite outside the search perimeter. But just when they thought no one had seen or heard anything, detectives spoke with a local woman who provided the first clue.

"It might be nothing, but I saw a woman jogging up and down the street out here. I don't know her. Never seen her before."

"Go on," said Detective Sergeant Brian Doig of the Morris County Prosecutor's Office, who had a pad and pen in hand.

"Well, you know, I guess she could have been someone living a few blocks over, but usually they just jog through and back. This woman jogged up and down the street a few times. I thought it was kinda odd. Always early in the morning. But I didn't see her every day."

"When did you first see her?"

"Oh, let me think. . . . I'm not sure. January, maybe February. I remember it was cold."

"Can you describe her?"

"She had blond hair, in a ponytail, maybe forty; I can't be certain about her age. She could've been forty-five. She was in good shape, like she runs a lot, and she had on a nice jogging suit and sunglasses."

The neighbor gave the detective a description of the mysterious jogger's hair, clothes, and even her shoes, although there was nothing distinctive about the woman's appearance. When asked, the neighbor explained that she'd even seen the jogger that very morning, but didn't watch to see if she went inside a house or a car. "She just jogged by." The neighbor sat down later that day with a skilled sketch artist, who etched out a composite of the mysterious female jogger. The same sketch artist would sit down with another neighbor days later to draw a composite of the woman's partner. The neighbor said she'd seen a man around 5:30 a.m. on the day before the disappearance, stepping from a white taxi-cab outside a house under construction at the end of the cul-de-sac. Authorities didn't know it then, but the composite drawings turned out to be uncanny likenesses of the real kidnappers.

Another neighbor, when asked if she'd seen any vehicles that she didn't recognize, at first said no as everyone else had, but a few days later telephoned Detective Sergeant Nunn, who'd left his card with her. She provided a significant clue.

"It was a white van, a business-type van. I'm not sure what model. No, it didn't have a business name on the side; just plain white," said the woman questioned over the telephone. "It was parked in the circle, and then pulled up the street. It sat there for maybe five or ten minutes. I'd say it was half past seven ... No, I couldn't see who was driving. I looked out later and it was gone. I thought it was probably workers waiting to get started on the house being built at the end of the street."

It wasn't a lot of information, yet it was a beginning. Detectives soon discovered, however, that there were more than 70,000 white vans registered in the area. And the number of forty-something-year-old blondes? Incalculable.

* * *

Though the Resos had lived on Jonathan Smith Road since the summer of 1986, they were not known by many of their neighbors. This wasn't a Sunday-barbecue, get-together-with-your-neighbors type of community. Many residents relocated from out-of-state and had busy careers like the Resos—high-level senior executives at Merck, Bell Labs, BP/Castrol, AK Steel, and Exxon, who'd worked all over the world and were now on the home stretch toward retirement.

A neighbor, Dannette Merchant, who was a physician's wife that had never met the Resos, described those who lived in the neighborhood: "A lot of people are corporate executives. They travel a lot or they work long hours. When they get home, they want to relax. They don't want to socialize. And our children are not at the ages that we meet people that way anymore. It's all very private."

Some inquisitive individuals may have met others for the first time as they cautiously walked down the street and attempted to talk to officers and catch a peek at the crime scene. They were met by uniformed officers like Morris Township patrolmen Bruce Starnes and Tom Nunn and two large Exxon security men in business suits and ties wearing beepers who denied them access. The curious were instructed to remain clear of those trying to do their jobs behind the yellow crime scene tape that stretched along the meandering perimeter of the property. Many residents didn't leave; they just stood and watched. Others returned home to telephone family, friends, and spouses already at work, to relay what they'd seen and heard. Some were concerned for their safety, and it possibly even crossed some minds how this incident, whatever it turned out to be, might affect property values.

Just as neighbors had grown comfortable with the echoes of officers' voices and shouts of orders down the street, the blades of a state police helicopter thudded over their heads like thunder, carrying binocular-wielding officers just over the treetops. It was unsettling. The helicopter flew for almost an hour in a tight grid pattern over the Reso residence and immediate area, searching for anything or anyone out of the ordinary. It would soon be joined by Helicopter Emergency Air Response Team (HEART) helicopters brought in from FBI field offices in New York, Philadelphia, Boston, Baltimore, and as far away as Miami. A New York SWAT team and the FBI's special operations group (special ops) also would be deployed.

Federal authorities typically do not begin investigating a missing person until at least twenty-four hours have passed, thereby creating a presumption that an individual who does not reappear has been transported across the state line. In this case, the FBI quickly mobilized because the missing executive was an Exxon president and because in the long history of Morris County, there'd never been a reported kidnapping for ransom. Local authorities needed the Bureau's help. Even so, Morris County Prosecutor W. Michael Murphy Jr. made it clear to Assistant Special Agent-in-Charge Jere Doyle on the day of the disappearance that because no evidence had yet been found indicating the kidnappers had carried Sid Reso across state lines, it was the FBI that would be assisting the Morris County Prosecutor's Office and the U.S. Attorney's Office, not vice versa. From a practical standpoint, however, the FBI was the lead agency due to its seemingly unlimited technological and investigative resources.

By early afternoon, FBI agents joined local authorities interviewing neighbors, mail carriers, and those making deliveries and repairs. Eventually, more than two hundred and fifty FBI agents and another fifty state and local officers and detectives would be assigned to case number 7-NK-74530, codename SIDNAP—the most that had been assigned to any U.S. kidnapping case since the disappearances of Patty Hearst in 1974 and Adolph Coors III in 1960. In fact, the disappearance of Sid Reso would become the biggest kidnapping case in the state of New Jersey since the baby of Charles and Anne Lindbergh was kidnapped there in May 1932, almost sixty years earlier to the day.

Soon, reporters arrived. The cars and vans bearing their stations' call signs and logos lined the curb farther up the street. Many were topped with dishes and antennae. Local newspaper reporters with identification lanyards, pads, and miniature recorders crowded around, mingling with radio announcers and crews setting up cameras as coiffed television newscasters jockeyed for the best viewpoint around the property. They captured images of the house, mailbox, driveway, and street sign. They photographed investigators milling about and rangers on horseback trotting by. They hoped for a photo of Pat Reso stepping outside, but that was not to be. Soon news helicopters joined law enforcement in the sky, though their pilots had been instructed not to encroach upon the restricted search area. Their images, videos, and headlines would appear in papers and magazines and on radio and television channels all across the country and even in faraway countries like England, Italy, and Japan by late afternoon and evening.

"It's so upsetting," one woman told a reporter, who fearfully asked not to be identified. "It's not every day you have a hundred people dropping on the street and helicopters flying overhead. You usually only see company limousines and realtors driving by." The woman told reporters she'd been questioned by police and the FBI. She said that she knew Sid Reso, though not very well, despite having been neighbors for six years. Afraid for her family's safety, the woman continued: "If they can do it to him, they can do it to us." Dr. Stanley Baer agreed. "We're going to be careful for a while." Many neighbors hired private security. Others like Janet Boni, who lived across the street from the Resos, had more simple concerns: "We're not getting our paper, and our deliveries haven't been getting through."

Neighbors who'd remained outside observed a myriad of activity, though they learned few details. They only knew the president of Exxon International was missing. They began to wonder with greater curiosity what was happening behind the scenes, especially inside the Reso home with its window blinds and curtains drawn, cordoned off by uniformed police. *Was Sid Reso dead? Was he kidnapped? How was Mrs. Reso? Was the criminal still on the loose?* Rumors of blood on the driveway, though false, spread as did other gruesome gossip, some true, but most exaggerated or completely fabricated.

"The neighborhood is just trying to figure out who would try to hurt this wonderful man," said Jackie Deskovick, a rare native who lived down the street with her husband, Dick, a builder and co-founder of a local bank. "It was just so eerie . . . to think that someone did come into the neighborhood, if that is the case . . . "

"I met them at a dinner party held by the Deskovicks," said next-door neighbor, Brigitte Privitere, whose husband Lou was a senior vice president at Merck and who like Sid had worked all over the world. "I never saw them outside . . . Pat Reso had become a bit withdrawn after the death of one of her sons."

The reporters soon became such a nuisance that neighbors refused to talk to them. "We decided to change our phone number," one neighbor said. "First, I got calls from reporters in the county, then the state, all over the place, as far as Europe."

Reporters didn't limit their questions to neighbors. They quickly located family members and friends and quizzed them over the telephone.

"He is one of the most level-headed people I've known in my life . . . He's not the kind who would pick up and take a fly . . . We're concerned; it just looks like an abduction," said Jerome Reso Jr., a cousin who lived in the Reso family's hometown of New Orleans. "Sid's a genuine, nice guy. It's hard to find the right adjectives to describe someone like him."

"He's well-respected but perhaps not as visible as others in the organization," said George Friesen, at that time a stock analyst for the Deutsche Bank Capital Group in New York. "He's very cerebral and controlled."

"A fine man, a pleasant man," said Joe Carlson, a spokesman for Exxon. "He's a warm, caring person with a knack for putting people at ease. I don't know anybody who doesn't like Sidney."

Despite all the activity along Jonathan Smith Road, it wasn't until the afternoon that law enforcement and Exxon acknowledged to reporters that Sid Reso was missing. Reso's secretary, Barbara Cruikshank, who'd worked for Exxon for thirty-three years, had spent the morning telling reporters, "I don't know anything about that," when asked if her boss was missing. Finally, Exxon released a statement: "Mr. Reso was reported missing after leaving for work earlier this morning. Mrs. Reso is fine. Any calls should be directed to the public affairs department."

A spokesperson for the Morris County Prosecutor's Office also began addressing reporters' questions. "At the present time, the investigation is being classified as a missing persons matter," Lois Ferguson said. "So far, we've got nothing."

Notwithstanding all the FBI agents, local detectives and officers, dogs, horses, and helicopters, authorities knew little more than they did when first called to the scene that morning. They'd learned that Sid Reso was a quiet, private man, who was well-liked and didn't have any known enemies, and was devoted to his family and his Roman Catholic faith. They also learned that an unknown jogger had been seen on the street that morning. That was it. There was no ransom note, no phone calls—nothing to indicate that Sid Reso had been abducted.

"We simply do not know what happened to Mr. Reso," said Morris County Prosecutor Mike Murphy. "We do not know if it was a voluntary or involuntary disappearance. At this juncture, we have exhausted all leads in the immediate area."

Though authorities weren't telling reporters, all believed Sid Reso had been kidnapped. And sadly, so did his wife, Pat.

* * *

The home of Sid and Pat Reso was exquisite. In 1986, when Sid Reso was promoted to vice-president of Exxon International, he and Pat moved from Houston to New Jersey and selected an exclusive private neighborhood in the Buckingham II subdivision of Morris Township to build their home. Morris County has one of the highest incomes per capita in the entire country. When the house was completed in June that same year, the one-story,

5,000-square foot, French colonial brick house sprawled atop a picturesque four-acre lot. The beautiful green grass, shrubs, and trees were highlighted by white dogwoods, yellow forsythia, and pink azaleas. It had a three-car garage and a lovely wraparound rear deck with planters and a gas grill, surrounded on all sides by dense mature trees teeming with squirrels, raccoon, and deer that provided a natural privacy barrier hundreds of feet deep.

With a net worth estimated to have been over $15 million in 1992, Sid Reso could have purchased a house many times larger and more extravagant, but it was more than enough for the modest man from Louisiana and his wife. Its five bedrooms, six baths, and finished basement provided ample space for the Resos and their three adult daughters and one son who occasionally visited from Houston, St. Louis, Washington, D.C., and Sacramento. And the living room, with its vaulted ceiling and skylight, its white-washed brick fireplace, and beautiful furnishings provided a luxurious yet comfortable area to relax or entertain. But on that Wednesday, the living room was being used for a purpose never conceived by the builder or its owners—a command post, full of Morris County detectives and FBI agents with dozens of phones, two-way radios, computers, fax machines, copiers, maps taped to walls, tables covered with papers, and drawing boards listing tasks and clues in various colored ink. The command post in the living room would soon swell into the dining room, foyer, study, and Sid Reso's home office. Antennae and dishes also would be attached to the roof.

Pat Reso had been interviewed by Chief of Detectives Richard Riley and Deputy Chief of Investigation John Dempsey from the Morris County Prosecutor's Office earlier that morning. Following her questioning by detectives, Pat telephoned each of her children and told them that their father was missing, though she hadn't been able to reach her youngest daughter, who was finishing law school at American University in Washington, D.C. All heart-wrenching conversations between a mother and her children. FBI agents would be dispatched from field offices near each child's residence to interview them, as well as Reso's two brothers, Robert and Warren, his sister, Mary Agnes Brauner, and his eighty-four-year-old mother, Josephine Agnes Reso (Sid Reso's father had died twenty-five years earlier).

By early afternoon, it was once again Pat's turn to be questioned—this time by federal agents. She sat upright at the kitchen table with a cup of chicory coffee as FBI Special Agents Gail Chapman and Ed Petersen prepared to question her. Petersen withdrew a missing person form that would be used to enter Sid Reso's personal information into the FBI's National Crime Information Center database.

"I see you have a photo of Mr. Reso," Agent Petersen said. "Thank you. We'll send out a bulletin with this photo and a description. Can you give us his height, weight, eye and hair colors? We can pull it from DMV, but it might be more accurate coming from you."

"Yes, well, Sid is five-foot seven, and right now he weighs a little over 170 pounds. The doctor put him on a diet after his heart attack." Pat paused and sighed. "Let me see, he has blue eyes and his hair is mostly gray with a touch of red."

"Are these eyeglasses the same ones he wore this morning?" Petersen asked, looking down at the photograph Pat had given him.

"Yes, they're horn-rimmed with large lenses."

"Tell us, does Mr. Reso have any distinguishing marks or tattoos? You mentioned he had a heart attack. Does he have a scar from heart surgery?"

"No, he did have a myocardial infarction about three years ago while in Colombia, but Sid didn't have to have surgery. They moved him to a Miami hospital where he underwent an angioplasty. Since then, he's been treated with medication for high cholesterol, and put on a special diet with multi-vitamins and an exercise regime. He also takes a daily aspirin to thin his blood. And no, Sid doesn't have any tattoos; he wasn't in the service. Korea was over and he was in his thirties when the Vietnam War was going on. But he does have a birthmark about the size of a quarter on his right knee."

"I see. Does he have to take his medication every day?"

"He should, and he's pretty good about it, but it's a cumulative-type thing, so it's all right if he misses a couple days here or there."

"Can you tell us what he was wearing when he left your house this morning?"

"Yes. He has on a gray pinstripe suit, a white dress shirt with a maroon tie, I believe, with black wingtips."

"What kind of watch?"

"It's a gold Rolex with a white face."

"Was Mr. Reso wearing any other jewelry?"

"His gold wedding band."

"Okay, now let's . . . are you okay, Mrs. Reso? Do you need a break?" asked Agent Petersen, who observed Pat as she sipped coffee from a cup.

"No, I'm fine."

She wasn't. Her hands trembled; the FBI agent had seen her coffee cup quivering. A physician from Exxon had arrived to give her something to relax, although he couldn't administer the medication until the questioning was over.

"Okay, tell us about this morning, from the time you woke up to the time your husband went missing. Just walk us through it, if you can."

Pat slid to the edge of her chair and clasped her hands in her lap as she answered. She'd already told county detectives, but she was eager now to tell the FBI.

"It was just our typical weekday morning. Sid sets the alarm for 6:30 usually, like he did this morning. He hopped in the shower and I fixed breakfast. We ate around seven; maybe a little later. After breakfast, he picked up his briefcase and overcoat and then I walked him to the door to the garage." Despite her anxiety and nervousness, Pat spoke calmly and to the point.

"What time was that?"

"That was about seven thirty." Pat stood and sighed heavily. "Excuse me, would you like more coffee?" she asked as she stepped over to the kitchen counter.

"No, thank you. Okay, after your husband walked out the door, what did you do? Did you see him drive away?" asked Agent Chapman, a serious-toned professional.

"No. I saw him back out and the garage door close. Then, I went into the living room with my coffee and sat and looked out at the beautiful morning. It's my quiet time. That's where I go to read my Bible and pray and meditate. When I was done, I went into my bathroom and took a shower. When I came out, I heard the phone ringing—"

"And what time was that?"

"I'd say just after 8:30," she replied, though phone records later revealed the exact time to be 8:49. "It was Sid's secretary calling. She said that Dave Kingston, he works with Sid, told her that Judy, that's his wife, had called him and said she'd noticed Sid's car still in our driveway. The Kingstons live cattycorner across the street. I didn't know it then, but Barbara had already called me when I was in the shower and left a message asking if Sid had left and—"

"Barbara?"

"Sid's secretary, Barbara Cruikshank. C-R-U-I-K-S-H-A-N-K."

"Okay, then what'd you do?"

"I was a bit confused. I told Barbara that Sid had left over half an hour ago, but to hold on and I'd check anyway. I thought maybe he could've had car trouble or something like that. So, I went outside, because you can't see the end of the driveway from the house, and I hurried up the hill. That's when I saw Sid's wagon at the top of the drive. The driver's door was open just a bit, and the motor was running. Then my mind raced. I thought Sid might be in some kind of distress because of his heart condition," she said. "But he wasn't inside. So I opened the front door with Kleenex and removed the keys from the ignition and closed the door. Then I ran—"

"Excuse me, you say you used Kleenex?" Agent Chapman asked.

"I always carry Kleenex in the pocket of my housecoat, and I didn't want to smudge any fingerprints that might be on the door handle."

Chapman scribbled on her notepad, pursing her lips as she wrote. "Okay, go on."

"Well, I hurried back to the house and told Barbara, she was still on the line, I told her to send security right away. I also called the Morris Township police. Then I hung up and went back to the car and opened the rear door. That's when I saw Sid's briefcase and coat laying on the backseat with the birthday card I'd asked him to mail. I just stood looking at them and started to shake. I had a really bad feeling. The key in the ignition with the motor running was the biggest clue to me. Sid always takes the key even if he's just getting out of the car for a minute. He's fanatical about keys. I just stood there frozen with fear. I don't remember anything more until Charlie and the security men came."

"Who's Charlie?"

"Charles Roxburgh. He's a vice president and works with Sid. He's also a close friend."

"Okay. And what time did they arrive?"

"I'm not sure. Maybe 9:30, a quarter till?" The FBI confirmed the time with the corporate security division of Exxon International. It was 10:10 a.m.

Sid Reso's secretary, Barbara Cruikshank, later recalled that Pat was "hysterical" when she returned to the telephone that morning. Cruikshank confirmed what Pat had told agents—that

Exxon security left immediately for the Reso home, accompanied by Del Miller, one of Sid Reso's drivers, and Reso's co-worker and friend, Charlie Roxburgh. "And then it all started," Cruikshank said, referring to the kidnapping investigation.

Pat answered a few more of the agents' questions, explaining that she didn't hear anything unusual that morning and didn't see any sign of a struggle. She listed the names of people who'd been to their house recently, particularly those making deliveries and performing repairs. She told the two agents that her husband had plans to fly to Dallas the following day for Exxon's annual shareholders' meeting being held that week. She also explained that Sid's heart condition was stable, though she still worried about him.

Agents asked Pat about her husband's recreational habits and where he'd been and what he'd done to the extent Pat could recall. She explained they'd gone into the city (New York City) the weekend before to see the Broadway plays, *Jake's Women* and *Death and the Maiden*, and dined at Il Capriccio in Hanover, one of their favorite restaurants. On that Sunday, she explained further that Sid had played golf with Charlie Roxburgh. Later, the FBI would interview Roxburgh as well as the Reso children, the domestic help, and others as the investigation widened. Polygraph tests were also administered to many.

"That's all we need for now, Mrs. Reso. Thank you," Agent Chapman said, who eventually became the case agent and would speak with Pat Reso daily. "Please rest. We'll call on you if we hear anything or need to follow up." Agent Petersen hadn't shown Pat Reso what he'd written in large capital letters on the Bureau's missing person form: POSS ABDUCTION/VICTIM IS EXXON EXEC. But Pat didn't need to see it—she knew the minute she'd seen the keys still in the car's ignition that her husband had been taken.

As the two agents left the kitchen to return to the sprawling command post, the Exxon physician stood from his chair. "Okay, here's something to help you rest."

After taking a sedative, Pat stretched out in her first floor master bedroom. The blinds and curtains had already been drawn. As she later recalled, "I was out of it most of the time those first few days."

The initial fifty-member task force made up principally of FBI agents and detectives from the Morris County Prosecutor's Office continued questioning neighbors and anyone making deliveries and repairs in the area. It was discovered that a boyfriend of one of the domestic help had a prison record and was questioned. Some associates of Sid and Pat Reso's son also were questioned. Agents interviewed Sid Reso's two chauffeurs and administered polygraph tests to them, even though neither had driven Reso that day. Everyone checked out.

Quickly, the FBI's search spread nationally and even internationally. The task force questioned Sid Reso's secretary briefly, reviewed his calendar, and checked his phone messages. Agents and detectives also began checking with Exxon security personnel around the world for a complete list of Reso's appointments and travel. "We're basically trying to relive the last few months of his life," said Morris County Prosecutor Mike Murphy. Exxon quickly set up two 24-hour hot lines for the public to call with any information.

Though there was nothing definitive that first day to indicate the Exxon president had been abducted, such as a note, phone call, or other evidence of a taking, the FBI and other authorities operated under that assumption. It was only a matter of time before the kidnappers made contact, they thought. Trap and trace devices that could register incoming telephone numbers and recording devices should a kidnapper call had already been connected to the Reso home and Sid Reso's office. Agents, detectives, and county attorneys who spoke to the press that Wednesday, however, did not disclose their expectations of a ransom call.

"Right now, we're involved in what I'd say is routine but necessary investigative work," said John O'Reilly, Assistant Morris County Prosecutor. When asked about the receipt of a ransom note, O'Reilly emphasized: "No, we haven't received anything to indicate Mr. Reso has been kidnapped. That is a rumor that has been the subject of media inquiries, but it is not true and it is not based on fact."

Later that afternoon as the command post inside the Reso home buzzed with phone calls, squealing fax machines, and conversation, Pat remained in her bedroom, secreting herself behind a closed door as if hiding from the outside world that had intruded into her life and her home. She rose from bed and sat at a large bureau where she removed a small journal. She'd only written in her diary once, several years earlier when visiting a friend in Nantucket. She'd begun her diary back then with the words of one of her favorite writers, Amantine Lucile Aurore Dupin, known by her pseudonym, George Sand: *The old woman I shall become will be quite different from the woman I am now. Another I is beginning.*

On that Wednesday, still a bit groggy, Pat began slowly writing her second entry—a conversation with her absent husband, as if writing him a daily letter. She wrote Sid that she and the children were fine and not to worry and that they were praying for him to return home soon. She would keep up the writing vigil twice a day until Sid was found. "I speak directly to Sid," Pat said. "That's my link to sanity . . . I've tried to . . . send as positive a message to him as I can because I know that he is a very optimistic, positive kind of person."

Pat hoped that writing loving entries in her diary directly to her husband would make her feel nearer to him. It did. She also hoped that her writing was not the beginning of another I. She preferred to remain Mrs. Sidney J. Reso.

* * *

Around 7:30 that morning, an hour and a half before Pat Reso discovered her husband's abandoned station wagon, a white 1991 Dodge Ram cargo van sped from the Reso driveway to the end of Jonathan Smith Road, slowed, turned right onto Jacob Arnold Road, and then took another right onto Gaston Road before turning west on New Jersey Route 24.

"Pull in here," the male kidnapper directed from the passenger seat. The woman steered the van left into Lewis Morris County Park about a mile from the Reso house. "Park over there."

"I know, I know," she said, it being all part of the plan they'd agreed on. She pulled the van into the Old Army lot, a small and secluded spot in the park.

"Did you kill him?" the woman asked.

"What? I told you. No. He just got it in the arm."

"Jesus Christ, Artie, why'd you have to—"

"Shh!" He whispered, pressing his index finger to his lips. "He can hear us."

"But—"

"What do you want me to do, kidnap a doctor? It's a superficial wound is all. We'll stop and get something to bandage 'im up. Stop worrying."

But she was worried. Now they'd have to take care of a wounded man. What if he got really sick or even died?

She jumped out of the van in her black sweatpants and navy North Face windbreaker and glanced about the small parking lot to see if anyone was watching. The lot was empty. She hurried to the front of the van where she knelt and removed the stolen plate that had been clipped over the real license plate, XV88DK, registered to a Hackettstown rental car company. She then hurried to the rear of the van and did the same.

While his female partner was outside, the man slid over to drive. When she rejoined him, he pulled the van onto Route 24 heading west. They discussed with whispers and hand signals what to do about their wounded passenger as they drove. When the male kidnapper wasn't checking his side mirror or looking into the cargo area, he busied himself with the radio, switching from channel to channel, first FM and then AM, for any word about their morning's misdeed. There was nothing.

They could hear groans from the wooden box behind them. Sid Reso's blood had sprayed on one side of the van's white metal interior and a spot on the floor glistened in the faint sunlight that penetrated the rear cargo area. Blood also oozed out of his arm into the bottom of the rough-hewn box. Tape was still wrapped tightly over Reso's mouth, stifling his attempts to speak. They also heard a thumping sound. It was the soles of Reso's dress shoes bumping against the end of the crude wooden box.

"Be still!" yelled the man from the front seat, the pitiful clamor adding to the stressful situation. The shooting had upset both kidnappers; it only complicated an already risky plan.

The van traveled past other motorists, pedestrians, bicyclists, and even a policeman in a patrol car. None could have imagined that the plain white van that just passed carried the president of Exxon International bound and bleeding inside a crate in the back.

The van passed through Mendham, a town of about nine thousand that is seven miles due west of Morristown, and then through Chester, a small town of about six thousand that is five miles farther west. The countryside is wooded and hilly. Both kidnappers grew quiet as they journeyed onward. Only an occasional thud or moan from the back disturbed the eerie silence, a silence that seemed only to heighten the tension inside the van. As the man drove, a faint smile crept across his face. His hostage's condition would not stop him from getting the ransom. He'd soon be filthy rich.

The winding two-lane highway weaved farther into the remote countryside. It would be another thirty minutes before the occupants of the van reached their destination.

* * *

Sidney Joseph Reso was born on February 12, 1935, in New Orleans, Louisiana. As a youngster, Sid Reso had been a Boy Scout and had served as president of the Catholic Youth Organization while attending the all-male St. Aloysius High School (now named Brother Martin). Only two months before his disappearance, his high school honored him as their Alumnus of the Year. He flew down to accept the honor and to reunite with old friends. "That's how down to earth he is—an easygoing guy," Sid Reso's cousin, Jerome Reso Jr., told reporters.

During his last two summers while attending college at Louisiana State University, young Reso worked as a roughneck on oil rigs in the Gulf of Mexico. The rig supervisor, P.J. Trahan, told reporters that "Sid was always a prince of a fella and I knew from the word go that he would do well."

In 1957, Reso graduated from LSU with a degree in petroleum engineering and as a member of two honor societies. He would not forget his alma mater. He served on the board of directors of the LSU Alumni Foundation and was a major contributor to the university. And LSU never forgot Sid Reso. He was inducted into LSU's College of Engineering Hall of Distinction in 1983.

After graduation from LSU, Reso's dream was to become a corporate oilman, so the twenty-two-year-old joined Humble Oil and Refining Co., a predecessor of Exxon Company, USA, the refining and marketing arm of Exxon Corporation. He was assigned to a dry oil field in an isolated spot west of New Orleans called New Iberia. "The joke around the company was that Sid was being exiled to New Siberia because there wasn't much going on there," Murray Hawkins, an LSU professor, recalled. "But when Sid got there, he got busy and found a bunch of oil that hadn't been tapped by wells, about seven million gallons."

That discovery helped the young engineer begin his climb up the Exxon organizational chart, a climb that continued for thirty-five years. It wasn't an easy climb, but Reso's vision, hard work, and willingness to move his family around the country and the world paid off. By 1988, he was among those at the top. He was now the president of Exxon International. With its 35,000 employees in sixty-eight countries, Sid Reso presided over a company that produced three-quarters of all profits of its parent, Exxon Corporation, and stood responsible for Exxon's worldwide oil and gas operations outside the U.S. and Canada. The presidents of Esso U.K., Esso France, and Esso Japan as well as many others reported directly to him. His influence was felt in so many places for so many years that those in the oil and gas industry dubbed him, "Mr. Exxon."

Everyone expected Sid Reso would soon be crowned the next CEO of Exxon Corporation in Irving, Texas. Afterward, when he reached Exxon's mandatory retirement age of sixty-five, Sid and Pat planned to retire to Indian River Shores, Florida, where they owned a winter home on posh Orchid Island and frequently played golf at John's Island Club.

Pontificating about Sid Reso's disappearance, Ivy LeBlanc, president of Reso's Catholic high school in New Orleans, told reporters that "[Sid is] strong on playing the hand that's dealt you." Indeed, a very difficult hand had been dealt to Sid Reso on April 29 and it was only going to become much tougher in the days ahead. How Reso, his family, and legal authorities could play such a terrifying hand of fate was mostly out of their control, though not entirely. Unfortunately, those dealing the hand were Reso's kidnappers and time would prove that few could be crueler.

* * *

Tree branches extended above a narrow two-lane road that twisted along the rolling hills of Washington County, dotted with modest houses bearing weatherworn wood siding that rested very near the countryside road. The temperature had already reached fifty degrees and the sun peeked through early morning clouds, showcasing thick woods along the roadside alive with purple aster and marigolds, redbuds, dogwoods, and pawpaw.

The rural scene made quite a lovely outing in late April as the blooms burst forth throughout the budding laurel-colored trees, yet the two kidnappers in the white van didn't notice. Their eyes were transfixed on the droning roadway ahead while their reluctant passenger could see only darkness. The kidnappers had not spoken for several minutes and the commotion in the back had calmed. Even the radio's volume was barely audible. Only the whine of the motor and the tires on the road filled the interior, nurturing the icy contemplation of those in the front seats.

Nearing their destination, the kidnappers turned left on Newburgh Road and after a short distance made another left on New Jersey Route 57. They pulled into the Mansfield Township Shopping Center just past the intersection. In 1992, there were no surveillance cameras in the parking lot. Extra lighting had been installed on poles to illuminate the parking area at night in an effort to discourage robberies and sexual assaults, but that was all.

The kidnappers had decided that the woman would go inside ShopRite to purchase gauze, tape, scissors, distilled water, hydrogen peroxide, Tylenol, plastic cups, and Evian bottled water. They'd treat their hostage's wound when they arrived at their hideaway.

"Remember, just act natural and don't talk to anybody."

The man stared out the windshield as his female partner walked into ShopRite. He maintained a close watch on the supermarket's doors and windows from his location while she shopped. As the lookout sat and waited with a wounded hostage in the back, he began to fidget. A few more minutes passed. He started the van's engine and withdrew the large .45-caliber pistol from his coat, resting it on his lap. He thought it was taking her way too long for such a simple task.

Inside, his partner went over to the pharmacy section to begin collecting the items they'd agreed on, instinctively checking the prices of different brands. She glanced up at the shoplifting cameras and responded awkwardly. When she finished shopping, she placed the items on the checkout counter and only nodded when asked if she found everything she needed. She paid with cash and slouched out of the store, her head tilted downward as she marched in short, quick steps across the parking lot.

"Where've you been? Anybody recognize you?"

"No, but I saw those damn cameras and they saw me," she replied. "I don't like it, Artie."

"Shh. Stop using my name," he whispered.

They pulled onto the highway once again, this time traveling south on Route 57, even though their destination was north. Along the eight-mile drive, the driver did his best to calm his compatriot. "Believe me; nobody will ever know we were there."

They soon reached the Port Colden Mall outside of Washington, New Jersey. There, the woman stepped out and got into a 1985 white Jeep Cherokee she'd parked in the lot earlier. They both then traveled up Route 57, past the Mansfield Township Shopping Center where they'd just stopped to buy medical supplies, and turned right, pulling up to a chain-link gate. Beside the six-foot high gate stood a brown sign with white letters, *Secure Storage*, along with a telephone number. The total trip had covered thirty miles and taken nearly fifty minutes. They'd been vigilant in obeying all traffic laws and maintained their speed below the posted limits. Still, they had taken a terrible risk. Engine trouble, a flat tire, or an unavoidable accident could have spelled an immediate end to their undertaking and to their freedom.

The man cranked the van's window down and entered a three-digit code, 591, into the gate's keypad attached to a metal post. He'd received the private code when signing a four-month lease for a storage unit two months earlier. There were no cameras at the complex, though the entry of his code registered electronically inside the office on a desktop computer. It was 8:23 a.m. The woman in the Jeep shortly arrived and likewise entered the same code at 8:27 a.m. The electronic gate could only be opened by renters between the hours of 7:00 a.m. and 9:00 p.m. Rarely was an employee present. This was a self-storage facility.

Secure Storage had been built only five years earlier just beyond the southeast boundary of Hackettstown, New Jersey. Five prefabricated taupe barracks with brown corrugated doors and shallow-gabled rib steel rooves stood on an asphalted ten-acre rectangular lot surrounded by a six-foot chain-link fence topped with barbed-wire. The Musconetcong River flowed literally a stone's throw behind the storage compound, flanked by spawning forest and farmland. Crows could be heard cawing above the sound of rippling water. It was a secluded place.

Once inside the fenced gate, the white van turned left at the office and slowly made a right into an alleyway between the third and fourth rows of units. The driver already knew where to find his rented space, having inspected it weeks earlier to insure that it would satisfy his needs. The woman parked her Jeep Cherokee away from the office and storage unit and walked, not wanting her Jeep to be associated with the van or the storage unit. Rental spaces were ten feet high from concrete floor to metal roof and available in eight sizes. They had selected a ten-foot wide by twenty-foot deep unit, about the size of a one-car garage, for $125 a month to house their unique belonging until it was time to let him go; if they let him go.

The kidnappers slipped on gloves, ski masks, and sunglasses. The male driver stepped out of the van and unlocked and raised the corrugated rollup door to unit 619, its number stenciled in white on a red placard above the door on building 6. It rattled loudly as it slid up, startling the kidnapper who hurried back to the driver's seat should someone appear, but they did not. He gripped the gear shift on the van's steering column and eased the van backward until the rear bumper rested inside.

The man folded open the van's rear doors while the woman slid between the two front seats into the rear compartment. On the man's signal, she pushed the heavy crate as he pulled from the outside, the homemade wooden box screeching along the van's metal floor on its way out. They heard muffled cries from inside the box, akin to "hey" or "help me." They also heard what sounded like Reso bumping his right elbow on the box's side, despite the placement of a blanket to muffle such attempts. The large man leaned down and whispered a warning to be quiet as they continued to slide the heavy box out and lower it to the concrete floor.

"Pull the van out then park it sideways in front of the door," the man directed. "I'll keep watch." As soon as the van's rear bumper cleared the unit, he slid the door down from the inside to conceal their payload, leaving only a few inches open at the bottom for light and fresh air to circulate.

His female companion parked the van only inches from the door and then stepped from the van. "Let me in," she said, rapping lightly.

The door slid up and she walked inside. He illuminated her way with a flashlight. There was no bulb inside and almost no light seeped in from the outside. The woman noticed her partner had scooted the wooden box toward the rear of the unit, now resting parallel to the compartment's front and rear panels. The man withdrew a set of keys. He used the keys to open the padlocks at the head, foot, and right-hand side of the box and then lifted the lid and folded it over the left side. As he did, the woman reflexively stepped backward against the wall, her masked face hidden in the darkness.

Inside lay Sid Reso, a man who'd harmed no one, especially

the two kidnappers in whose hands he found himself bound and gagged, lying prostrate and helpless before them. He was a smart man and it was obvious what they wanted. Exxon executives had been briefed on the dangers of kidnapping, though usually it was of concern only when traveling outside of the country. As much as he wanted to escape, Reso probably realized that was impossible, at least for the time being. All he could do was wait and hope that his captors would release him once they received the ransom money.

Staring down inside the box, it had to have been difficult for the kidnappers to believe that they'd held Reso captive for merely an hour. So far, they'd made a mess of it. Their flashlight revealed the Exxon executive squirming and murmuring in the shadows of the box, his eyes and mouth bound firmly with gray duct tape. His suit coat was on and his tie and pocket handkerchief that Pat Reso had straightened that morning were still in place, though now spattered with blood from the gunshot. The left sleeve, completely saturated in moist blood, revealed a powder burn and a ruffled hole.

"Hand me that sack," said the man, who removed the contents of the grocery bag. He raised Sid Reso at the waist and cut the bloody sleeve from the wrist to the elbow as Reso grunted and tried to speak. "Be quiet," the man ordered. "We're trying to help you." He rubbed the wound with distilled water and peroxide as his patient yelped and twitched his injured arm. The large man then wrapped Reso's wrist and elbow with gauze and taped it. The bleeding had stopped, though the area surrounding the wound was reddening and the forearm was beginning to swell. The kidnappers did not elevate his wounded arm. Instead, they cuffed Reso's arms *behind* his back. They also didn't apply ice or administer antibiotics; just simply cleaned the exterior wounds and wrapped his burning, pulsating forearm in gauze.

The man told his partner that it was a "superficial flesh wound." He'd been a police officer and part of a corporate security team so he had some knowledge of gunshot wounds, though he was being generous in his description. The entrance and exit wounds were anything but superficial. At almost half an inch wide, the lead bullet had ripped muscle, capillaries, and bone as it passed in and out of Sid Reso's left forearm. Mangled tissue mixed with bone splinters surrounded the exit wound that protruded above the elbow.

The male kidnapper cut Reso's Rolex off his swollen and bleeding wrist and also took Reso's wallet, containing an Exxon credit card. Then he removed the tape from Reso's mouth so the woman could place a cup of lukewarm water to his lips.

"Let me go . . . please," Reso pleaded, struggling to speak. "My family . . . they—"

"Don't talk. Just drink," the man said. The woman never spoke a word.

"What do you want from me?"

"We don't want anything from you," the man replied. "We're not going to harm you (though they'd already shot him). We just want money from Exxon. Then we'll let you go. Now drink."

The taste must have been bitter because Sid Reso refused to continue drinking, possibly believing he was being drugged despite being told it was a crushed Tylenol tablet and a multi-vitamin mixed with water. Much of the odd concoction spilled on his chin and down his neck. He received two cups of water. When done, the kidnappers wasted no time taping his mouth shut again and lowering him back into the box. They did not want to converse with their hostage.

The stocky man stood and closed the lid. He then clicked and tested each of the padlocks to make sure they were securely locked. The kidnappers were uneasy about leaving their prisoner alone that first day, afraid that someone might discover him. Nevertheless, they left. Reso heard what sounded to him like a door of some kind sliding up and then down and a vehicle driving away.

He lay there for three and a half hours completely alone and in pain inside the coffin-like crate before he heard a car stop outside and then the door lift. The woman had returned only to raise the door a few inches to help ventilate the unit. She stayed outside, but could hear muffled noises escaping the darkness within. It sounded as if Reso was trying to talk to her, though he didn't know who was there. She didn't speak and would not enter without the large man present, but he'd caught the commuter train into New York City, and wouldn't return until the early evening. The woman's silence must have further tormented the suffering Exxon executive.

The two kidnappers did visit the storage unit again before closing time that first day, their entries at the gate registering at 8:18 and 8:30 p.m. They changed Sid Reso's bandage and gave him two more cups of lukewarm water that contained three Tylenol tablets, one multi-vitamin, and two sleeping pills that the woman had crushed and mixed with the water in the corner of the storage unit. They didn't give him any food. The kidnappers had decided not to feed Reso during his captivity because, according to the female kidnapper, "it would cause problems." He'd already urinated on himself while lying in the box. His pants and undershorts and a portion of the sleeping bag beneath him were saturated. The kidnappers would not allow Reso to stand or step out of the box, nor would they give him a change of clothes.

Initially, the kidnappers had planned to hold Sid Reso inside an apartment, but abandoned the idea because neither would be able to stay with him around the clock and they were afraid a meddlesome landlord or a scheduled exterminator might discover him. They didn't have the money to lease an apartment anyway. They'd briefly considered renting a U-Haul truck and parking it in a vacant lot or campsite with Reso in the back, but dropped the idea due to the possibility of discovery. Then one day in February while driving to visit a friend, the male kidnapper saw a storage space in a rural area beside the highway. He convinced his female partner that a self-storage unit would be the perfect solution. At first, they considered placing Reso in the back of a U-Haul truck and parking the truck inside a storage unit in Wall Township south of Sandy Hook Bay. They decided against it once they discovered that none of the units' doors were high enough to admit a truck of that size. The male kidnapper instead elected to build a wooden container, stuff Reso inside it, and then place the crate inside the unit.

Though it may have seemed like a good idea in February when they rented the unit, it would prove to be unwise. The units at Secure Storage were not temperature-controlled and only had roofline openings to supply ventilation. That was barely sufficient to keep a stifling springtime space from becoming a baking oven. In late April, temperatures were already creeping into the sixties making it very warm inside the units during the daytime, particularly with the sun beaming down on the metal buildings. No shade trees stood within the storage perimeter. The kidnappers had not yet removed Reso's suit coat and had strapped him down inside a stuffy box lined with a pillow, a blanket, and a blue sleeping bag with only a few air holes drilled around the box's perimeter for circulation. Though that setup provided warmth at night, it would make the afternoons agonizingly hot.

But as the coolness of that first evening seeped inside the uninsulated metal storage compartment, Sid Reso surely thought about his wife, his four children, and his elderly mother. He knew they had to be terribly worried about him and that made a miserable situation a sorrowful one. His children would be arriving at his home that evening and the following morning to console Pat and to be consoled. Those at home may have felt as helpless as Reso did inside that terrible box. His family had already suffered incredible pain when his twenty-seven-year-old son, Greg, died five years earlier. Pat was just beginning to come out of her melancholy from that loss and return to her old self. But there was nothing he could do, except wait alone, entombed like a corpse in a narrow dark coffin, the gunshot wound burning and his back and shoulders aching from his hands being cuffed behind his back. As he dozed off from the sleeping pills, how could he have known that he lay only two and a half miles from the Hackettstown (New Jersey) Police Department, and what could he have done if he had known?

Chapter 2

"We have Reso." The call came into the main switchboard at the Exxon International offices in Florham Park, New Jersey. The time was 10:13 a.m. on Thursday, April 30, the day after Sid Reso's disappearance. Several employees were attending a retirement coffee party in a room adjacent to the switchboard. Spilling out into the hallway, they made so much commotion that Exxon operator, Alba Pytel, stood up and flapped her arms and hands signaling for quiet. Having not understood the shrill, almost mechanical sounding voice on the line, Pytel asked the woman to repeat herself.

"We are the Warriors of the Rainbow. Listen very carefully for information leading to Sidney Reso's whereabouts. Information can be found at the Livingston Mall parking lot number one, opposite of Sears. Look for the telephone pole with the yellow traffic barrier," the disguised voice said. The caller then hung up.

The operator had been alerted to the possibility of such a telephone call. She informed her supervisor, Brenda Braen, who telephoned Exxon security, who in turn notified the FBI in Newark, New Jersey.

The FBI immediately dispatched Special Agents Larry Sparks and John Turkington, who raced to the mall to retrieve the envelope. While the agents were en route, a reverse toll edit revealed the call originated from a payphone near an AMOCO gas station on McCarter Highway in Newark, fifteen miles away. Other agents rushed to the payphone to investigate and collect evidence.

Within minutes, the agents arrived at Livingston Mall, a two-level indoor shopping center with orange brick and stained limestone trim built in 1972, only two miles from Exxon's Florham Park office. They sprang from their car in the Sears parking lot and quickly discovered a white envelope taped behind a yellow guardrail surrounding a light pole. They photographed the location of the envelope and the surrounding area before carefully removing the gray duct tape and the envelope. Both were bagged. A forensics team would arrive shortly to dust for fingerprints and scan the area for cigarette butts, footprints, and tire marks, and to vacuum for fibers and other trace evidence. The agents questioned mall employees, security, and patrons to determine if they'd seen anyone standing near the light pole that morning or the night before. Unfortunately, the mall did not have cameras in the parking lot.

Agents Sparks and Turkington interviewed Ms. Pytel who told them that the caller's voice sounded disguised and serious. She said it sounded like a woman, but there was nothing distinctive about the voice. She'd heard a hissing noise in the background as if the statement had been prerecorded. The Exxon operator repeated the message to agents and said it ended with "Warriors," but she couldn't understand what followed the unusual word.

The FBI copied the ransom note. An agent then drove more than two hundred miles to Washington, D.C. to deliver the original letter and envelope, along with the duct tape, to the Identification Division and Document Section of the FBI Laboratory for processing. To save time, Exxon allowed agents access to a company jet to make future deliveries to the lab. Besides analyzing the paper and font types, the lab promptly discovered a woman's bleached-blond hair stuck to the envelope seal and a carpet fiber on the envelope's stamp. The hair and fiber told the FBI that the kidnappers, though they'd successfully taken Sid Reso without being detected, were not infallible.

Within minutes, Supervisory Senior Resident Agent John Walker with the Garret Mountain Resident Agency, an FBI satellite office covering Morris County, informed Pat Reso of the ransom letter. Agent Walker was in charge of the command post set up inside the Reso house. Pat had expected the note, and may even have been a bit relieved to have received it, for the letter explained that Sid was being held for ransom and that upon payment, he would be released unharmed. The note read:

The major industrial entities continue their thoughtless programs which are destroying the earth and harming countless forms of life. Destruction of the land, sea and air continues at unprecedented rates . . .

We propose to make industry pay for this continuing campaign. To ensure your contribution we have seized the President of your International Division.

. . . your share will be $18.5 Million.

Gather the money in used $100 bills.

Obtain a portable cellular telephone with a 201 area code.

Place an ad in The Star Ledger Pets section under Birds saying "Rare International birds — call 201-XXX-XXXX" using the cellular telephone number with the last 4 digits reversed.

We will contact you with delivery instructions.

Mr. Reso will be held in total isolation with no food or water. If you do not fully comply he most certainly will die . . .

Any involvement by the police, FBI, or media will be extremely counterproductive. We will not negotiate . . .

Fernando Pereira Brigade
Warriors of the Rainbow

The telephone call made that morning to the Exxon operator

had not been part of the kidnappers' original plan. They had intended to leave the envelope in the front seat of Sid Reso's station wagon. Because of the struggle inside the van, the kidnappers sped away, which gave them no choice but to tape the envelope to a shopping center light pole the next day.

With delivery of the ransom note, the kidnappers had set the exchange in motion. Incredibly, the ransom letter asked for the highest ransom ever demanded in a U.S. kidnapping: $18.5 million ($34 million today). It also carried a major threat: "Mr. Reso will be held in total isolation with no food or water. If you do not fully comply, he will most certainly die."

The FBI immediately initiated plans to comply with their demands, but also began checking its files on environmental extremists. The Bureau had no information about a group called Warriors of the Rainbow. Still, such groups often popped up overnight and Exxon had few friends among those concerned about the environment.

To the FBI's criminal investigative analysts, often called criminal profilers, who formed the FBI's Behavioral Science Unit in Quantico, Virginia, something about these kidnappers didn't add up. What's more, according to Dr. Murray Miron, a psychologist adviser to the FBI, who conducted a psycholinguistic analysis of the letter, the ransom demand was written by someone with "impulse control dysfunction" whose "motivations are psychopathic rather than environmentalist." The bottom line, according to Dr. Miron, was that "Sidney Reso's life is in considerable jeopardy."

* * *

Even though no one had ever heard of the Fernando Pereira Brigade or the Warriors of the Rainbow, the self-proclaimed environmental terrorists did appear to have some foundation in fact.

On July 10, 1985, the Greenpeace ship, *Rainbow Warrior*, was anchored in Auckland, New Zealand, preparing to lead a peaceful protest against French nuclear testing in Moruroa Atoll. The trawler had been christened after a Native-American proverb, "When the planet is sick and dying, the people will rise up like warriors of the rainbow."

Before the Greenpeace trawler left port, agents from the French government illegally planted two underwater mines on the hull of the *Rainbow Warrior*. The first bomb exploded, severely damaging the unmanned vessel. A Dutch freelance photographer traveling on the Greenpeace ship ran back aboard to retrieve his camera gear before the ship sank not knowing that a second mine had been set to detonate within minutes. The second bomb exploded. He drowned aboard the sinking ship. The photographer's name was Fernando Pereira.

On March 24, 1989, the petroleum tanker, USS *Exxon Valdez*, struck Bligh Reef in Prince William Sound, one of the most pristine coastal areas in the world. More than eleven million gallons of crude oil spilled from the cracked single hull, covering 1,300 miles of coastline and over 11,000 square miles of ocean water with the toxic sticky substance. The largest oil tanker spill in U.S. history was considered by many to be the most devastating human-caused environmental disaster ever until the BP Deepwater Horizon oil spill in the Gulf of Mexico in 2010.

And in the summer of 1991, only months before Sid Reso's kidnapping, Greenpeace had anchored *Rainbow Warrior II*, the vessel that replaced the sabotaged *Rainbow Warrior*, in Port Valdez, Alaska, as a peaceful protest against Exxon.

The FBI gathered this information within hours of retrieving the ransom note from Livingston Mall and immediately contacted Greenpeace to interview the international environmental organization's chief representatives. The Warriors of the Rainbow's connection to Greenpeace initially seemed overwhelming. Greenpeace representatives, however, emphatically denied any knowledge of the self-proclaimed terrorist group and strongly denounced the kidnapping, fearful of repercussions it might have on Greenpeace's environmental activism. Greenpeace's admonishment was a position shared by other environmental groups interviewed by the FBI and reporters. "It's terrible the way this paints the environmental community," said a New York environmentalist who insisted on anonymity. "Greenpeace goes in for stunts, not acts of violence."

The FBI understood how quickly radical groups can splinter from peaceful environmental groups. Greenpeace was ruled out as a suspect straightaway. The Bureau began investigating groups such as the Sea Shepherd Conservation Society, Animal Liberation Front (ALF), and Earth First!, some of whose supporters had committed violent acts to further their organizations' agendas, though mostly acts that interrupted business or caused property damage. The FBI also contacted peaceful organizations to find out if any militant activists might be bouncing about as suspects in the environmental grapevine. None could furnish any possible suspects.

The FBI's investigation of environmental organizations was covert. Spokespersons for the FBI and the Morris County Prosecutor's Office simply told the media that they were treating the disappearance as a "high-intensity" missing persons case and that so far, they were "stumped." As the FBI's investigation report made clear at the time: "Although for public consumption, the FBI is handling instant matter as a missing person case, the possibility exists that Reso was kidnapped by environmental activists/terrorists due to Reso's position, given environmental activists' continuing concern over the Exxon Valdez oil spill in Prince William Sound, Alaska, and the Exxon oil pipeline leak in the Arthur Kill [aka Staten Island Sound], New Jersey/New York."

A report from the FBI Behavioral Science Unit, however, noted: "Despite the documented actions of the more extreme environmentalists, the kidnapping of a ranking executive represents a leap in criminality far in excess of a precedent for such groups."

It now appeared that Sid Reso may have become the first recorded kidnap victim of eco-terrorism.

* * *

The FBI wasted no time complying with the demands in the ransom note. As soon as agents received the kidnappers' letter that Thursday, they contacted Cellular One in New York and obtained a "cellular telephone." In 1992, the novel cellphones were much larger and heavier than today with a flexible rubber antenna protruding from their tops. Both battery life and signal range were extremely limited. The kidnappers erroneously believed that cellphone calls would be much more difficult to trace than those made on a landline. Actually, the FBI had developed specialized communications technology and electronic tracking methods that made it easier to track incoming cellular calls than regular telephone calls.

Working with Cellular One and New Jersey Bell, the FBI erected several antennae atop the fourteen-story Headquarters Plaza, the tallest office building in Morristown. Additional communications and electronics equipment were installed in a county building in Morris Township. (Like many communities in New Jersey, Morris Township looks much like a donut that completely surrounds Morristown as its donut-hole.) The FBI also duplicated the cellular phone so that if a kidnapper called the FBI cellular phone, wherever it was, it would also ring a landline inside the command post so that the conversation could not only be heard, but trapped and traced and recorded. It was one of the first uses of phone cloning in law enforcement.

The FBI placed an ad that same day with *The Star-Ledger*, the most circulated newspaper in New Jersey. As directed in the ransom note, the ad appeared in the BIRDS section of the classified advertisements on Friday, May 1, and set out the cellular telephone number, 201-404-3176, with the last four digits reversed:

INTERNATIONAL
RARE BIRDS
CALL 201-404-6713

During this time, Exxon withdrew $18.5 million from its accounts in Chemical Bank in New York and transported the money by Brink's armored truck to a bank in Morristown. The bank president insisted that his small town bank was not equipped to hold that much cash securely, so the bank delivered the money by armored truck to the Reso home. Two uniformed men stepped from the armored truck, opened the rear doors, and unloaded three large trunks into the Reso garage. The money consisted solely of used $100 bills. The serial numbers of all 185,000 bills had been recorded at the New York bank and some of the bills had been marked. The total ransom weighed a bulky 407 pounds. If an agent had stacked all of the $100 bills on top of the others beneath a brick paperweight, the stack would have risen more than sixty-six feet into the air.

It would later be discovered that the staggering ransom figure originated from news reports a month earlier that Rockwell International had agreed to plead guilty and accept a fine of $18.5 million for mishandling poisonous wastes near Denver, Colorado. The enormous fine had been big news in April, covered by newspapers and magazines around the country. The male kidnapper, who was an avid reader of periodicals, spotted the article in *TIME* magazine at a local library and admired the impressive figure.

It was a lot of money, yet represented merely a single day's profit for Exxon in 1992. Besides, Exxon carried kidnapping insurance on its high-level executives like many large corporations that transact business in dangerous parts of the world; only Morris Township would be the last place Exxon would have considered kidnap insurance to be necessary.

The kidnappers also were busy preparing for the ransom drop. They purchased a small, inexpensive tape recorder from a Radio Shack store at the Flemington Circle Shopping Center. They then drove to Secure Storage. The electronic registry in the office logged their entry at 8:38 a.m. It was Friday morning, May 1. They parked, slipped on their gloves, masks, and sunglasses, and unlocked and raised the door to unit 619. Sid Reso heard the door slide up, though he likely had not yet deduced that he was being held in a storage unit. The kidnappers heard him make a muffled noise, as if attempting to talk. They closed the door, leaving no more than a foot of space for air to enter. It was stuffy inside and carried a revolting smell. They clicked on a flashlight.

The male kidnapper inserted keys into the three padlocks on the wooden crate, one on the right side and the others at the head and foot. He gently opened and then lowered the lid made of five-eighths of an inch plywood over to the left side of the box. The smell that smacked the male kidnapper in the face was indescribable. Sweat and urine mixed with blood and feces that had baked inside a wooden oven overnight filled the entire space with an odor that would make anyone want to vomit. Even so, the kidnappers would not allow Sid Reso to stand and would not clean him or the blankets and sleeping bag that lined the inside of the box, nor would they change Reso's clothes.

The sight of Sid Reso inside that wooden coffin-like box had to have been just as sickening. Though the male kidnapper had served as a police officer, this was his first kidnapping, and observing a bloodied man lying in that box had to make a plot that looked good on paper turn sour in real life. Still, there was no hesitation by either kidnapper. The burly man reached in and raised Reso from the waist. He discovered that Reso had been able to work the tape away from one corner of his mouth. The kidnapper removed the crinkled tape.

"Please . . . My arm. Can you—"

"We're gonna give you some water with vitamins and change your bandages. We can't take you to a doctor, sir, but we'll be releasing you very soon. We're working with your company right now to get the ransom."

"Leave the tape off my—"

"Just drink," the man said as the woman held a cup of the lukewarm and bitter concoction. They then uncuffed his hands and removed the bandages from his arm. It looked bad. The wound was bruised and red and the forearm and wrist were swollen with red streaks running up and down the forearm. It was infected. The exit wound looked even worse. The man cleaned both wounds with peroxide and wrapped Reso's arm with fresh bandages. The Exxon president grunted repeatedly. Tylenol does little to relieve pain from an infected gunshot wound, especially from a .45-caliber bullet, and topical peroxide is of little use. Reso needed intravenous antibiotics and pain medication.

Between sips of water, Reso pleaded for the kidnappers to remove his suitcoat, tie, belt, and shoes to make him more comfortable. The large man agreed. He also acceded to Reso's request to move his handcuffed hands from his back to his front. He next withdrew a tape recorder and held Reso's shoulders as he told Reso what to say. The woman held the flashlight.

"Okay, say what I've told you. Don't say anything else. No tricks."

Sid Reso attempted to repeat the kidnapper's words. He was in a lot of pain, straining from the continuous pangs shooting through his arm into his left shoulder. The playback was barely audible so he was told to repeat it. This time it was louder, though not comprehensible. They tried again. At last, they had instructions that could be understood, though people who knew

Reso would never have believed it to be him. The mild-mannered man with a steady deep voice conveyed anything but that on tape. His voice was high-pitched, breathy, and agitated.

The man stretched tape over Reso's mouth and lowered his head and torso back onto the pillow and sleeping bag. He snapped the three latches and clicked the padlocks shut. In a few minutes, the kidnappers raised the door and left the storage facility again, leaving Reso completely alone in the stuffy and dark confined space with only his thoughts to keep him company.

They returned ten hours later, at 6:21 p.m., to allow in some fresh air and give Sid Reso two cups of water with the mixture of crushed Tylenol, vitamin, and sleeping pills. After leaving Secure Storage around 6:45, the kidnappers drove into Lewis Morris County Park, the same park they'd used to switch license plates on the day of the kidnapping. The sky was darkening and the park was empty. The sounds of birds had been replaced with an eerie cacophony of crickets, croaking frogs, and a whip-poor-will whose lonesome call filled the night air.

Park attendants usually closed and locked the gates at dusk, although that night the kidnappers had been lucky, the gates weren't locked until 10:30 p.m. They dropped an envelope containing another ransom letter near the sign at the entrance to the park and then drove to a shopping center at The Hills in Bedminster. They used a payphone outside King's Food Market to call the cellular telephone number they'd retrieved from *The Star-Ledger* advertisement the previous day. It was 9:27 p.m. on Friday, May 1. Sid Reso had already been held captive for sixty-two hours.

The cellular phone rang inside the FBI command post at the Reso house. Special Agent Ed Petersen was selected to pose as Jim Morakis, the public affairs manager for Exxon International, since the ransom note had been addressed to Exxon International and had instructed that no police be involved. Petersen answered, sounding much like Morakis.

"Hello . . . hello . . . hello?"

There was a pause, then a click and a hissing sound.

"Go to the main entrance of Lewis Morris Park and look on the ground for a letter," were the instructions recorded in Reso's voice and played into the payphone's mouthpiece.

"Hello . . . hello?"

"Go to the main entrance of Lewis Morris Park and look on the ground for a letter."

"Can you repeat that please? Can you repeat that please?"

The kidnapper hung up.

The FBI recorded the telephone call and quickly traced it to a payphone at the intersection of New Jersey Routes 202 and 206, in Bedminster, New Jersey. Within minutes, FBI agents swept into the parking lot to view the payphone. No one was around. Agents questioned people in the payphone's vicinity, but no one had seen anything. A forensics team soon arrived and photographed the ground and the payphone and dusted the phone for prints. The telephone receiver was eventually cut away from the box and, with the help of the telephone company, the coin box was emptied. Each coin would be fingerprinted. The FBI checked the prints, but the kidnappers had wiped their coins and wore gloves. The payphone's call records also were examined for the previous three days in case the kidnappers had practiced using that payphone, but all numbers checked out. A telephone detail soon arrived and processed all additional payphones not only in that park, but Burnham Park nearby. They finished at 1:25 a.m.

While agents processed the scene, Special Agents Ed Petersen and Tom Cottone arrived at the entrance to Lewis Morris County Park. Shining flashlights, they discovered the envelope on the ground near a large rock on which was attached a bronze plaque displaying the park's history. Agent Cottone slipped on gloves and picked up the envelope from the ground and placed it in a plastic bag.

The two agents returned to the command post where the letter was opened, read, and copied, and another agent delivered the envelope, letter, duct tape, and dental stone casts of tire treads to the FBI Laboratory in Washington, D.C. aboard an Exxon jet.

Within hours, lab specialists had completed checked the letter and envelope for prints and fibers. There were none. They determined that an IBM Selectric II, primarily manufactured during the 1970s, typed the letter. The paper's watermarks revealed when the paper was produced and to what stores in New Jersey and New York the paper had been distributed for retail sale. Agents compared the letter and envelope with the ransom note found at Livingston Mall the day before. They matched. Agents checked them against those in the FBI's anonymous letter file, but found no matches. The command post also forwarded a copy to the Behavioral Science Unit at Quantico, Virginia, where agents Steve Mardigian, Gregg McCrary, and others would conduct a psycholinguistics analysis as part of their criminal behavioral study of the kidnappers.

The typed ransom letter was a long one—fifteen paragraphs. The first note had been twelve paragraphs. Not typical for kidnappers who tend to prefer brevity. It covered one full letter-sized page and part of another. The letter read in part:

We strongly believe that it is the responsibility of industry to create a new awareness of the hazards of environmental neglect. It is imperative that the destruction of the eco-system be stopped . . .

Our goal is to have several industries and major corporations contribute toward the achievement of this end.

. . . we are organized so that our pick up team know nothing about Reso's location or of the other team members. We have arranged a signal and if it is not received Reso's fate, as well as the fate of . . . 2 additional Exxon employees NOT NECESSARILY senior executives . . . will be your responsibility.

Any attempt to follow the money will result in immediate action. Attempts at electronic surveillance will have the same result.

The delivery will be done by Patricia Reso and her four children . . .

Assemble the money at the Reso residence. Distribute it equally into 10 Eddie Bauer large sport duffle bags.

They are to use the white Subaru station wagon for delivery . . .

Next, have a jump capable 9 passenger aircraft with an unarmed Exxon pilot at the private aircraft terminal at Newark Airport. The plane must be fueled and have a range of 1500 miles.

. . .

You will receive further delivery instructions.

. . .

Warriors of the Rainbow

FBI agents and Reso family members once again were pleased they had been contacted by the kidnappers. The first seventy-two hours after a kidnapping are critical, and the continuation of communication during that time is crucial. Once again, the letter chastised Exxon for its environmental transgressions. The note threatened action against other Exxon employees and boasted of their surveillance activity of the home of K. Terry Koonce, president and CEO of Exxon Research and Engineering Company at the Florham Park complex. Yet, the Koonces had not leased the house at the stakeout location since September 1990. In fact, Koonce was living in Houston and his wife was selling their home in Morristown when the letter arrived. The kidnappers had pulled the address from an out-of-date telephone directory.

"The fact that they offer these details as proof of their diligence and terrorist expertise again implies a certain naiveté if not even sloppiness of trade craft," remarked criminal psychologist Dr. Murray Miron. "However, the letter implies a singular disregard for life and the lack of any capacity for empathy," continued the respected independent advisor to the FBI. "I hold to the conclusion to treat them as psychopaths rather than demented ideologues."

Though the kidnappers again spouted several useless comments in the latest ransom letter, the note did provide further directives. The only question was when the exchange would take place. Everyone would have to wait for further instructions.

The FBI played the recording of the phone call for the Reso family in order to confirm that it was Sid Reso's voice.

"I can't be one hundred percent certain," Pat said, "but that doesn't sound anything like Sid." Her children agreed.

That concerned the FBI and the Reso family. Though they believed the letter's writers were the genuine kidnappers, they had not received a photo of Sid Reso in captivity or a recording of Reso stating that he was all right. The kidnappers had included Reso's Exxon credit card with the first ransom note, but that didn't guarantee that he was still alive. Yet, Reso *was* alive and being held only twenty miles away and it was his distressed voice on the tape.

The kidnappers read in the newspapers the following day that the FBI wanted proof that Reso was alive. Eager to pick up the ransom, they planned to record two more messages with Reso's voice to provide that proof.

Sid Reso was already in poor condition. It was May 1, which meant higher temperatures. The high of sixty-eight degrees that day would reach eighty-three on the following two days, an unusual spike at that time of year that would send the heat inside the metal storage unit soaring. A person who is not accustomed to elevated heat, like Reso who sat in an air-conditioned office, can sweat several ounces of water each hour. The kidnappers had been giving Reso a mere two cups of water twice a day, less than fifty ounces for the entire day. With the temperature inside the wooden box to approach one hundred degrees the following two days, more water and ventilation would be necessary for the fifty-seven-year-old executive with a heart condition and an infected gunshot wound to survive.

So far, the kidnappers had done their research and pulled off a successful, albeit sloppy, kidnapping. With the ransom drop only two days away, however, Sid Reso's life depended on his kidnappers taking better care of their golden goose.

* * *

This was not the first time an Exxon executive had been kidnapped for ransom. The one that garnered the most news coverage (until the Reso kidnapping) occurred in Argentina on December 6, 1973. To those at Exxon in 1992, the kidnapping case was hauntingly familiar.

In the early 1970s, kidnappings were occurring in many parts of the world, including two of the most famous: J. Paul Getty III, the Italian-raised grandson of oil-magnate and one-time richest man in the world, had just been taken in Italy. His family was negotiating with captors. Three months later, Patty Hearst would be taken by the Symbionese Liberation Army in California.

It was a particularly violent period in Argentina in 1973. Militant groups kidnapped or assassinated more than 190 individuals in Argentina that year, collecting $34 million in ransom. It was during this dangerous time that Victor E. Samuelson, from Cleveland, the general manager of an Esso

Argentina refinery in Campana, fifty miles northwest of Buenos Aires, was taken from the refinery cafeteria by a dozen armed and masked men. His kidnappers proclaimed to be members of the People's Revolutionary Army, a band of guerilla fighters who supported the Marxist-led Workers' Revolutionary Party in Argentina during the late 1960s and 1970s.

The guerrillas threatened to execute Samuelson unless they received $10 million cash, plus another $4.2 million in food, clothing, medicine, and other relief to be distributed among Argentine flood victims. It was the largest ransom ever reported up to that time for the release of a hostage. Though Italian mafia had initially asked $17 million for the release of J. Paul Getty III, negotiations had brought that figure down to about $3 million. Consequently, the $14.2 million demanded from Exxon for Samuelson seemed sensational.

Exxon countered with an offer to pay half, which only infuriated the kidnappers. Guerrillas led Samuelson out and stood him before a group of men shouldering long guns. Like a suspenseful Hollywood script, Exxon agreed to pay the full amount minutes before Samuelson would have been executed by firing squad. After 144 days in captivity, the guerrillas bound and blindfolded Samuelson inside a wooden box and dumped him on the lawn of his children's pediatrician on April 29, 1974. "It's not an experience I'd recommend for anybody," Samuelson said after his release.

Nearly two decades later, Exxon now faced a similar kidnapping, though this time the president of its international division had been taken on American soil; a rarity. Still, the similarities were striking. In both cases, terrorists demanded millions to be paid in used $100 bills. Guerrillas placed Samuelson in a wooden box and nailed the lid shut when they released him (though the FBI did not yet know the kidnappers were holding Sid Reso inside a wooden box). Samuelson was released on April 29; Reso was kidnapped on April 29. The similarities could have been mere coincidences, yet the FBI wondered if the terrorists were somehow connected or perhaps were copycats. Just in case, the Bureau researched details of the Samuelson abduction.

To the FBI's Behavioral Science Unit, however, there was something different about these so-called environmental terrorists. Their profile was beginning to take shape. Despite an exhaustive search, no one had ever heard of a group called Warriors of the Rainbow. An agent in Dallas had discovered in the June 1991 issue of *Outside Magazine* that a documentary, *Warriors of the Rainbow*, about the sinking of Greenpeace's ship, was being advertised for release in the spring of 1992. That's all there was on the subject.

Whether real or not, the FBI wondered if the Warriors of the Rainbow were as dangerous as they boasted. The People's Revolutionary Army had been a determined group of guerrilla fighters in a faraway country, but even they allowed Samuelson to read books and newspapers, draw, and listen to the radio in captivity. When he was released, Samuelson admitted he was fed and well-treated. But what about the Warriors of the Rainbow? Who were they and would they really murder and display Reso's body as threatened in the last ransom note? Would they kidnap or kill other Exxon executives as they claimed? No one knew and that's what made the situation seriously unpredictable. Even though Morris Township, New Jersey, was not Argentina in the 1970s, circumstances were proving every bit as dangerous for Sid Reso.

* * *

On Saturday, May 2, a pleasant breeze swept across tree tops inside the Morris Township neighborhood of Washington Valley while bright clouds drifted across a crystal blue sky. The hissing sound of water sprinklers on manicured lawns and birds fluttering inside trimmed trees greeted graying couples as they strolled along their subdivision streets in pleated white tracksuits draped with pastel sweaters. The days were getting longer, staying light until almost eight o'clock, and the temperature had crested at a balmy eighty degrees. Summer would come soon, a welcome relief from the harsh winter, which would carry the promise of vacations to the mountains and coastlines of Europe and to the faraway islands of the Pacific.

But as those same couples ventured down one cul-de-sac, the sky seemed to darken while the sun passed behind graying clouds as if afraid to shine. Even the birds seemed to restrain their songs with shushed beaks along this stretch of roadway.

Two hundred feet from the end of the lane on which typically cruised sleek German, Italian, and Japanese automobiles, more than a dozen boxy American-made cars, some bearing stark official insignias, still crowded the curbside and the driveway at 15 Jonathan Smith Road. The residence that once was as charming as any in the neighborhood now bore remnants of crime scene tape, a conspicuous hole that once had gripped a mailbox post, windows shrouded by blinds drawn during daylight, and heavy communication antennae braced atop an asphalt-shingled roof. Just like that, all the pleasantness of the morning had disappeared, especially with the sight of men shouldering large, black, automatic weapons standing guard in the shadows of the thick-wooded property. It was as if the strolling couple, who moments earlier were enjoying the color and beauty of the Land of Oz, had crossed into a black and white world of fear. With their nerves waning, they advanced their pace, tarrying no longer than necessary to escape this dreadful strip of Jonathan Smith Road.

Twenty miles west, a man wrested from that same neighborhood could only see darkness and endure the stinging sensations of thirst, hunger, and pain. He did not know when he'd be released to stroll about his own neighborhood again. The kidnappers had only told him "soon." Hours later, he perhaps thought soon had arrived when he heard a metal door rise and then close. It was 1:18 pm on Saturday, May 2. Sid Reso's fourth day of captivity.

The kidnappers stepped in with their faces cloaked by masks and their eyes concealed behind dark sunglasses. They left the unit door open a few inches. The Exxon president struggled to breathe in the fresh air. The smell of blood, sweat, urine, and feces had spread throughout the storage unit, and enveloped the kidnappers as they stepped inside. They worried that the smell might seep outside and be noticed by a Secure Storage employee.

The two masked visitors assumed their positions inside the unit and began their regular duties. It was eerily becoming almost routine. The man inserted the keys into the wooden crate's padlocks with gloved hands and the woman knelt in a corner mixing Tylenol and vitamins with water.

The two pulled Reso up inside the box and removed his bandage. His wounds were growing worse. Reso's arm showed clear signs of infection, an infection that had now spread throughout his body. The lead bullet had ripped pieces of cloth from Reso's suit coat and dress shirt and deposited the fibers along the inside of his forearm. The foreign material, together with lead and powder from the bullet, untreated with antibiotics for four days, created a serious problem.

The man wiped Reso's arm with hydrogen peroxide and applied a new bandage over the wound. This meager dispensation continued to be Reso's sole form of medical assistance. The kidnappers noticed that their hostage's forehead also exhibited fresh scrapes and bruising as though he might have tried banging his head against his coffin's lid in an attempt to alert someone outside. His hands also showed signs of beating and scraping.

"Here, we have some tangerine slices for you," said the man in a disguised voice as the woman held a slice near Reso's mouth. He could smell the citrus, yet shook his head and turned away, refusing the only food offered to him in four days. A simple milkshake from a fast-food drive-through would have served him better.

"Please . . . it's so hot. I need water."

"That's why we're here, sir." The man then shined the flashlight on the woman. "Give him some water."

Reso drank the first cup and then a second.

"We need you to make more recordings," the man said, withdrawing a small tape recorder from his jacket. "Two more, in fact. This is what I want you to say . . . " he began, ordering Reso to give directions to a restaurant in the nearby community of Summit. Still blindfolded with duct tape, the weakened Reso did as he was told. The kidnappers played back Reso's breathy instructions.

The captors were satisfied with the first message. "Now we want you to say something about the riots in Los Angeles so they know you're okay," the man said, again using a disguised voice.

A series of riots, lootings, arsons, beatings, and killings in Los Angeles ignited on April 29, the day of Reso's kidnapping, after a jury acquitted four white L.A. police officers involved in the videotaped arrest and beating of African-American Rodney King. The riots were still continuing that Saturday, though the U.S. Army and Marines and the California National Guard had been called in to restore order. In fact, national news coverage of Reso's kidnapping had taken a back page to the riots that were consuming print space and the airwaves. Gary Penrith, Special Agent-in-Charge of the FBI's field office in Newark, had been in Los Angeles when the riots broke out and his duties there prevented his return to direct the investigation of the Reso case until Saturday, four days after the kidnapping.

Because Reso knew nothing of the riots, the kidnappers told him what had been splashed across the newspapers and television screens and coached him on what to say. He repeated it into the recorder.

Sid Reso tried to speak to the kidnappers. He surely reminded them of the intense heat, the difficulty breathing with tape over his mouth, and the effects of the gunshot. The male kidnapper didn't want to talk to Reso unless absolutely necessary; to do so required him to disguise his voice and created the risk that he might accidentally give away clues to their identities or location. The woman never spoke.

"When can I go home?" Reso asked. He sounded weak and ill. "You said soon."

"Yes, soon, maybe even tomorrow," the male kidnapper replied.

Reso nodded. "Hot . . . It's—"

The man pulled tape from the roll and placed it over Reso's mouth. The conversation was over. He lowered Reso's shoulders and head into the box. Reso grunted in pain. The kidnappers then exited the storage unit to put their plan for the ransom drop into motion.

The male kidnapper had told Sid Reso the truth. Once payment was safely received, they would release him the next morning; at least, that was their intention, so they said. First, they needed a rental car, something plain like a Chevy in a lackluster brown or maroon color. They didn't want to drive their white Mercedes-Benz or white Jeep. Someone might spot them in the area of the drop. Unable to find a rental car locally, the kidnappers drove fifty miles east to Newark International Airport and parked. When the kidnappers approached a car rental counter, a representative of the agency explained that they couldn't rent a car to a local resident who didn't have a return plane ticket. Frustrated, the kidnappers abandoned their plan to obtain the ransom money that night. They would have to wait until Sunday, and so would a languishing Reso.

Before they retired for the evening, the kidnappers returned to Secure Storage presumably to give Sid Reso water and change his bandages again, but their trip had taken longer than expected. The man rolled down the Mercedes' window and attempted to enter the code into the gate's keypad. It was denied. He tried again. It was denied again. He then realized that it was nearing ten o'clock. The self-storage compound closed at nine. He backed out and drove on.

The two kidnappers ate dinner at their hideaway later that night, watched some television, and went to bed, nervous, yet excited about their plans for the ransom drop and hostage release the following night. Though sleep initially came with difficulty, the kidnappers dozed off with full stomachs on a comfortable bed in a room with a pleasant temperature. It had been nine hours since they gave Sid Reso water and it had been a warm day. It would be another thirteen hours before they would enter storage unit 619. Their $18.5 million hostage would just have to survive the best he could until then.

* * *

When the armored truck arrived at the Reso home that Saturday to unload three trunks full of four hundred pounds of $100 bills into the garage, the Brinks driver asked Agent Tom Cottone to sign a receipt for the $18.5 million of cash as they stood on the Reso driveway. The agent refused to accept the unique home delivery until the money could be counted. It would take nearly six hours for four agents to count the money, divide it into bundles, package it in plastic, and insert $1,850,000 into each of the ten Eddie Bauer sport bags. The ten bags holding $18.5 million were placed in the corner of the Reso garage near a set of golf clubs and some fishing gear.

When Special Agent-in-Charge Penrith learned that the money was parked in the garage and several of the agents who'd been working long hours had been given Saturday evening off, he instructed Agent Walker to call in support immediately. Penrith didn't know if the Bureau was dealing with two or three kidnappers or a small army that could ambush the Reso home and grab the money.

Agents carried the bags of money inside and dumped them in a bathtub in a spare bathroom downstairs. According to Penrith, when he learned the money was in an unguarded bathroom used by federal agents and local detectives and officers, he grew fearful that the temptation to grab a package or two of money might prove too great for even the most honest of law enforcement. He ordered the money moved into the basement where SWAT and technical agents were posted. A log was maintained of who entered and exited and the times they did so. Penrith later recalled seeing the bags of money covered with an electric heating blanket. He was told that the money was warmed to make the bundles more visible from an aircraft using thermal imagery during a possible upcoming ransom drop. Overly concerned, Penrith called an engineering friend and asked if money could burn beneath a heating blanket. The friend laughed and assured Penrith the money would be just fine and snuggly.

Four of the ransom bags were green, three purple, and three blue. The kidnappers later specified that all bags had to be green, perhaps for camouflage purposes, or perhaps because green was their favorite color. Members of the FBI's Behavioral Science Unit found it revealing that the kidnappers had specified Eddie Bauer, a premium-brand. Most kidnappers simply say "bag," "laundry bag," or "case," with absolutely no interest in the brand. Agents took note of the odd request. They were formulating a profile of the kidnappers that was beginning to reveal an interesting theory.

* * *

Since Sid Reso's disappearance, Pat and her four children had been living under the same roof with forty to sixty agents and detectives, twenty-four hours a day. The command post with its tables, chairs, maps, boards, files, phones, computers, fax machines, and support personnel had continued to swell to the point that it had consumed most of the downstairs, making it awkward for Pat and her children. The upstairs where the children stayed and Pat's downstairs master bedroom remained off limits. But Pat preferred having the agents and detectives in her home where she could observe them working on her husband's case.

FBI agents and Morris County detectives were impressed each day with the family's fortitude and optimism, which made them want to work even harder to bring Sid Reso home safely, so much so that they often had to be ordered to go home and sleep.

Nonetheless, the endless waiting drained the Reso family both physically and emotionally—sitting about all day inside the home waiting for word about Sid, hoping that every phone call would bring good news, yet also fearing it might bring bad. Pat and her children continuously supported one another during this time. When one of them was weak, the others lifted that person's spirits. The family would pass the day consuming lots of coffee and tea and reading books and magazines. Of course, the television provided a welcome distraction as did music played from speakers throughout the house. Occasionally, they sat outside on the deck and talked, reminiscing or sharing their worries, while they pitched food to deer and raccoon.

On one of those early days, they shared their dreams about Sid as law enforcement carried out their duties around them. One daughter told her mother and siblings how she'd asked her father during a dream, "Are you being beaten up or anything?" She said replied, "Well, a little, but you know it's not so bad, please don't worry." Another daughter described a dream where Sid said, "Mom has always wanted me to grow a beard. Well, maybe she'll be happy now." Everyone laughed. Pat also joined in. "I was talking to your father on the telephone and I told him that we all loved and missed him and he told me that he was fine and would see us soon . . . And last night I dreamed your father and I were having dinner at the Grand Café. We were having such a wonderful time there. It's our comfort place."

Desmond Lloyd, owner of the Grand Café, a French restaurant in Morristown, would have agreed with Pat. "Mr. and Mrs. Reso are a lovely couple," Lloyd told reporters. "Nothing pretentious about them at all . . . They often come in on Friday evenings and sit at a table near our classical pianist . . . They hold hands. I would say they seem to be very much in love."

Undeniably, the Resos were very much in love. They'd met while attending a Catholic Youth Organization dance in high school at the age of seventeen. Within a month they were going steady, and four years later, they married when Sid was a junior at Louisiana State University. They'd raised five children: two sons and three daughters, and they'd moved around much of the world, taking their children with them. And they'd helplessly watched and cared for their older son as he succumbed to AIDS in March 1987, one month after famed pianist, Liberace, died of the disease. Pat stayed with her dying son every day and Sid stayed with him every weekend. And when Pat spent months in bed in a body cast after surgery to correct her scoliosis, Sid visited her every day, except when he was out of the country. Through it all, the good and the bad, they had remained close and loving. Pat believed this ordeal would be no different; and no one praised Sid more than Pat.

"Sid's always been there for his family. He was there when all five of our children were born, through all of their illnesses, and the important moments in their lives. And no matter how busy he is, he comes home from the office every day, and he goes with us on every vacation. He enjoys his family around him."

Obviously worried and upset as they sat sharing stories, they truly believed Sid would be home soon. Though the family had lived for years with the possibility that their husband and father could be kidnapped and held for ransom, that had been while living abroad and even then it had seemed like a remote possibility. After all, he'd worked in England and Australia; not exactly hotbeds of terrorist activity.

Pat went to bed that evening and wrote an entry in her diary. She still wrote twice each day; once after her meditation session in the morning and then before she retired to bed. Each night, she'd also say a prayer for Sid. She prayed as sincerely and passionately as anyone could for her husband's health and safe return. She'd then doze off. Her last waking thoughts were always of Sid, and she'd continue to think of him in her dreams. He was never far away.

Pat didn't realize it, but her husband also wasn't physically far away. Inside the dark, warm space of unit 619 at the Secure Storage facility just outside of Hackettstown, twenty miles from the Reso home, lay a wooden box in the center of a concrete floor that for four days and nights, Wednesday through Saturday, had served as Sid Reso's tomb of torture. He had been isolated and alone, essentially buried alive—unable to see, barely able to breath, lying in filth, hungry, thirsty, hurting, worrying, and despondent. Most likely, he spent most of his waking hours worrying about his family.

As Saturday night turned to morning, the tomb was warm and quiet. Sunday would present everyone with excitement and challenges.

Chapter 3

It was Sunday, May 3—ransom day. The kidnappers slept in, ate breakfast, and then the female kidnapper drove ten miles to Aries Rent-a-Car in Hackettstown, arriving around 10:30 a.m. She rented a red 1991 Chevrolet Lumina, plate number GRI82U. From there, she drove a short distance and picked up her partner before passing through the Secure Storage gate at 10:55 a.m. They wanted to give their water/vitamin/Tylenol concoction to their hostage, change his bandages, and let in some fresh air before putting their plans into action that day. It had been twenty-one hours and forty minutes, almost a full day, since they'd last attended to their hostage held in solitude. No fresh air; no water.

The Mayo Clinic reports that generally a person should drink sixty-four ounces of water each day, but hot conditions and fever can increase a person's need for fluids substantially. The kidnappers had given Sid Reso a paltry two cupfuls, or sixteen ounces, of water over the last forty hours and thirty-six minutes, with only a few minutes of fresh air during that time. Whether or not they realized it, the kidnappers had employed "hot box torture," a form of punishment sometimes inflicted on prisoners of war in violation of the Geneva Conventions, the brutality of which has been portrayed in several films. They'd done so by forcing a wounded and feverish fifty-seven-year-old executive with a heart condition into solitary confinement inside a box, within a poorly ventilated and hot metal shed, with no food, no medical care, and virtually no water. Their inattention and seemingly indifference so far had inflicted unimaginable pain and suffering on a man valued at $18.5 million to the kidnappers, who were worth only about $200 themselves.

But it was Sunday and they were there now. By Monday morning, they figured their captive and the wooden box would be gone, replaced by ten large green Eddie Bauer bags full of green money. The idea that they could be extremely rich by morning made them both excited and nervous. It had been five days since taking Sid Reso and their plan had called for the swap to be made the night before, but they'd been unable to rent a car. It was still the weekend, however, and that meant they were on schedule. Despite a serious case of butterflies, they were confident in their plan's success.

The FBI was just as confident in its plan's success. And unlike the kidnappers who were attempting their first ransom exchange, the FBI is an agency of professionals, experienced at successfully resolving innumerable kidnappings throughout the world. There is little that the FBI hasn't seen before, and the Bureau wanted to send a clear message to criminals and terrorists that snatching someone in the United States for ransom could never succeed.

FBI agents continued their preparations while awaiting word from the kidnappers. The latest ransom note had demanded that the ransom money be placed in ten Eddie Bauer bags, which the FBI had already done. Only agents did one better. With permission from a federal magistrate, agents planted tracking devices in the linings of the bags and in some of the bundles of money.

The ransom note also demanded that when the kidnappers gave the signal, the money must be delivered in a white Subaru wagon (they mistook Reso's VW wagon for a Subaru). More tracking devices were planted inside the station wagon and also in the cellular phone that the FBI used to speak with the kidnappers.

The kidnappers had also demanded that a nine-passenger aircraft with jump capability be fueled and ready at the private aircraft terminal of Newark International Airport. The FBI believed the kidnappers might use the plane to escape with the bags of money on board, or require someone to toss the bags of money out of the plane at a designated location. Perhaps they might even parachute out with the money midflight as the infamous skyjacker, D.B. Cooper, had done in 1971. After some consideration, however, the FBI largely disregarded the demand for a plane, believing it to be purely diversionary. Sensible criminals would never risk being exposed on an open tarmac within the crosshairs of FBI snipers. And an airdrop could easily be tracked.

Special Agent-in-Charge Penrith and Agent Walker explained the Bureau's plan to Pat Reso and though she understood there were risks, she believed she had no other choice. She also believed Sid would have told her to trust the FBI. And so, the family anxiously waited with FBI agents and county detectives for the kidnappers to signal that the exchange was on.

* * *

"MERCEDES TEAR GAS SYSTEM HURTS 15 AT MORRISTOWN DEALER," read the headline in *The Star-Ledger* soon after Sid Reso's kidnapping. A 1992 Mercedes-Benz sedan owned by a consumer finance company was undergoing routine maintenance at a Morristown dealership when canisters of CS tear gas in the front and rear wheel wells and a smoke bomb in the rear inadvertently dropped and exploded.

Sid Reso had been offered a daily limousine driver, but most often refused it. For him, protection wasn't really necessary in New Jersey, U.S.A. Though Exxon refused to comment on its security measures, Reso's limousine driver likely would have been armed and trained in the detection and avoidance of assault and kidnapping situations. His most frequent driver, Del Miller, claimed to be a former state patrol officer with military experience. At a minimum, the limousine would have been equipped with a phone to alert company security and local police in the event of a threat.

"If I want to kidnap you, I watch your house and office. It is that simple," says Fred Burton, a former State Department special agent who is chief security officer at Stratfor in Austin, Texas. "Unless you are looking for pre-operational surveillance, you will never see it."

That's exactly what happened to Sid Reso. Perhaps he had become a bit too relaxed in his routine. He hadn't noticed that the kidnappers jogged past his house, and also parked a van down the street. The female kidnapper had even kicked Reso's newspaper to the passenger side of the driveway on more than one occasion, including the morning of the kidnapping.

For a busy executive like Sid Reso with many things on his mind, however, those seemingly innocuous actions could easily have been overlooked. That's why it would have been best to use Exxon's trained driver. "For the most part," Burton points out, "executives are creatures of habit, pre-occupied with business and oblivious to their surroundings. Predictable patterns and habits can be deadly."

Special Agent-in-Charge Penrith later used Sid Reso's actions and inactions as a teaching aid that he called, "Lessons Learned for Corporate Management." In it, among other things, Penrith pointed out that companies should expand their use of drivers for top corporate management and must do a thorough background check of all drivers either by their own corporate security or through an extremely reputable agency.

While Sid Reso lay inside what surely resembled a coffin to him, he likely wished he'd used an Exxon driver. Though he was in no way to blame, the Exxon executive may have felt a bit guilty that if he had been more observant of the danger signs, his wife and children would not be going through agonizing worry. But it was too late for Reso; he'd already been snatched. There was nothing he or Exxon could do to wind back the clock. Yet, other companies and their executives could and that's why the Mercedes that accidentally gassed a car repair shop had been equipped with tear gas and smoke bombs. Companies everywhere, nationally and internationally, were hiring security consultants and reevaluating their existing security measures — especially Exxon.

"Tragedy forces behavioral change," noted Burton, "like company-mandated security programs."

Indeed, many U.S. companies began providing their most valuable executives with James Bond-type limousines that ordinarily would be used in kidnapping hot spots outside the United States. The vehicles were equipped with emergency alarms, bullet-proof glass, armor-plated door and floorboard inserts, run flat/self-sealing tires, fuel tank protection, tear gas and smoke bomb releasing mechanisms, and possibly even road tack dispensers and electrified door handles. These super-vehicles were driven by security-trained individuals equipped with firearms and special communication devices, who could evade would-be kidnappers or otherwise escape from a dangerous situation quickly.

Because Reso's kidnappers had threatened in more than one ransom letter to kidnap or harm other Exxon executives, like Terry Koonce, Exxon International beefed up its security in several ways, including the hiring of local off-duty police officers to guard not only the Reso home, but the Koonce houses in Houston and Morristown, as well as the homes of other Exxon executives, and even the renter of Koonce's former home. "They sign up for it, just like when King's Food Market needs someone directing traffic," Morris Township Deputy Police Chief Ed Rochford said.

Local officers were accustomed to providing extra security not only for executives, but for celebrities like Whitney Houston, who lived in nearby Mendham, ten miles from the Reso home. Several officers had already volunteered to work Whitney Houston's wedding to Bobby Brown at Mendham that July, where security would be heightened as a result of the Reso kidnapping.

Exxon was doing a lot more than guarding executive homes,

which according to FBI notes included checking the backgrounds of everyone at Exxon, even "down to the parking lot attendant." But Exxon wasn't broadcasting exactly what those increased security measures were. "It's not security if you talk about it," Exxon public information officer, Jim Morakis, said. "If there's somebody out there like Sid Reso's kidnappers—God forbid there is—anything we say might be helpful to that individual."

Companies that had not already increased security for their high-level executives would soon do so when, amazingly, four weeks after Sid Reso's kidnapping, Charles Geschke, co-founder of the multinational software giant, Adobe Systems Incorporated, would be kidnapped at gunpoint from the company's parking lot in Mountain View, California. Geschke would be held for four days before the FBI freed him and arrested the two kidnappers.

Unlike Geschke's kidnapping, four days had already passed and Sid Reso had not yet been freed. The FBI still believed it would get its chance. Indeed, it would. The kidnappers would be calling again on the fifth night.

* * *

It was time. The man and woman left Secure Storage that Sunday morning to run some kidnapping errands. The man returned in the Chevy Lumina at 12:34 p.m. followed by the woman four minutes later in the Mercedes. They brought with them cleaning products and other supplies they'd picked up at a Jamesway discount store in Washington Township.

The big man lifted Sid Reso out of the box and stripped him of his soiled and smelly clothes. It was the first time Reso had been out of the box since the first day of the kidnapping. He'd been in the same clothes since they snatched him, yet they still hadn't brought him a change of clothes. Instead, they left him in his disgusting underwear, crusted in feces and dried urine and sweat. The smell was almost more than they could endure.

The two began sponging and wiping him down. Lying on the concrete floor outside the box, the kidnappers could clearly see how much Reso's complexion had turned pale or even gray. It was then that the female kidnapper wanted to end it, maybe telephone Reso's family and give directions to where they could find him. However, after she and her partner discussed it in the Mercedes out of sight of Reso, they decided to continue with their plan. So, after they'd finished cleaning Reso, they began cleaning up the storage space. The unit's door remained open a few inches above the concrete floor to circulate fresh air and help dissipate the odor of chemicals.

The kidnappers were jittery and frazzled that morning as they cleaned; even more so than usual. Still, they were optimistic. The two had spent weeks talking about how they'd spend the money. Perhaps a mansion on the bay in Hilton Head with an enormous sailboat moored at a private marina like they once owned, and new white his-and-hers Mercedes just as before. There'd be country club memberships and travel to Europe. Maybe they'd sail around the world. And no more cleaning; there'd be plenty of household servants and gardeners to whom they'd be benevolent yet firm, lest they be taken advantage of.

When they were done, the kidnappers left Reso inside while they carried out garbage bags stuffed with dirty clothes, empty water bottles, plastic cups, wrappers, and used bandages they'd gathered while cleaning. They'd burn them later, but first, it was time to put their ransom drop plan into action. Reso would not be coming out; not yet.

The Mercedes followed far behind the rented Lumina as the two kidnappers drove to an Exxon station (now a Raceway) in Summit, New Jersey. The man pulled into the station as the woman drove past and parked nearby where she could watch him. He adjusted the volume on a small tape recorder so that Sid Reso's instructions on the tape would be understood. Then he put on rubber gloves and took a deep breath as he stepped out of the Lumina in the dark. Traffic whizzed past him as he crossed the street, trying to stay outside the glare of street lights. Once across, he crept along a hedgerow and stuck an envelope in bushes in front of the Villa Restaurant (now The Broadway Diner). He casually walked back to the Exxon station where, still wearing gloves, he picked up the receiver of an outside payphone. It was 8:00 p.m. He punched the numbers 2-0-2-4-0-4-3-1-7-6 on the phone's touch-tone keypad as he nervously listened to the tones change with each punch of the phone's buttons. The cellular phone, manned by Agent Petersen still posing as Exxon public information officer Jim Morakis, rang twice and then—

"Hello?"

The man placed the tape recorder near the phone's mouthpiece and clicked the PLAY button: "Down Route 24 through Morristown, Chatham, Madison, to River Road. Take a right at the Exxon station on River Road. There's a restaurant off the street. Go to that restaurant. Go to a phone booth in the parking lot. There await our call." Sid Reso sounded out of breath and in distress on the tape.

"Please don't hang up," Petersen said with a Jersey accent. "We are trying to meet your demands. The quality of your tape messages are not clear. Hello? . . ."

The man clicked off the recorder and hung up the telephone.

The FBI tapped and traced the call as originating from a payphone at the Exxon station on 36 River Road in Summit, which sat directly across the street from the Villa Restaurant. Agents and local police sped toward the gas station. Apprehension wasn't the purpose. Agents wanted to trail the caller hoping he'd lead them to Reso.

Just before authorities arrived, the man hopped back in the Lumina and proceeded to the Summit train station followed by his female partner. In the parking lot outside the old-fashioned station with its deep-red brick façade and black shingled roof in a very busy part of downtown Summit, the man stepped out of the Lumina and taped the envelope containing the latest ransom letter to the back of the payphone. He next reached in his pocket to retrieve the cassette tape with Reso's voice talking about the L.A. riots. "Damn." He'd left the cassette in the Mercedes. He got back in the Lumina and drove to a nearby parking lot where the woman in the Mercedes waited. They rolled down their windows.

"I left the cassette in your car. Go back and tape it under the station payphone over the ransom envelope. I'm going on to Short Hills. You know what to do." Another train station was located in Short Hills.

"Okay."

The woman was frustrated and a bit worried. He was making mistakes. First, he'd shot their hostage in the arm and forgotten to leave the ransom note in the driveway. Then they'd made a worthless trip all the way to the airport the day before only to learn they needed a plane ticket to rent a car. And now, he'd forgotten the cassette tape on the night of the drop. But that wasn't the worst of it. He'd seemed so sharp and confident when he outlined the plan to her. They'd discussed it over and over and it seemed so simple, and with his background, she was convinced, and had believed in him, as she always had, but now—

She did as she was told. She went to the Summit train station and slipped her hand that held the cassette beneath the phone box shelf, pressing the duct tape firmly against the dusty metal.

Back in her car, she pulled away and drove a short distance to park near another payphone. By this time, the man had arrived at the train station in Short Hills, three miles away, where he also parked and waited in an unlit portion of the lot. Both kidnappers were now far away from the River Road Exxon station when FBI agents and county detectives converged to find no one near the payphone.

"Did you see anybody talking on that payphone there in the parking lot?" an agent asked, showing his FBI badge and pointing toward the payphone.

The cashier, customers, and even passersby who were asked that question may have thought for a second or two, but the answer was always, "no." Pressed by the agents, the cashier offered up maybe seeing a van, although he wasn't sure.

While agents and detectives remained at the scene to process the payphone, Special Agent Ed Petersen, posing as Exxon spokesman Jim Morakis, along with Special Agent Tom Cottone and Morristown Police Chief Robert O'Connor, loaded into Sid Reso's station wagon. As the car pulled out of the Reso driveway, it was trailed overhead by FBI aircraft. Special ops arrived ahead of them and stationed themselves in the area surrounding the Villa Restaurant to conduct surveillance.

Pat and her four children remained at home and waited as agents and detectives buzzed about the Reso house, coming and going, answering phones in the command post, drinking coffee and bottled water in the hallway, and slipping outside for a smoke, bringing the cigarette aroma back inside with them. All those with seniority were there, such as Mike Chertoff, Mike Murphy, Gary Penrith, and Jere Doyle. It seemed a bit chaotic to the Resos, though the agents and detectives knew their jobs. Everyone in law enforcement had been working long hours and even volunteering for overtime. This had become a bit personal. Agents and detectives wanted to bring Sid home for Pat and the kids, and they wanted the kidnappers in jail. So, they waited.

Agents Petersen and Cottone with Chief O'Connor pulled into the parking lot at the Villa Restaurant, sitting on 55 River Road, a busy two-lane street, in Summit. It was 9:10 p.m. Agent Petersen exited the station wagon and stood beside the two phone booths located there. He was wired both electronically and emotionally. The temperature had dropped below fifty degrees and it was chilly. At first, Petersen leaned against one of the phone booths, then after a few minutes, he began pacing about while Agent Cottone watched and relayed updates to the command post. Everyone was tense.

Fewer than two miles away, the female kidnapper stood near a payphone at the Summit train station gathering her nerve to call the phone booth at the Villa Restaurant. In a few minutes, she'd make the call and play a tape recording of Sid Reso's voice directing Jim Morakis with Pat (not realizing they'd be Petersen, Cottone, and O'Connor) to an envelope in a clump of bushes outside the restaurant. A letter inside the envelope would further direct them to the Summit train station to retrieve yet another note and a cassette tape from underneath a payphone there. The cassette tape would contain Reso's voice discussing the L.A. riots to prove he was still alive, and the letter would direct Morakis and Pat to board the eastbound train carrying the cellular phone and the ten Eddie Bauer bags bulging with ransom money. Once on the train, they'd receive another call on the cellphone instructing them to disembark at the Short Hills train station just long enough to leave the bags of money on the platform and then reboard the train and continue east. The male kidnapper, who was parked in the shadows of the train station, would then drive up to the platform, load the bags in the Chevy Lumina, and leave, much wealthier than he'd been minutes earlier. When safely away, they'd call Jim Morakis and tell him where to find Sid — presumably.

That was the kidnappers' plan. The woman rehearsed it in her mind as she got ready to call the payphone outside the Villa Restaurant. This was it; the night they'd planned for six months. By tomorrow, they'd either be rich or behind bars.

Agent Petersen continued standing beside the restaurant phone booths waiting for the call while Agent Cottone remained in the station wagon with Chief O'Connor. A cold Petersen stomped his feet and clapped his gloves. Nine o'clock became ten o'clock. Passing traffic quietened as the hour grew later. It was forty-five degrees now and the lawmen anxiously continued to wait for the payphone to ring. Petersen paced about, trying to stay warm, eager to receive the call and catch the kidnappers. Ten o'clock became eleven and then midnight. The VW station wagon was now the only vehicle in the parking lot. A frustrated Petersen turned and looked at Agent Cottone and shook his head. Cottone relayed the situation to the command post and was told by Agent John Walker to wrap it up for the night. Something had gone wrong.

Exxon International Vice President Charlie Roxburgh, who was also at the command post, insisted that he be the one to tell Pat that the kidnappers had not called. The news devastated Pat and the children. The FBI had been confident and that confidence had inspired the family. Agents had not guaranteed success; nonetheless, they'd left the impression that the whole kidnapping mess could be over that evening. As Agent Petersen later recollected, "We were ready and waiting and waiting and then nothing. That phone never rang. We were crushed."

The last thing anyone expected from the kidnappers that night was silence. Silence couldn't mean anything good. Had the kidnappers lost their nerve? Had they spotted special ops watching the area? Had something happened to Sid?

Everyone that night wondered what could have gone wrong. Strangely, so did the kidnappers.

The answer was simple.

Chapter 4

Monday morning was not embraced by the Reso family, yet the sun still rose, the birds still sang, and regrettably, the smell of nicotine and aftershave lotion still filled the air inside the Reso home. Pat and her children had expected Sid to be sitting with them in the living room that morning, praying, drinking coffee, sharing the story of his ordeal while exchanging hugs and kisses in a home occupied only by Resos. But Sid was not home and the house was still buzzing with agents, detectives, and officers. Everyone in the Reso house that morning was disheartened over the failure to make contact with the kidnappers at the Villa Restaurant the night before. No one could understand what had happened.

The kidnappers believed they knew what had happened: the FBI bungled the job. The female kidnapper had punched in what she believed was the number for the restaurant payphone shortly after nine o'clock the night before. When no one answered, she'd tried again and then again, but still nothing. Frustrated and confused, she'd driven to a Chinese restaurant on Morris Avenue in nearby Springfield, New Jersey, southeast of Summit and waited in the rear parking lot. That was the prearranged location to meet her fellow kidnapper should something go wrong. When he didn't show, she'd started her car and drove along a highway while uneasiness gripped her by the throat. She pulled into a motel parking lot on New Jersey Route 22 in Springfield that served as their second prearranged meeting spot. She fretted while she waited. Several more minutes passed. Again, her partner didn't show. She tried to remain calm, but it wasn't working.

"I'm telling you," she recounted to her partner later, "I thought you'd been arrested for sure and that's why nobody was answering the Villa payphone. And I knew if you'd been arrested, it wouldn't be long before I was." She could see the frustration and anger building in his eyes, although it wasn't directed toward her. He believed the FBI must have gone to the wrong payphone or showed up too late to answer.

"I just knew they were coming for me," she continued. "But when I didn't see flashing reds or any suspicious cars, I left the motel and headed back to the Chinese restaurant."

And that's what she had done. Her hands trembled as she sped to their first prearranged location again while her lungs forgot to expand and contract. She at last exhaled so strongly that she'd fogged up her side window after spotting the red Chevy Lumina pass by with her male compatriot at the wheel. She was thrilled to see that he wasn't being chased or followed. He appeared to be headed to the motel, having missed her at the Chinese restaurant. She turned around once again and caught up with him at the motel. They rolled down their windows.

"Dammit, Jackie. Where've you been?" the man shouted. "Why didn't they show?"

"I called three times, but nobody answered," she replied.

The man shook his head in disgust. "You sure you dialed the right number?"

"I promise I did everything like you told me, Artie."

Confused and scared, the kidnappers decided the attempted ransom pickup was a bust and left for the night. Consequently the next morning, the male kidnapper believed it had been the FBI's fault.

It would be determined weeks later that his female partner had not dialed the number correctly. It was she, not the FBI, who'd bungled the job. She suffered from dyslexia. She also carried the telephone number of the Exxon station across the street from the Villa Restaurant with other phone numbers, including the restaurant's number. The phone numbers for the Exxon station and the Villa Restaurant were, according to Agent Tom Cottone, a single digit apart. Cottone recalled hearing the payphone at the Exxon station ringing, but Petersen didn't want to leave his assigned post at the Villa payphone.

But for her mistake, it is likely that the kidnappers would have been captured that night and the entire matter would have been over on Sunday, May 3. It would be just one of many fortuitous events brought about by the kidnappers' bungling. As a consequence, on that Monday morning, the kidnappers were not rich, Sid Reso was not home, and everyone was rattled.

* * *

A fire blazed along the banks of the Musconetcong River on the night of Sunday, May 3, exposing a large man's silhouette as he tossed wood and bundles into the budding flame five miles away from Secure Storage. He also pitched objects into the river. The man stared into the flames and reassured himself that he'd conceived a masterful plan, and that he was a smart man with experience. Yet, if that was true, why were so many things going wrong?

The kidnapper tossed more objects into the fire and watched as red cinders spiraled upward into the cool night air. Was his plan going up in smoke, too?

* * *

Three days had passed since the unsuccessful ransom exchange at the Villa Restaurant and no one could describe to Pat's satisfaction that Wednesday why the kidnappers had been quiet during those three days. Special Agents Walker and Chapman tried to explain that the FBI hadn't spooked the kidnappers at the Villa Restaurant Sunday night, though it proved to be of little consolation. Later that day, Gary Penrith, Special Agent-in-Charge of the FBI field office in Newark, arrived at Pat's home to discuss the status of the case and, just as important to Penrith, to show he cared. Penrith would later admit in a letter, "In more than twenty-four years of law enforcement, I cannot recall being part of any investigation which touched me personally in the same fashion as this case did."

After a few observations about the morning weather and the traffic, Penrith turned to the reason he was there. "I know this is difficult and I realize being patient is easier said than done, Mrs. Reso, but we cannot assume that just because the kidnappers are quiet, your husband has been harmed. There're a number of likely reasons for this pause."

"I've been racking my brain thinking of possibilities," Pat said, looking directly at Penrith, "but most of them are not good."

"I can tell you that there could be legitimate reasons, at least in the minds of the kidnappers. Simple fear of apprehension for one. They could have gotten cold feet at the last minute."

"Well . . . I—"

"Maybe they saw something that spooked 'em and they want to lay low until things cool off." Penrith took a sip of a soft drink that Pat had offered him earlier.

"Well, maybe," Pat said, sounding exhausted.

"And you know, it could be as simple as a kidnapper got sick. What I'm trying to say is it could be almost anything. It doesn't necessarily mean anything nefarious." Penrith knew, but did not say, it could as easily mean something bad, very bad.

"I know," Pat said shaking her head in agreement, though sounding unconvinced.

Penrith placed a hand on her shoulder and gave her a pat. He looked up and saw a painting on the wall, a framed reproduction. "You know, the original is in the Louvre in Paris," he remarked. Pat glanced up with surprise. Penrith's private art collection, including pieces adorning the walls of his Newark office, rivaled those in some small museums.

In fact, Gary Penrith may have been the most unique FBI agent in the Bureau's history. A man who inherited wealth created by his grandfather, Penrith joined the FBI in 1968 and was paid nothing compared with what he could have earned in the private sector. Despite the hard work and low pay, he was a dedicated agent. Some might say that Penrith's sparkling Rolls Royce, later traded for a chauffeur-driven limousine in Newark, his gold Rolex watch, and his tailored suits that would make even Exxon management envious, would soften any sacrifice; but Penrith had chosen a career in public service and he was anything but soft. The forty-nine-year-old agent with graying hair and large eyeglasses may have worn a kind-looking face, but he had become one of the most outstanding investigators and administrators the Bureau ever produced. He ran the hard-hitting New Jersey FBI field office with resolve and an impressive record of arrests. He was not someone to be taken lightly.

When Penrith decided to join the FBI, he bounced about in his quest to climb to the top of the Bureau, much as Sid Reso had done at Exxon. He'd been assigned to field offices in Houston, San Francisco, Dallas, and San Diego, and had a stint in Washington, D.C., as deputy assistant director of the FBI's intelligence division. He'd also worked famous cases like the kidnapping of troubled heiress, Patty Hearst, the illegal activities of the Black Panther Party, and the mysterious skyjacking by D.B. Cooper.

Penrith had requested to be assigned to Newark, a place shunned by most agents despite being the sixth-largest FBI office in the nation at that time. While in Newark, he'd overseen the investigation and arrest of Giovanni Riggi, a Jersey mobster and one-time boss of the DeCavalcante crime family. His hard work paid off when he was appointed special agent-in-charge of the Newark field office in August, 1990 (one of only fifty-six field offices in the nation). Like Reso, Penrith was one of the best at what he did.

Penrith reassured Pat that Sunday night's disappointment at the Villa Restaurant had nothing to do with his agents or the Bureau. "Like I said before, it could have been anything, but try to remain optimistic. We'll catch these crooks and do everything to bring Mr. Reso home safely."

Penrith admired how strong Pat Reso had been so far; much stronger than most. He actually felt sorry for Pat and her family and understood what they were going through. He'd learned to empathize with many crime victims, drawing not only from his professional life, but also his personal life. In 1964, his father was murdered during a robbery in the garage of his Chicago home. In 1966, an attempt was made to kidnap Penrith's son, Alex, from their home. And Penrith's wife, Lynne, who'd worked in FBI support for eleven years, had been the victim of an assault. He knew what pain and suffering at the hands of criminals were all about.

When Penrith finished speaking with Pat Reso that Wednesday, she walked him to the door, though first, they stopped at the command post. With Pat standing beside him, Penrith praised and encouraged the agents and detectives for their long hours and dedication. Then he left; more determined than ever. The kidnappers did not realize it yet, but Penrith and his team were a group the kidnappers absolutely did not want tracking them.

Nonetheless, Penrith was experiencing tremendous pressure not only from the CEO of Exxon Corporation, but his boss, FBI Director William Sessions, and his boss's boss, U.S. Attorney General William Barr. If that wasn't enough, there was someone else even more powerful who wanted immediate results. It seemed that Sid Reso was a personal friend of another oilman who lived in Houston, Texas, though at that time the oilman was living in his second home on 1600 Pennsylvania Avenue— President George H.W. Bush. And President Bush, who'd once served as Director of the C.I.A. and knew something about gathering intelligence, wanted his oil buddy found, and found now.

* * *

The FBI continued actively investigating environmental groups. Though the Behavioral Science Unit had studied clues that were beginning to point the Bureau in a different direction, the FBI still considered the environmental language of the ransom letters problematic. The Earth Summit, a United Nations conference of 172 nations discussing how to reconcile worldwide economic development with protection of the environment, was being held in Rio de Janeiro in June. The references in the ransom letters to the summit couldn't be ignored. Consequently, the FBI command center in Newark faxed a general command to FBI field offices all over the country:

> WILL CANVAS ALL LOGICAL SOURCES RELATING TO ENVIRONMENTAL ACTIVITIES FOR INFORMATION ON AND CURRENT ACTIVITIES OF THE FERNANDO PEREIRA BRIGADE AND WARRIORS OF THE RAINBOW, AND EXPEDITIOUSLY FORWARD THE RESULTS TO NEWARK.

The FBI is always very thorough in tracking down and tightening loose ends, and operation SIDNAP was no different. The Bureau had to satisfy itself that there were not any terrorist groups that could harm Sid Reso or any other Exxon executive. The FBI would soon have its answer.

* * *

"DID ECO-TERRORISTS SEIZE EXXON EXEC IN N.J.?" read the headlines of the *New York Post* on Thursday, May 7, 1992. The newspaper went on to describe, according to an anonymous "top law-enforcement source," that authorities had received a ransom note and two phone calls from an environmental terrorist group calling itself the Warriors of the Rainbow. Someone had leaked the contents of the ransom letters.

Despite the news report, authorities maintained their strategy of keeping the public in the dark. "I've been involved in this case from day one," FBI spokesman Bill Tonkin declared, "and have no knowledge of that." Exxon spokesman, Jim Morakis, echoed the FBI when he told reporters, "I don't know anything about it." Everyone referred reporters to the Morris County Prosecutor's Office. Lois Ferguson, a spokesperson for that office, also claimed no knowledge. (Each morning, the spokespersons for the FBI, the prosecutor's office, and Exxon met to discuss the status of the case and their strategy for disseminating information consistently.)

Because of the details set out in the *Post* article, and the sincere concern for Reso's safety, Morris County Prosecutor Mike Murphy felt compelled to call a press conference outside his office. He stood before a swarm of men and women holding microphones and cameras:

"As you know, a New York City daily newspaper has printed unconfirmed allegations regarding communications from a group maintaining that they have Mr. Reso in their custody. Absent a current photograph or a voice recording, this office cannot reach the conclusion Mr. Reso is in the custody of any particular group."

"Furthermore, we believe it is ill-advised for any media organization to publish uncorroborated and unidentified sources of information about a matter which has the potential to affect someone's well-being. For this reason, you will appreciate that law enforcement authorities cannot discuss the progress of our efforts except to say we are exerting all our energy and resources to locate Mr. Reso. The Reso family has demonstrated great character and an inspiring depth of faith regarding the return of Mr. Reso. It is the desire of all parties that he be returned unharmed in an expeditious fashion. Thank you."

Reporters began shouting out questions, but Murphy refused to answer and walked away.

As difficult as it might have been for her, even Pat Reso maintained the ruse in order not to say anything that might anger the kidnappers and endanger her husband. It had been eight excruciatingly stressful days since Sid had been taken and, worse, four days since the failed attempt to exchange ransom for Reso at the Villa Restaurant. Pat must have been about to go out of her mind with worry.

From her living room, Pat sat erect in a high-backed chair with reporters kneeling and standing before her interested in her response to the *New York Post* story. She'd requested Exxon spokesman, Jim Morakis, with the FBI's consent, to set up the news conference inside her home.

Pat Reso was a thin woman with a long face and gray hair. She dressed conservatively and wore large eyeglasses that were the style at that time. She was reserved, though firm, and enunciated her words in a composed manner.

"Do you believe your husband has been kidnapped by environmental terrorists as reported?" one journalist asked.

"If, indeed, there is an environmental group involved," Pat began without any discernable emotion, "they should know his feelings and concerns about the environment. If they did, they would not have chosen him. His love of nature has been evident to us as a family, always." Reporters held their tape recorders closer as she spoke softly. "Sid has often told our children about his deep concern for the environment in connection with his work. He has said that to be outside in touch with nature is a great healing for him. And while at Exxon, he has always said, 'No business objective will take precedence over having respect for the environment.'"

"How are you and the family holding up?" asked one reporter. The question was cliché, but Pat answered graciously.

"Every day, there is a sense of something that takes over and you're able to do it," she said, sighing. "I can't tell you how the day goes."

The *New York Post* story had also connected Warriors of the Rainbow to the Greenpeace ship that had been sunk by French government agents. The *Post* had done so without accusing Greenpeace of any wrongdoing. Still, Greenpeace felt compelled to release an immediate and strong rebuke through its executive director, Steve D'Esposito: "For twenty years, Greenpeace has steadfastly adhered to the principle of non-violence. This tragic allegation does a real disservice to legitimate environmental organizations working to protect our global environment . . . As an organization which itself has been the victim of violence, we condemn the use of violence in the name of environmental activism."

Agents of the FBI's Behavioral Science Unit read the *New York Post* report that had become part of the investigation file in Quantico, Virginia. They were about to release their profile of the kidnappers.

* * *

The chain-link gate to Secure Storage slowly opened at 7:48 on Monday morning, May 4, as the male kidnapper drove his rented Chevrolet Lumina inside followed six minutes later by the female kidnapper in her Mercedes. Once again, she parked away from unit 619 and walked. The man opened the rented Lumina's trunk and removed some supplies. He unlocked the storage unit door, raised it, and walked inside, closing the door behind him.

The night had been cool and the day would be a comfortable sixty-two degrees. Sid Reso would have enjoyed the past weekend. The weather had been perfect for golfing, though being from the South, Reso had preferred fishing year round and dove hunting in the autumn. He'd fished for crappie in March and maybe some brook trout, although this time of year brought out the small-mouth bass in some of the local lakes and reservoirs, and that had been Reso's favorite fishing.

His kidnappers weren't interested in fishing. They were still trying to figure out what to do with the prize catch already in their net. They'd been busy the past couple of days revising their plans to get the ransom following what they still believed to have been an FBI mistake at the Villa Restaurant.

They left the storage facility later that morning and drove the burgundy Lumina one hundred ten miles on the Garden State Parkway to the southern tip of New Jersey. They took exit 58 and continued driving into the southernmost parts of Ocean and Burlington counties. It turned out to be a day trip to run what best can be described as a kidnapping errand. In fact, it was the most important errand since they'd snatched Sid Reso from his driveway.

The kidnappers returned early in the evening, but did not go back to the storage unit. Rather, they went to their hideaway and while the woman prepared dinner, the man burned additional items removed that day from the storage unit. The following morning, they returned the Lumina to Aries Rent-a-Car after thoroughly cleaning it, and then visited the storage unit in the Mercedes. Records show they entered Secure Storage at 2:01 p.m. that Tuesday, May 5.

While the FBI and the Reso family waited for any word, the kidnappers had no intention of contacting them—for the moment. They were busy amending their plans and convincing themselves to continue with the ransom pickup. If only Jim Morakis had answered the payphone at the Villa Restaurant, they thought, this would be over. For now, they'd lie low.

As the kidnappers zipped about south and north and back again for a week, doing things that only they knew at that time, Pat Reso and her children continued to wait for word, any word that might end their torture. As telephones, fax machines, and FBI agents and detectives harried about inside her home, Pat felt as if she could explode with the questions everyone wanted the answers to: *Why hadn't the kidnappers called? Was Sid okay?*

Rather than sit around the house helpless that Saturday, May 9, and wonder, Pat decided to take action. She asked Jim Morakis to contact *The Star-Ledger* and the public television program, *NJN News*, in an attempt to attract the attention of the kidnappers or anyone who might know where Sid was being held. It was difficult for her because she preferred staying out of the spotlight and was a naturally private and reserved person. With the help of Exxon and the FBI, Pat also requested NBC to script Robert Stack presenting the Reso case on an episode of *Unsolved Mysteries*. The network agreed. The episode aired four days later.

On that Saturday, May 9, Pat met a reporter with *The Star-Ledger* at the Delbarton School, a Roman Catholic prep school in Morris Township. Pat wore a plaid pantsuit and off-white turtleneck as her four children and Exxon security escorted her into the school. Her blue eyes appeared sunken and weary and her hair a bit grayer. At least this interview was for print, not video.

"My primary concern is his safety and return," she began telling *The Star-Ledger* reporter. "If someone has him, I need to know he's well and safe. Our need for him as husband and father is great. Please, I want him home."

"Please consider how much my husband's eighty-four-year-old mother has had to endure through this awful time," Pat continued. "I appeal to anyone who may know of his whereabouts: Please send him home. This gathering of my children here with me seldom occurs, as they live all over the country. Please allow him to spend Mother's Day with us all." Mother's Day was the next day, May 10.

"Sid is a decent, kind family man who thinks of others first. I can't understand why anyone would want to hurt a man like that."

When asked about her husband's health, Pat calmly

responded: "I worry a great deal because of his heart attack, if he's under tremendous stress, and if that's having an impact on his well-being."

In closing the interview, the reporter asked if there was anything else she'd like to say to the kidnappers.

"Yes. Our youngest daughter's graduation from law school is next Sunday. Please let him go to the graduation."

When wrapping up the interview, Pat and the reporter spoke about the fact that she and her children had terrific senses of humor and that had helped a lot. It didn't help, however, when on the following day, the *New York Post* published a cartoon of Sid Reso being held captive by oily seals and birds pointing a pistol at his head saying, "Alright Reso. I'm gonna take off the tape. But remember, no funny stuff." Pat was furious.

So was Exxon. Jim Morakis wrote the editor of the *New York Post*, rebuking his decision to print the cartoon. In his letter, Morakis wrote: "This shameful attempt to create humor from the disappearance of a decent and honorable man, with all the contingent pain and stress it has caused his family . . . sets a new low standard for journalistic treatment of such abhorrent events."

After her interview with *The Star-Ledger*, Pat returned home. The Channel 9 crew soon arrived, picked a cozy backdrop, and set up lights, microphones, and a camera. When everything was ready, Pat sat down for an interview with an anchor at *NJN News*.

"I'm taking things minute by minute, hour by hour, day by day," Pat told the reporter. "Yes, I do," she answered when asked if she believed her husband was being held by environmental terrorists. "I'm asking myself daily to forgive them, and I want them to know if somebody does have Sid, I have no malice. Let my husband come home," she said, speaking directly into the television camera.

After more questions, the reporter closed the interview with a tough one: "Do you think you'll ever see your husband again?"

Pat didn't hesitate. "He's got a strong faith," she began. "He's courageous, he's honest, and he's good, and so if anybody can survive any set of circumstances like that, it's Sid. Yeah, I'll see him again."

Pat Reso loved her husband and he was all those things in her eyes and the eyes of many. But it all depended on the kidnappers. She had done all she could that day. She hoped and prayed that Sid could be home with her and their children on Mother's Day. All she could do now was wait and hope that the kidnappers watched or read her interviews and would call to make the exchange.

The telephone didn't ring.

* * *

Special Agents Steve Mardigian and Gregg McCrary of the FBI Behavioral Science Unit were experts within the Bureau. Their specialty was criminal investigative analysis or what many refer to simply as criminal profiling. Though it had its rudimentary beginnings in the nineteenth century when London physicians attempted to predict the movements of Jack the Ripper, it was the FBI that made the discipline a useful analytical and investigative tool.

According to Agent McCrary, "The basic premise [of criminal investigative analysis] is that behavior reflects personality." To reach an opinion, the FBI profilers conducted a comprehensive analysis of the victim, the crime scene, the nature of the crime, the investigative reports, and all forensic and laboratory examinations. Still, specialists in the Behavioral Science Unit admitted that criminal profiling oftentimes can be more art than science. "Early on," McCrary later recalled, "it was just a bunch of us basing our work on our investigative experience [rather than empirical psychiatric data], and hopefully being right more than we were wrong."

The FBI profilers had been working for days on the Reso case, and despite the words and actions of the kidnappers, they were beginning to believe that most of those words and actions were diversionary. The profilers would soon report to the FBI field office in Newark that they believed the kidnappers were not international environmental terrorists at all, but were simply local amateurs. They would report that they also believed there were only two, maybe three, kidnappers, who were: Caucasian, suburbanites, middle-aged, most likely husband and wife with children and a dog, and in dire financial straits. The husband most likely had prior law enforcement experience, and may have even worked for Exxon. He also was likely narcissistic.

At first glance, some might think the profilers either had a crystal ball or they'd been working way too much overtime. Not so. After reviewing and evaluating everything at their disposal, the agents' conclusions were based solely on the evidence gathered so far.

These were first-time kidnappers rather than a group of trained terrorists for several reasons, according to the deductions of the FBI profilers. For one thing, they were perhaps the chattiest kidnappers ever encountered. Their ransom letters were numerous and lengthy and tended to be repetitive. Sid Reso's kidnappers also didn't want publicity. What terrorist group doesn't want publicity to shine light on its cause? Most take responsibility in the press not only for kidnappings or assassinations committed by them, but oftentimes for those they didn't commit. The kidnappers also seemed much more interested in money than their proclaimed cause. What's more, a chemically-treated blond hair had been found beneath the seal of a ransom envelope, and a dog's long brown hair had been found stuck to duct tape that held another envelope. Most international terrorists roaming about the globe kidnapping executives and otherwise wreaking corporate havoc don't regularly stop by the hair salon to bleach their hair or tote their pooch along with them.

The amateur kidnappers also lived nearby, the profilers postulated, because all phone calls so far had been made from payphones in the surrounding three-county area, and all ransom notes had been placed at obscure locations known primarily by local residents. The kidnappers also had demanded that the FBI publish the cellular number in a New Jersey newspaper, *The Star-Ledger*, rather than a newspaper of national or international circulation, like *The New York Times* or *Wall Street Journal*.

The blond hair indicated Caucasian race as did a linguistic analysis of the kidnappers' disguised voices and letters. Additionally, a neighbor had described a mysterious female jogger as white with blond hair, and another had described a man exiting a taxi on Jonathan Smith Road as white with blond hair and a beard. The descriptions seem to fit the profilers' emerging analysis.

Members of the FBI's Behavioral Science Unit suspected Reso's kidnappers were husband and wife because so far there'd only been two kidnappers, one male and one female. A local amateur couple is more likely to be husband and wife than males and females who are a part of a criminally-experienced and trained team. The profilers knew, however, that husband and wife teams generally don't commit violent crimes (Bonnie and Clyde weren't married). Instead, they tend to be involved in fraud and embezzlement, or other elaborate schemes to con people out of money. Still, they believed these were New Jersey husband and wife kidnappers who'd obviously gotten themselves into a financial mess and were looking for a big score, which pointed toward them being middle-aged.

Those in the Behavioral Science Unit also believed the kidnappers were living in the suburbs or were yuppies (slang at that time for young urban professionals). The ransom letter demanded that the money be delivered in Eddie Bauer bags. The kidnappers also were familiar with restaurants and other places frequented by middle-to-upper-income suburban dwellers. They figured the dog was likely a golden retriever because of the long brown dog hair discovered stuck to duct tape retrieved by the FBI, and because golden retrievers tended to be very popular among yuppies. The FBI began reviewing dog licenses issued in the area while agents and detectives canvassed local veterinarians, pet stores, and groomers asking if any had seen the blond woman or man depicted in the police sketches.

Narcissism is present in many criminals. The ransom letters' language indicated the writer's belief that they were smarter than law enforcement. Support for this conclusion came when, at first, the kidnappers warned not to get the FBI or police involved. After it became clear they were involved, the kidnappers nonetheless continued with their scheme. Their letters basically pushed aside any concern that the authorities were on the case and made it clear that they, not the authorities, were in control.

The most intriguing and perhaps frightening attribute of these kidnappers within the developing profile was that the male kidnapper had law enforcement experience either with a government department or a private security force. Language used in the letters indicated some experience with crime detection, such as the use of the terms "bona fides" and "prohibited left turn." Even more, the selection of Sid Reso and Terry Koonce as their targets could indicate the male kidnapper had some current or past association with Exxon. In response to this part of the profile, the FBI immediately ordered the seemingly impossible task of reviewing thousands of employee records, from top to bottom.

The Bureau's profilers likely would acknowledge that there was some gut instinct involved in the profile of Sid Reso's kidnappers. Some of their deductions could be incorrect or partially correct. For example, two or more kidnappers who are part of an environmental terrorist group could be holding Sid Reso inside a local motel room. That could explain the local nature of many of their actions; after all, they kidnapped Reso in Morristown, not in Pakistan. Just because the FBI had only heard from a male and a female kidnapper didn't necessarily mean that there couldn't be a third or even fourth kidnapper taking care of Reso at their hideaway. There could be several. Certainly, there were other possibilities. Nonetheless, those in the Behavioral Science Unit had carefully reviewed the evidence and believed that their evolving profile was correct—the only greener future this self-proclaimed environmental group was concerned about was ten bags of cash in their bank account.

Chapter 5

No one noticed the orange flames and gray smoke rising above a solitary trash barrel on the Musconetcong River bank or the large man stoking it. The property on which the barrel and the man stood belonged to Arthur L. and Daphne Seale, retired residents of a rural area called Changewater between Lebanon Township and Washington Township, New Jersey. Houses along the Hunterdon County side of the river are widely separated by acreage and cloaked by thick stands of trees that afford not only privacy for residents, but on this evening, secrecy for one.

The Seale house was among the finest along that stretch of river: a contemporary cedar-sided house with a brick, tiered patio, nestled on five acres and concealed along the heavily treed country road. The house's privacy rivaled that of the much nicer Reso house twenty miles away. Only a mailbox remained visible at the entrance to a long asphalt driveway that disappeared as it curled through large trees and underbrush toward the house's garage. The driveway entrance was recognizable to passersby only because a homemade sign with a painted white seal and a misspelled word stood near the mailbox that proclaimed, "The Seales of Possom Hollow," lived there.

"Tell Artie supper's ready," Daphne Seale said that night. She was Art Seale's mother and had worked many years as a school secretary before retiring. Now she performed community work, volunteered at the Red Mill Museum Village, and was a member of the Hunterdon Hills Garden Club.

Jackie Seale, who'd just returned from a walk, stepped out the back door and yelled for her husband to come in for dinner. She waited as she held the door for Brandy, the family's golden retriever. She could see her husband standing beside the light of the fire still tossing objects into the flames. He turned and waved.

"He's coming," Jackie told her mother-in-law, who replied, "What's he burning anyway?"

"Just some papers and stuff about a marina business he's thinking about starting. He doesn't want anyone to steal his ideas."

"The boy knows what he's doing, Mother," Art Seale's father, Arthur, remarked. "You can't be too careful with corporate secrets these days. He learned that on the force."

The elder Seale was an intelligent and quick-witted sixty-six-year-old retiree drawing social security benefits and a pension from the Hillside Police Department. Living beside the river, the retired policeman now spent most of his time trying to catch trout rather than crooks. He'd joined the Hillside police after serving in World War II and was well-respected in the community. He'd once headed the Hillside detective bureau before rising to deputy chief of police. His superiors and fellow officers said that the elder Seale was a "solid guy" who could have been chief of police if he'd not lost the promotion to a fellow veteran officer. As one neighbor described him and his wife, "They were the nicest people you ever wanted to meet. They'd do anything for you."

The back door closed and in walked Art Seale, a husky man at five-foot ten-inches and 200 pounds. He had sandy hair and at forty-five years of age still carried the look of the all-American boy next door.

Arthur Dixon "Art" Seale and Irene Jacqueline "Jackie" Szarko had eloped in September 1967. They'd both grown up in Hillside, New Jersey. She'd been a bit pampered in her youth, being the daughter of a family who'd inherited some land and operated Szarko's Liquor Store on Liberty Avenue. A "half-hearted" student who had "not learned to apply herself" according to some teachers, she'd attended Vail-Dean School in Mountainside where she began using the name Jackie rather than Irene in the ninth grade. She met Art Seale while he attended

Admiral Farragut Academy, a military prep school in Pine Beach, New Jersey (whose most famous alumnus is the first U.S. astronaut in space, Alan Shepard). He played football and she was a cheerleader. Both were athletic and attractive. He seemed intelligent, quiet, and a bit serious. Classmates in his yearbook had called him, "Dreamer," a label that still fit him in his forties. She was described by her classmates as "bubbly and chatty" and "a real sweetheart."

Jackie Seale had attended Boston University for a year where she was a homecoming queen finalist. She dropped out to marry Art Seale, but then went on to Kean College in nearby Union, New Jersey, and earned a Bachelor of Arts degree in education. She worked as a substitute teacher for the Chester School District for $35 a day, and then left teaching to work as a business manager and bookkeeper at Tewksbury Wine Cellars in Tewksbury, New Jersey, for $14,000 a year.

Not long after high school, Art Seale joined the Hillside Police Department in 1968 where he served as a police officer until he injured his knee chasing a burglary suspect. He resigned from the force in 1977 to draw a disability pension. Few had anything good to say about Art Seale's performance as a policeman. Hillside's mayor, James C. Welsh, who'd been the police commissioner during Art Seale's tenure, remembered Seale as an "aggressive cop" who received several reprimands and two suspensions. "I recall he used excessive force and used his gun on a number of occasions, certainly more than he should have." Once while trying to arrest a teenager, according to newspapers, he hit the boy's mother in the face with his pistol barrel for arguing with him. "He just seemed to have a low boiling point." Another time, he "roughed up a local man at gunpoint for a minor violation and scared the hell out of him," Welsh remembered. As deputy chief of police, Art Seale's father likely saved his son's job on more than one occasion.

After leaving the Hillside Police Department, Art Seale found a job in 1978 at Exxon International in nearby Florham Park working as a driver for its executives. He later accepted a fairly high-paying promotion at Exxon as a security supervisor and then security manager. He became a familiar face among Exxon executives and staff in the hallways. Exxon terminated Seale's employment in 1986 with a buy-out of his contract as part of a corporate restructuring.

"How's the job search coming, Jackie?" the elder Seale asked over dinner, who'd already talked to his son about his job possibilities.

Since moving in with her husband's parents in the fall of 1989, Jackie Seale had held a handful of jobs, such as a sales manager at the Four Sisters Winery in Belvidere earning $7 an hour, a receptionist at Title Lines in Far Hills, and a receptionist at Acres Land Title Company in Milburn for $425 a week. None of her jobs lasted long. Most recently, she'd applied for the executive director position at the Hackettstown Chamber of Commerce, although she lost out to a woman with more experience. Art Seale hadn't fared much better. In addition to his disability pension, he'd earned some money working at Intertel, a security consulting business, until he was eventually terminated. His three-page résumé exaggerated his qualifications, including listing a bachelor's degree in economics from Rutgers University. In actuality, he hadn't earned a college degree of any kind.

With little income, Art Seale relied on his parents' credit cards and their help to pay his son's college tuition bills and his children's medical bills, in addition to providing a roof over the heads of his wife and two children. Understandably, the elder Seale was frustrated with his son and daughter-in-law's lack of financial progress.

Art and Jackie Seale, with their two teenage children, had lived with the elder Seales since becoming deeply in debt to several creditors, including the I.R.S. With his son and his family seeking refuge in their home for the last two and a half years, the elder Seales had run out of patience. Four adults, two teenagers, and a dog in a one story, three-bedroom, and two-bath house with a basement was tough, especially when the elder Seales had expected to be enjoying a quiet retirement on a fixed income. So, in December 1991, Mr. Seale gave his son six months to be out of the house and back on his own supporting his family. Art and Jackie Seale didn't take the June deadline well. But now they felt they had devised a way out.

As everyone settled down for sleep that Sunday night, May 3, Art and Jackie Seale lay in bed in their basement bedroom. The nightstand drawer was filled with his latest reading: *Pakistan Travel Survival Kit*; *The Secret Money Market: Inside the Dark World of Tax Evasion, Financial Fraud, Insider Trading, Money Laundering, and Capital Flight*; and a *Wall Street Journal* advertisement, "No Income Tax! No Wealth Tax! No Questions Asked About Source of Funds! No Identity to be Disclosed!" Also inside the nightstand was a piece of paper on which he'd scribbled out a letter to be typed on the large IBM electric typewriter that sat in the corner of the basement.

Jackie Seale flipped through a magazine in bed beside her husband. "We've just gotta get out of here . . . Think we can still do this?"

"It'll still work. Nothing's really changed. Here, listen—tell me what you think," Art Seale said, opening the nightstand drawer and removing a marked-up sheet of paper: "We had hoped that it would not be necessary to hold Reso for a long period, but we may have been wrong . . ."

* * *

It had been eight days since the bungled phone call at the Villa Restaurant. The kidnappers still had not contacted the Reso family or Exxon to follow up on their ransom demands. According to Secure Storage records, they'd entered the storage unit five times since then, but whatever their reasons were for the delay, only they knew.

As a precaution and perhaps because it was believed that the money was no longer needed, a Brinks truck loaded up the ransom from the Reso house and carried the load of cash to Chemical Bank in New York on May 11 where it was deposited back into Exxon's accounts. The departure of the intended ransom money seemed only to intensify everyone's disappointment. Morale was at a low point. "Because Pat Reso sensed the feelings of agents in the command post," Jim Morakis recalled later, "they naturally tried not to show it, but after all those days, their mood was very low . . . The silence was so deafening."

Indeed, those days of silence were agonizing for Pat and her children, but she remained strong. Her faith supported her. She and Sid had managed to attend church weekly wherever in the world they happened to be, and now she attended daily. The Reverend Martin Rauscher, who formerly served at the Resurrection Parish Roman Catholic Church in Randolph where the Resos attended, said about Sid and Pat: "Some people come forward whenever you ask for help. That's the kind of people [the Resos] are . . . Quiet and low-key people who aren't interested in thanks or notoriety."

Pat Reso was an extraordinary person, but she was only human. Her husband had been missing for ten days now. During the first three days of the ordeal, the kidnappers had called three times and sent two letters, but then failed to call that night at the Villa Restaurant when it meant the most. Since then—nothing.

In her diary, Pat asked Sid how he was, where he was, and what was going on as if he could complete the following page with a comforting answer. Pat tried not to show her intense fear; but no matter how often Pat and her children prayed and buoyed one another with hope, dark thoughts kept creeping in, slowly attempting to pump the remaining hope out of them. Yet, Pat refused to cap her well of hope. Sid would be coming home—she knew it.

Days later, Exxon decided to offer a reward. After all, the Exxon corporate empire had more cash and assets than many countries. Exxon spokesman Jim Morakis released a statement to the news media on Wednesday, May 13, offering a "substantial reward for information resulting in the safe return of missing President, Sidney J. Reso." Two telephone numbers were listed. The hotlines would be staffed twenty-four hours each day by law enforcement.

"We're looking for help," Morakis told reporters. "We're asking anybody who has seen anything or knows anything to come forward. All we're doing is asking for the public's help."

When asked about Exxon's reward offer, FBI spokesman Bill Tonkin said, "That is an Exxon decision, made by the Exxon Corporation. The possibility exists, however, that it may aid our ongoing investigation into the mysterious disappearance and possible abduction of Mr. Reso."

"Is Reso still alive?" one reporter asked Tonkin.

"We have no reason to believe he is not," the FBI spokesman replied.

Despite contrary statements to the press, agents and detectives believed something catastrophic must have happened. The FBI had assigned more than two hundred fifty agents to the case who investigated alongside another fifty state and local detectives and officers, yet they'd been unable to uncover a meaningful clue as to the identity of the kidnappers. They feared Sid Reso was dead and the kidnappers had escaped, scot-free, never to be heard from again. They hoped they were mistaken, yet logic and experience pointed toward that terrible conclusion. Agent John Walker, who was still in charge of the command post, shared those fears with Pat, just to help her prepare for the worst.

Refusing to slow down, the FBI's New Jersey field office and resident offices continued working the ever-expanding Reso investigation, which included checking out more environmental groups and Exxon employees while still handling the office's other cases. Exxon International had provided the Newark FBI office with the names, addresses, phone numbers, and social security numbers of past and present employees, more than 10,000 of them over the last five years, as well as the vehicle descriptions and license plate numbers of those authorized to park in Exxon's lot. The FBI hoped that a connection between a disgruntled Exxon employee and Sid Reso would emerge. None did. (The Bureau would later discover that the five-year lookback at employee records had missed Art Seale's departure from Exxon by only weeks.)

It was beginning to appear that unless the kidnappers made contact again, the Reso case would fall into the cold files, ultimately to be forgotten.

* * *

Art Seale first conceived of kidnapping an Exxon executive six months earlier, in December 1991, not long after his father told him to be out of the family home by June. In his mind, he was desperate. The Seales had searched for high-paying jobs the last two years without success. They had skipped out on several creditors owing more than $700,000. They could no longer pay for their son's college or a therapist for their troubled daughter.

Despite their failures, their dreams of living the good life were stronger than ever. Art Seale considered crime as the best way out of his financial predicament, though he would later say that it was his wife who "suggested one desperate act" to get money. He considered robbing a bank or an armored car, but was afraid of a shoot-out, so he settled on kidnapping. He first considered executives from Allied Chemical and AT&T, but was unsure whether the companies would be willing to pay a large ransom. Seale eventually settled on an Exxon executive as his target. He had worked for Exxon where he'd learned the company's security measures used to protect its high-level executives. He'd recently telephoned former colleagues at Exxon inquiring into the company's current security, who obliged him as a professional courtesy among security men. But the primary reason Art Seale selected Exxon was because he'd read that Exxon had paid $14.2 million for kidnapped employee Victor Samuelson's release in Argentina almost two decades earlier — that meant Exxon would likely pay a large ransom again.

According to Art Seale in the FBI report, when he told his wife of his kidnapping plot that December, the mother of two teenagers agreed to join his scheme without hesitation. He would later say she was a "full and willing participant."

In January, the husband and wife kidnapping team commenced putting their plan into action.

"Jackie, go over to the library and find the home addresses for K. Terry Koonce and Sidney J. Reso. Then we'll go over to their houses and look things over." Most of the Seales' research on Exxon and environmental organizations was conducted at the New York Public Library or at the Hunterdon County Library near their home. They also had used the latest Exxon Annual Report to locate Sid Reso's address.

Once the Seales settled on Reso because of the secluded location of his house, they'd park their car in a condominium complex at the intersection of Sussex and Ketch Roads a few blocks away or at a dirt pullover on a curve along Gaston Road. From there, they walked and jogged up and down Jonathan Smith Road more than a half dozen times each in January and February 1992 to conduct surveillance. Jackie Seale usually wore a white or navy North Face windbreaker and black sweatpants while Art Seale wore a gray sweat suit. With their blond hair, tanned faces, and designer outfits, the middle-aged couple looked like every other neighbor in the wealthy community. Art Seale also hid out in a house under construction at the end of the cul-de-sac to observe the Reso home.

The two monitored what time Sid Reso left each morning and whether he drove himself or rode in a company limousine. They determined that when a limousine came to pick up Reso, the punctual limo driver always passed a specific point around the corner at 7:20 a.m. If he didn't drive past by 7:20 that meant Reso would be driving himself. The Exxon executive usually drove more often than not, typically leaving between 7:15 and 7:45 for the fifteen minute drive to Florham Park. The Seales noted that Reso always stopped at the end of his driveway to pick up his morning newspaper. He did so casually without suspicion and his routine rarely varied.

By mid-February, their plans had progressed. While Art Seale's parents visited their grandson at college, Seale went to Channel Lumber in Chester, New Jersey, and paid cash for plywood, two-by-four-inch studs, screws, nails, rope, eyehooks, latches, and locks. Jackie Seale assisted in building the wooden box in the garage while the elder Seales were away. As part of its construction, Art Seale drilled a series of air holes about the size of an index finger around the top and sides, spaced about six-inches apart. He and his wife lined the bottom with a sleeping bag and a pillow, with a blanket to throw over Reso. Then—

"We need to test it out," Art Seale declared. He stepped into the box, sat down, and stretched out, placing his arms alongside of him. "It's not so bad," he said as he wriggled. "Close the lid to let me see the clearance."

"It was confined, but not restricted," Art Seale would later say in an attempt to minimize the box's horror. "It was not a place you'd want to go to, but it was not a torture chamber."

When completed, the box's dimensions were six feet, four inches in length, three feet in width, and three feet, six inches high. The crude box was slightly larger than a coffin, though Art Seale repeatedly referred to it as a "secure container" that was the size of a "small closet," albeit a horizontal one.

With help from his wife, Art Seale slid the completed box

on blankets to the door of his parents' basement. From there, they slid the box down the stairs and into a corner where they concealed it with a blanket and boxes.

A week later, on February 22, Art Seale signed a rental agreement for unit 619 at Secure Storage. Then on March 31 while his parents had gone out for the day, Jackie Seale rented a white Dodge cargo van from Thrifty Rental in Bridgewater, New Jersey. The Seales pushed and pulled the heavy box up the basement stairs and outside into the van. They then drove to Secure Storage and unloaded the empty box into the unit. It had to have been a haunting scene—the coffin-like box lying in the middle of an empty storage space waiting for its victim.

As the FBI report later noted, the Seales planned "to kidnap Mr. Reso during the middle of the week, obtain the ransom payment by the weekend, and release Mr. Reso in an unpopulated area of northwestern New Jersey." To accomplish this, the Seales rented a van four times, on April 5, 12, 16, and 23, from different rental companies, including one in Hackettstown and two others in Plainfield, New Jersey. Each time, they drove to the Resos' Washington Valley neighborhood with the wooden box in the back and parked around the corner from the Reso house. There, they waited to see whether a limousine would pass to pick up Sid Reso that day. Each time, the Seales abandoned their plans when either a limousine showed or Reso did not drive away by 7:30 a.m.

On April 27, Jackie Seale rented a 1991 Dodge Ram van from Aries Rent-a-Car in Hackettstown using her mother's credit card. The following evening, Art Seale drove the van to Secure Storage and once again loaded the wooden box into the back. He also stole two license plates that night. Then on Wednesday, April 29, a day that Jackie Seale later recounted, "fit within the family's schedule," the Seales drove the van with the wooden box to Washington Valley at 7:15 a.m. and watched for the limousine. This would be their fifth and, as it turned out, final attempt.

When a limo didn't appear by 7:20, Jackie Seale stepped out of the van and jogged around the corner to pass the Reso driveway for a last minute look. She noticed the newspaper lying on the driver's side of the driveway. When she turned to jog back, she kicked the newspaper to the passenger side so that when Sid Reso pulled to the end of the driveway, he'd have to step out of his car to pick up the newspaper.

After returning to the van, Jackie Seale drove to the end of Jonathan Smith Road where she turned around in the circle and parked on the wrong side of the street next to a railing about two hundred feet from the Reso driveway. She and her husband could clearly see the garage door to the Reso home through the bare trees. They waited wearing dark masks, sunglasses, gloves, and long dark coats. Both were armed. At about 7:30, the garage door to the Reso house rose and Sid Reso backed out. Jackie Seale reportedly shouted, "There he is!"

That had been sixteen days ago. Sid Reso had not been seen since by anyone other than the kidnappers—and the kidnappers had not been heard from for eleven long days. Perhaps they'd decided to quit before they were discovered. But if so, where was Sid?

* * *

The kidnappers didn't know when to quit. At 10:30 a.m. on Thursday, May 14, eleven days after the Villa Restaurant failure, Exxon Corporation in Irving, Texas, received a letter. It was addressed to Exxon CEO Lawrence Rawl, postmarked May 12, from New York, New York. Executive secretary, Tamara Brazile, opened the envelope and was stunned to see the ransom note inside. Though she knew about Sid Reso's kidnapping, the Exxon offices in Texas had not been a part of the ugly affair in New Jersey. She immediately took the letter and envelope down the hallway to the office of Exxon president, Lee Raymond, since

Larry Rawl was not in the office that day. Raymond read the letter and instructed his secretary to connect him with Exxon security at Florham Park, New Jersey, who advised him to contact the FBI in Newark, which he did. Special Agent Stan Burke from the Dallas field office rushed over to Exxon and retrieved the letter. The agent then interviewed and fingerprinted both Raymond and Brazile to eliminate their fingerprints on the letter and envelope. The Dallas agent faxed the letter to the field office in Newark and forwarded the original letter and envelope via overnight mail to the FBI Laboratory in Washington, D.C. for analysis. All prints would be run through the Bureau's Automated Fingerprint Identification System (AFIS). There was no match.

The letter read in part:

We had hoped that it would not be necessary to hold Reso for a long period, but we may have been wrong.

We offered you the opportunity to end this quickly, but it didn't work. It is unclear [why] . . .

Tell Mrs. Reso that his pills were in a small white square pill box in his pants pocket. We have had no need for them yet.

Our council has decided . . . it is necessary to move Reso from your country. This has now been accomplished.

. . .

When you want Reso back . . . place an ad in the NEW YORK TIMES under Florida Real Estate stating "Central Florida Cattle Ranch, 160 acres call 201-404-6713" . . .

We will be in touch.

Warriors of the Rainbow

For a long time, Exxon had implemented security measures in its mailroom. It came with the territory. In Florham Park, mail was delivered at 7:00 a.m., 11:00 a.m., and 2:00 p.m. All mail was x-rayed before distribution to employees and, following Sid Reso's kidnapping, mail handlers wore plastic gloves. Reso's mail was opened and read by Exxon security before forwarding to Reso's secretary. After the receipt of the letter addressed to Larry Rawl, Dallas employed stiffer security measures for the distribution of its internal mail. The new protocols not only protected Exxon employees, but also preserved evidence related to Sid Reso's kidnapping.

The latest letter set out three key points. One, the kidnappers blamed the FBI for the "botched" exchange at the Villa Restaurant. This puzzled the FBI since Agent Petersen stood beside the twin phone booths that night as instructed, but no call ever came. Second, the letter informed Exxon that because of FBI interference it had been "necessary to move Reso from your country." Agents believed this was probably a ploy to avoid providing proof that Sid Reso was alive. The FBI also considered the possibility that this language really meant that Reso was dead; though it was still possible the FBI was dealing with eco-terrorists who had removed Reso from the United States. And third, the kidnappers instructed Exxon to place an ad in *The New York Times* to signal its readiness to pay the ransom for Reso's return.

Immediately, the FBI began preparations for another attempted ransom exchange. Three trunks of cash were again delivered on May 16 and the money was placed in a safe at a Morris County building guarded by a local officer. Helicopters and pilots went on standby. All recorders were checked and double checked as was all telephone tracking equipment. And as instructed, the Bureau placed an ad in the *Times* to run beginning Monday, May 18, which read:

CENTRAL FLA Cattle Ranch. 160 acs
Will trade—Current appraisal your responsibility
Previous offer not received
Call 202-404-6713

The FBI also dispatched Agents John Turkington and Richard Amato to the Summit train station to search for the cassette tape that the latest ransom note claimed was left underneath a payphone. Because Agent Petersen never received the call at the Villa Restaurant, the Bureau hadn't known to look for the cassette. They were anxious to retrieve it. Instead of finding an envelope with a cassette containing Sid Reso's voice, however, Turkington and Amato found only a piece of dirty duct tape dangling beneath the payphone's directory shelf. They checked with the station's lost and found, but there was nothing. The cassette was never located. The psychologist advisor to the FBI, Dr. Miron, astutely pointed out, "There are certainly additional ways of indicating the victim is still alive . . . [They] could send a picture of the victim holding a current newspaper." But the kidnappers wouldn't, and that troubled authorities.

Later that same day as the FBI addressed the specifics of the Rawl ransom letter, and before the FBI's ad appeared in the *Times*, the kidnappers made contact again. They'd been silent for eleven days, but now they couldn't shut up. Apparently, Art Seale didn't appreciate the headlines of *The Star-Ledger* published that day: 'NO DEALS' FBI wants proof of Reso well-being. The FBI and Exxon believed that no deal should be undertaken without proof that Reso was alive. As Dr. Miron put it, "The absence of some sort of definitive proof raises suspicions . . . of [the kidnappers] not having any goods to deliver."

So, at 3 p.m., from a payphone in the parking lot of the ACME Market in Washington Township, Jackie Seale called the reception desk at Rockaway Mall on Mount Hope Road in Rockaway Township, New Jersey, about fifteen miles from the Reso home.

A twenty-two-year-old sergeant with mall security, who'd filled in for the receptionist that day, answered the telephone.

"Welcome to the Rockaway Townsquare Mall, Rachel speaking, how may I help you?"

The caller answered, "Listen very carefully. There is a letter concerning the Exxon executive at pole number 33."

When the caller hung up, the security guard dialed *69 and *57 hoping to reach the caller or retrieve the number. Instead, she received a message that the call was out of the calling area.

The security guard telephoned the head of mall security who instructed her to contact the Rockaway Township police. Curious to see if the note was there, the guard went to pole number 33 in the parking lot near Macy's and spotted a white envelope taped behind a green New York Commuter sign. Patrol Officer Walt Ardin arrived and secured the area, instructing the head of mall security and two other mall guards to leave the premises. Officer Ardin also instructed two reporters from *The Daily Record* to leave the scene. They'd heard the commotion over a police scanner. Ardin retrieved the note just as it began to rain.

Rockaway police finally called the FBI, and at 4 p.m., Special Agent Richard Manning, Morris County Prosecutor's Office Detective Lieutenant Mark Prach, and Morris Township Police Detective Sergeant Nunn arrived and took possession of the note. The three lawmen spent the next two hours questioning anyone who'd spoken with the caller or visited pole number 33, which seemed to include everyone associated with mall security and management. No one had seen anyone taping the envelope to the pole or otherwise acting suspiciously in that area. Frustrated by the mall's delay, the FBI instructed the mall manager to call the FBI immediately should a similar situation arise. The same directive was issued to all shopping centers in the area. The New York Commuter sign was removed and the sign and photographs of fingerprints along with a brown paper bag found beside the pole were hand-delivered by an agent aboard an Exxon private jet to the FBI Laboratory in Washington, D.C. for analysis.

According to the security sergeant who received the ransom call, the voice sounded like an elderly female and was live rather than prerecorded. She also could not identify any noises in the background during the short call.

This ransom letter was addressed to "Mrs. Reso" and was the longest yet—two full pages plus a three-line addendum on a third page—atypical among professional kidnappers.

Like the previous letter, this ransom note scolded the FBI for the failed delivery attempt at the Villa Restaurant. This letter, however, provided Pat Reso and her children some comfort. It mentioned Sid several times in the present tense, using such phrases as, "He very much wants to come home," and "We sincerely hope that you and your husband can be reunited soon."

Pat's hope strengthened from the words of this latest note that she clutched near her chest. "The kidnappers wrote that they sincerely hope Sid and I will be reunited soon."

The letter did, however, describe several "setbacks." It blamed the FBI and police for interfering; for being more interested in apprehension than in Reso's return; for speculating to reporters that an environmental terrorist group was involved; and for failing to obtain a prior cassette tape of Reso's voice as evidence of his well-being.

The ransom letter closed with the harshest demand of Pat so far: "Mrs. Reso must immediately release a statement to the press indicating that she has received this communication. It must come from her and not the police or the FBI."

It seemed Pat's torture would never end. Though she confided in her children, closest friends, and priest, only she and her diary truly knew how torturous the ordeal was for her. Obviously, Pat wanted to do anything if it meant bringing Sid home. So, rather than simply release a statement to the press, Pat asked Jim Morakis, with the FBI's consent, to set up a television interview with Newark's WWOR-TV.

* * *

On Friday evening, at ten o'clock, May 15, Pat Reso appeared on Secaucus, New Jersey-based WWOR-TV, Channel 9, to read a statement. She looked directly into the camera, knowing the kidnappers were watching.

"I'm making a personal appeal to some people who I *want* to believe have my husband with them," Pat began calmly. "I know in my heart he's alive. I pray that he is healthy."

"I want you to know that I have received your message. But, it is important to me that my kids and I have assurance that he is safe and unharmed." This request had been recommended by the FBI.

"I am willing to do whatever is necessary to have him reunited with us. And I hope that he will be released very soon. I love Sidney and want him to come home to us."

Pat's voice remained steady and unemotional.

"Lastly, I am asking the news media to stop any speculation as to who you may be and what your goals are. I simply want my husband back with our family."

When she was done, she stood, unclipped the microphone from her jacket, shook hands and thanked everyone, and departed, escorted by Jim Morakis and a Morris County detective. She hoped her brief television appearance would satisfy the kidnappers' demand. It angered Pat that the kidnappers had forced her to plead for her husband's life, but she believed that soon she'd have Sid home and the kidnappers would be locked away where they couldn't trouble anyone again.

Two days after Pat Reso's plea on television, the Reso's youngest daughter graduated from American University School of Law on May 17 without her father present for the commencement. There'd been no word from the kidnappers. It was a bittersweet ceremony. She was close to her father and wanted him to be there to witness her accomplishment and to be a part of the celebration. "Wherever he is today, he's thinking of you," Pat told her daughter. "Your father would have been here if there was any way he could. He is so proud of you."

"I never thought Sid would be kidnapped here in America," Pat explained to reporters after the graduation. "As a couple, we never even discussed it, because neither of us was worried. Of course, security was always taken when we traveled internationally, but here, never, ever was it a consideration in our minds. Once we returned to the United States in 1978 after living in Australia and London, we never gave it a second thought."

That was very understandable; but it also was dreadfully unfortunate.

* * *

Another ten days passed without any word from the kidnappers. It had been twenty-seven days since Sid Reso was kidnapped; almost an entire month. Though Victor Samuelson had been held 144 days in Argentina, this kidnapping didn't feel the same. It was beginning to make no sense at all. First, a flurry of phone calls and letters received from the kidnappers and then eleven days of silence. Next, another flurry of calls and letters, including one demanding Pat's appearance on television, which she dutifully did, and then ten more days of silence. It seemed as if the kidnapping had become a sick game of cat and mouse and the cat had Alzheimer's disease.

Colleagues at Exxon felt terrible for Sid Reso and his family, yet a $117 billion multinational corporation with 35,000 employees operating in sixty-eight countries could not stand still. Reso had been responsible for all of Exxon's oil and gas production outside the United States and Canada, representing seventy-five percent of Exxon's total profits. The tiger's tail curled from Malaysia to Yemen and the North Sea. Exxon shareholders expected management to make certain that the company didn't miss a single barrel of oil drilled from an ocean platform, a gallon of gas pumped from a station, a Btu of natural gas tapped through a meter, or a loaf of bread sold at a convenience store. Shareholders and management weren't disappointed. Exxon made a *profit* of $15.5 million a day or $11,000 each minute in 1992. (While mind-boggling, compare that with an $86,000 profit each minute in 2008 and again in 2012.)

With the fall of the Berlin Wall almost three years earlier, Exxon moved to add drilling operations and gas stations all over Eastern Europe and even parts of Russia. "They are involved practically everywhere," said Alvin Silber, then an analyst for the now defunct Brean Murray, Foster Securities Inc. in New York. "Wherever oil is, you will find Exxon," another analyst said.

Since the day Sid Reso had disappeared, two executive vice presidents had run Exxon International. One oversaw upstream operations that consisted of oil and gas production, and another handled downstream operations that consisted of refining and marketing.

"Exxon has a deep bench, so if you lose somebody, you have someone to fill in," an anonymous source told *The Star-Ledger*. "Exxon, within the oil business, is regarded as the standard for all others," said Stephen Smith, then an oil analyst for the now extinct Bear Stearns Companies, Inc. of New York. "It is very deep in management talent."

Though Exxon wasn't telling reporters, the search for a replacement had already begun. Because Exxon International by its very name is an international company, a new president could come from anywhere in the world. Despite having devoted thirty-five years of his life to Exxon, Sid Reso was expendable just like everyone else in the company. He'd been trained and paid handsomely, but if he didn't return soon, movers would switch out his furniture and a decorator would replace his wall hangings and his personal effects with those of another Exxon devotee worthy of promotion. But Sid Reso's office was safe— for now.

Chapter 6

It was Monday, May 25th. Sid Reso had been missing four weeks. And it was Memorial Day. The temperature had risen to sixty-two degrees and, although the wind gusted at times, it was a beautiful, sunny day. As the unofficial start of summer, most folks who'd endured winter colds and spring allergies were ready to commence their favorite activities in the warmth of the sun. They dragged out their boats, golf clubs, fishing rods, grills, picnic baskets, and most anything else in their closets, garages, or attics.

The kidnappers were no different. They'd spent an enjoyable weekend with their family, perhaps grilling in the back near the river or boating. Unlike everyone else, however, Art and Jackie Seale also were reexamining how best to extort $18.5 million from Exxon. They were running out of time. The elder Seale had decreed that they be out of his house by the end of June. Though they still had thirty-five days, the kidnappers had become confused and afraid after the failed attempt at the Villa Restaurant. Their once seemingly foolproof plan had crumbled into no plan at all. They were floundering; sending ransom letters and making phone calls without any follow up, as if trying to regain their nerves. With Mr. Seale's ultimatum, they had no choice; they'd have to substitute desperation for nerves. So, at 5:46 p.m. that Monday, their holiday weekend fun was over as they drove into Secure Storage and entered unit 619.

Their scheme may have received a boost when, on the day before at 9:45 a.m., the owner of the Villa Restaurant, Joseph Dasti, and fifty-one-year-old gardener, Vincenzo Piscioneri, discovered a plain white envelope stuck in the shrubs near the restaurant sign. The envelope was addressed to: "Mr. Lawrence Rawl, Exxon Corporation, C/O Mrs. Reso." The owner opened it and, having kept up with the kidnapping in the news, instantly realized what he'd found. He telephoned police. The FBI dispatched Agent Steve Thornton and Morris County Prosecutor's Office Detective Mark Prach to retrieve the note and interview the two men.

This was the letter Art Seale had stuffed in the bushes at the Villa Restaurant the night before the attempted ransom pickup on May 3 when Jackie Seale punched in the wrong telephone number. It was the same letter that the kidnappers intended for Exxon's Jim Morakis to find after they phoned. Its purpose was to give Morakis directions to the Summit train station, where he'd find another letter and a cassette tape under a station payphone that would further instruct him to board the train with Pat Reso and the ransom money.

The find did explain a few things for the FBI. If nothing else, the kidnappers' insistence that they'd sent a letter and a cassette had some credibility now. It also served as a stark reminder, however, not only for the Bureau, but more importantly for Pat and her children, of that disappointing night. Pat didn't know whether the FBI or the kidnappers were to blame for the failed call at the Villa Restaurant. It didn't matter. She believed she should've had Sid back home that night. Instead, a torturous three weeks had passed.

Even more frightening, ten days had passed since she and Exxon had heard from the kidnappers. And worse, her children had just left New Jersey and returned to their homes. After all, they'd been with her for a month, neglecting their own lives. It was terribly difficult for them to leave their mother, though Pat understood. Who knew when the kidnappers would reach out again?

The command post had also left Pat's home. With dozens of agents and detectives commandeering the living room, dining room, study, Sid's home office, and even the foyer, not to mention using the kitchen and patio for eating and breaks, Pat's house simply had grown too small to house the expanding investigation. Everyone had packed up and moved out during the middle of May and set up a new command post on the top floor of a Morris County government building near the Morris County Police Academy in Morristown. Only a handful of agents and detectives stayed behind to man the telephones and recorders and to guard the Reso house. While it might seem that Pat would have welcomed their departure from her home, she didn't. For over a month, she'd seen how hard everyone was working, which comforted her. She feared "out of sight, out of mind" — that their departure meant they were scaling back the investigation, though Agents Walker and Chapman assured her that wasn't the case.

Not only were her children and the command post gone, but so were the news articles. News of Sid's abduction had been slipping out of the news columns for days. That weekend, *The Star-Ledger* only noted that the case was beginning its fifth week and printed these questions: *So where is Reso? Was it an abduction by ecoterrorists? Or was it a voluntary disappearance? Amnesia? Illness?* The newspaper also quoted Morris County Prosecutor Mike Murphy: "All I can say is that we are hoping for a break in the case and that Mr. Reso will be returned to his loved ones." That pretty much summed up the state of the investigation.

Like many holiday weekends, it was a slow news day all over. The L.A. riots had ended and it was time to rebuild, though race relations would remain strained as would be revealed two years later upon O.J. Simpson's arrest. Besides local fluff, the media had little to report other than President George H.W. Bush's Memorial Day radio address and updates on the 1992 presidential campaigns. The Gallup Poll had just released numbers that put Bush and Ross Perot in a dead heat, with Bill Clinton trailing by ten points. The major news story, however, had been late night TV host Johnny Carson's retirement three days earlier with Jay Leno making his debut appearance as the new host of the *Tonight Show* that Monday.

It all seemed so trivial to Pat. Nonetheless, she would be one of sixteen million viewers staying up to witness Leno's performance that night. She'd rather have been enjoying the long weekend with her husband. Sid most likely would have played some golf. Perhaps they would have gone into New York City for the weekend, or thrown a party as they occasionally did, with Sid insisting on serving his favorite New Orleans dish, Cajun gumbo. It was not to be.

While she waited that evening, Pat may have thought about their last weekend together, and hoped for more wonderful times, maybe even a European vacation. Perhaps she reminisced about their thirty-six year marriage, soon to be thirty-seven years on August 20. Their wedding had been at St. Anthony of Padua Catholic Church in New Orleans. It was beautiful and they were so young. Their fresh faces beamed with excitement and joy as they considered building Sid's career and their family together.

Born on July 22, 1934, and raised in New Orleans as an only child to parents in the restaurant and grocery businesses, Patricia Marie "Pat" Armond had married Sid on August 20, 1955, at the age of twenty-one. She had never really had a career other than as a wife and mother, which had been an enormous job with five children traipsing about the world following Sid's career, something she did with hardly an objection. Pat was kind, giving, and deeply loved her husband and children. She also depended on Sid, not only financially, but as the person who handled most things that arose in their family and their household.

Being from New Orleans with its French roots, Pat was a devout Roman Catholic, something that had been a tremendous comfort during the terrible ordeal. Since her husband's disappearance, she had attended church services every day no matter how low she felt. And not only had she been visited by many friends and fellow church members, she'd received thousands of letters from people all over the country and the world extending their prayers and well-wishes. She now wore a blue ribbon. She'd received it from Charlie Roxburgh. Many Exxon employees were wearing blue ribbons to remind one another to pray for Sid's safe return.

At least Pat didn't have to worry about finances as some might under similar circumstances with their income-earning spouse missing. The Resos were multimillionaires thanks to Sid's talent and hard work. Obviously, money was not on Pat's mind. Though she and Sid had lived nicely, they lived more modestly than many with less. Besides, at least two people wanted more money, which had led to Sid's predicament, and despite Exxon's willingness to pay $18.5 million, money had yet to bring Sid home. Pat, the faithful Catholic, may have recalled First Timothy of the New Testament: "For the love of money is the root of all kinds of evil."

Through it all, Exxon had stuck beside Pat. Sid Reso had devoted thirty-five years of his life to Exxon and Reso's loyalty would be returned during Pat's time of need. The mammoth multi-national corporation provided not only security guards, but the comfort and support of management and employees. Charlie Roxburgh talked to Pat and law enforcement almost every day. He also made certain that Exxon paid a catering service to deliver breakfast, lunch, and dinner to all those working in the command post. Exxon also continued to pay Reso's base salary of almost $60,000 a month ($110,000 a month today), and it also continued the perks, though unused now, such as a club membership and a limo driver. And there were the usual executive benefits like health, dental, and disability insurance, and, of course, life insurance. Exxon sincerely stood by Sid, Pat, and all the Resos. Yet, behind the scenes, it continued considering candidates to succeed Sid Reso as president — just in case.

* * *

Jackie Seale stood in front of yet another payphone in another parking lot on another day of another week. She'd selected a snappy outfit in which to make her ransom call that Tuesday morning. The color and fit of her day's ensemble showcased not only her athletic figure, blond hair, and tanned face, but also her baby blue Rubbermaid gloves that shielded her fingerprints.

She reached in her North Face windbreaker and withdrew a clean quarter and inserted it into the phone's coin slot. It clanked with a ding in the coin return. She tried again. It dropped through again. Once more; same result. It was her only quarter. "Unbelievable." The woman and mother of two, portraying an international eco-terrorist, looked around and spotted another payphone a few hundred feet away. She jumped in her Mercedes and whipped her frustration and her vehicle over to the next phone. She withdrew tissue and wiped the phone's ear and mouth pieces. Just before inserting the quarter, she also wiped the coin, recalling her husband's instructions to always clean the quarters before dropping them into coin slots: "They check 'em for fingerprints and lint. Remember, it's the little mistakes that will send you to prison."

Jackie looked up at the sky as if making a wish. She cleared her throat and raised a cupped-hand filled with nickels and slipped them into her mouth. According to the FBI report, her husband had suggested the coins when she'd complained of difficulty maintaining a disguised voice. She'd likely collected new, shiny nickels and washed them in a detergent-filled kitchen sink before placing them in a plastic bag that morning.

She inserted the quarter into the phone. This time, she heard a dial-tone. It was nine o'clock on the morning of May 26—eleven days since her last ransom call to the Rockaway Mall.

"Morristown Memorial Hospital, patient information, how may I help you?"

"You will find a letter about Sid Reso of Exxon in your mailbox outside," the garbled voice said.

"I'm sorry? What did you say?"

Jackie clanked down the phone receiver and hurried to her Mercedes. She wanted to get home before clouds rolled in. She'd planned a five-mile jog and a little sunbathing.

The hospital employee, like the ransom call-recipients before her, commenced the usual progression of calling her supervisor, who called security, who called the local police, who then called the FBI. Minutes later, agents arrived at the hospital and inspected all mailboxes outside and inside the hospital complex, including the hospital's offices on Mount Kemble Avenue. They found nothing. The FBI would later learn that Art Seale had not placed the unstamped letter in the mailbox outside the Morristown hospital as his wife had said over the payphone, but rather outside the Morris Museum a mile away. One of the Warriors had misunderstood the day's plan.

Ten hours later, a postal inspector discovered the unsealed and unstamped envelope at a post office in Whippany, New Jersey, two miles from the Morris Museum. It was addressed to "Lawrence Rawl, Chairperson, Exxon Corp." He notified the FBI. The letter had been picked up by a mail carrier from the Morris Museum mailbox and, lacking the proper postage, deposited at the West Jersey General Mail Facility in Whippany. Special Agent Tom Cottone and Morris County Detective Sergeant Brian Doig retrieved the letter and envelope.

```
Mr. Lawrence Rawl,
By signifying your willingness to comply with
our demands you have started an irreversible
path. All events must now occur according to a
preset schedule. Reso will either be released
in conjunction with an Earth Summit event or
his body will be prominently displayed. The
outcome is now up to you.
     . . . no individual is more important than
our cause and Reso will become an example if
```

necessary. If Reso dies as a result of your
lack of cooperation our next targets will take
us/more seriously . . .

Reso is now being held in relative isolation.
He has not seen any of us and cannot identify
any members of our group . . .

Instructions will follow.
WARRIORS OF THE RAINBOW

The kidnappers had sent another threatening letter, yet failed to
follow through. The letter stated that Sid Reso would die if the
kidnappers' demands weren't met, but it failed to include any
ransom delivery instructions. Five days later, the kidnappers
did it again. A letter addressed to "Mr. Sidney J. Reso, President,
Exxon," arrived at Reso's office in Florham Park. The letter
seemed to be little more than a written stutter. It stated, "This is
your last chance." Again, no ransom delivery instructions.

Special Agent-in-Charge Penrith and his agents may have
wanted to scream: *We know! We know! Give us the damn delivery
instructions already!* It may have seemed ridiculous, but it was
deadly serious.

The FBI concluded that the kidnappers were clearly
stalling, but Penrith and his team weren't sure why. Everyone
wondered if the so-called Warriors of the Rainbow even held
Sid Reso anymore. Sure, they'd inserted Reso's credit card in the
envelope with the first ransom note and had described his pill
box, but that didn't prove Reso was still alive and with them.
Following the mix-up at the Villa Restaurant, the kidnappers
had consistently refused to produce a photograph or a recording
that demonstrated Reso was alive. Their letters only reminded
Exxon that they'd already done so, once with Reso's voice giving
directions to the Livingston Mall the day after the kidnapping,
then directions to the second letter drop at Lewis Morris County
Park, and another time talking about the L.A. riots in an audio

cassette taped beneath a payphone at the Summit train station. But Reso's family didn't believe the Livingston Mall and Lewis Morris County Park recordings were of his voice, and the Summit cassette was missing by the time the FBI learned of it.

That left Murphy and Penrith with nothing, except vacillating kidnappers who refused to provide additional proof of Reso's health and well-being. The county prosecutor and the FBI special-agent-in-charge were afraid that meant only one thing. The Behavioral Science Unit agreed. Agent John Walker continued to relay those concerns to Pat. She appreciated Walker's candor, which she later expressed in a letter to him. But she wasn't going to give up hope—that was not Pat Reso.

* * *

The beginning of June in the Garden State brought fully-leaved northern oaks speckled with yellow finches doing their best to fulfill their duties as official state symbols. But June also brought the elder Seale's ultimatum. Art and Jackie Seale had to be out of his house by the end of the month. That meant no more stalling. The time had come either to get on with their criminal plans or, god forbid, rejoin the working class.

For most of their lives, Art and Jackie Seale had held jobs, owned their own home, and supported two children. They'd even thrived, at one time making a combined income of $100,000 a year during the 1980s. But that wasn't good enough. They'd wanted more.

On August 25, 1986, Art and Jackie sold their two-story, four-bedroom colonial house on five acres tucked away on a dead-end lane off Rogers Road in Far Hills, New Jersey. They received $385,000 for the house they'd purchased seven years earlier for $46,000 and later mortgaged for $135,000. They'd also quit their jobs. Art Seale received a buyout of his employment contract from Exxon, reportedly netting him more than $100,000. He also continued to receive his annual disability benefit of more than $10,000.

With $400,000 in cash, Art and Jackie Seale moved with their children that August to Hilton Head, South Carolina. This was the time of Gordon Gekko, the movie *Wall Street*, and the Decade of Greed. They purchased a beautiful home on an acre lot in one of the most desirable locations on the marsh. They paid $360,000 for a sprawling single-level cypress-sided home at 4 Willet Road, on Gull Point in the gated Sea Pines Plantation Resort, just off the Harbour Town Golf Links. Sitting in the back under palm trees, magnolias, and oaks dripping with Spanish moss while serenaded by sea gulls amid the aroma of the ocean surf, they watched the beautiful sailboats and yachts going out and coming into the private Gull Point Marina on Braddock Cove. The lovely sight inspired Art Seale to purchase a $90,000 38-foot French sloop called *Gallant* and moor it at the marina. They could see the main mast of *Gallant* from their backyard. It was one of the largest sailboats in the marina. There was just one minor, though temporary, snag: neither Seale knew diddly about sailing.

"They sure lived the good life down here," recalled Porter Thompson, a Hilton Head advertising executive, who taught Art Seale how to sail. "[Artie] was constantly looking for opportunities and considered himself a winner who wanted to look and live like a winner."

Continuing to act as though they'd just won the lottery, the Seales also purchased matching his and hers 1984 white turbo diesel Mercedes-Benz 300D sedans with wood-grain interior trim and gold-colored leather seats. Art also bought an Isuzu truck. They enrolled their son in the eighth grade and their daughter in the fifth grade at Hilton Head Preparatory School, which boasts being the preeminent private school in the area. They dined out and were frequently seen at the local marina with their children. Art Seale's skill at sailing improved and he often took the family to Florida aboard his luxury cabin sailboat.

"They used to talk about all the poor saps who lived back up in New Jersey," remembered Ron Walker, a local businessman. "About how they would do anything rather than live that nine to five rat race life again . . . They seemed to have a lot of contempt for the people who had to get up and go to work and then do it all again the next day . . . I envied them. They seemed to have it all."

The Seales did seem to have it all, except employment. Rather than looking for jobs like all the other "poor saps," Art and Jackie purchased an established outdoor furniture and home design business called "Sally Hunter Interiors" in the Hunter Building at 811 William Hilton Parkway near the entrance to the Palmetto Dunes Resort. They mortgaged their beautiful home to purchase the business for $425,000 from Bill and Sally Hunter, who received an $85,000 down-payment and financed the balance themselves. The Seales changed the name of the twelve-year-old furniture store to "Insiders," unwisely eliminating any patron goodwill, and hired local residents to help operate it. They talked about opening additional stores in Columbia, South Carolina, and on Florida's Gold Coast. Art Seale, the Dreamer, even talked about establishing a franchise even though he'd never operated a business of any kind before. The Seales appeared to be enjoying the good life at last.

"He was always looking for the art of the deal," Special Agent Jere Doyle told a reporter in 1992. "He considered himself a Donald Trump type . . . always pulling scams and deals . . . who thought he was better than everyone else."

But Art and Jackie Seale soon discovered they'd chosen an unstable time to purchase a business in a seasonal tourist area. Earlier that year, the nation's economy had fallen into a recession. Though the Seales' business was fine in the beginning, as that first year progressed, more and more money went out the door than came in. Then Black Monday struck on October 19, 1987. The Dow Jones Industrial Average dropped twenty-three percent, the largest single-day percentage drop in history. The Seales took out a $320,000 second mortgage on their home in an attempt to keep their business afloat. Workers at the store noticed the slowdown and witnessed Art Seale's frustrations boil over. He began throwing tantrums behind closed doors that soon moved into the showroom where once he reportedly threw a screwdriver at a designer in front of customers and employees. After a year in the business, the Seales found themselves laying off sales staff and liquidating inventory. Then came the bill collectors.

When a sheriff's deputy showed up at their bayside home to serve an eviction notice as part of a judicial foreclosure proceeding, the Seales realized their Hilton Head dream had ended. One night in the summer of 1988, Art and Jackie packed up their children and a few suitcases and skipped town in one of their Mercedes owing roughly $715,000 (or $1.5 million today).

Many who had befriended the Seales were shocked to learn of their midnight exodus. Roger Thompson, the gentleman who'd taught Art Seale how to sail, held unpaid bills of more than $30,000 for his advertising efforts.

"It became clear [Art Seale] didn't know as much about business as he said he did," Thompson said. "They became overwhelmed and left in the middle of the night with a lot of people down here holding the bag."

Besides Thompson, the Seales owed Hilton Head Prep for unpaid tuition, and owed $71,238 to Maryland National Bank for the fancy sailboat, which just happened to have mysteriously disappeared like its owners. Their vehicles had been sold or repossessed, except the Mercedes they vanished in. Eunice Waters, a decorator in nearby Savannah, was owed for work done for the Seales as was Berry Edwards, the owner of a landscaping company, who collected a past due account from the Seales just before they absconded, only to have the check bounce. The Seales also owed the local newspaper, *The Islander*, for advertising. Not to be left out, the IRS filed a lien for $29,000 in back employment taxes and soon added unpaid income and capital gains taxes pushing the total unpaid tax bill into the six figures. But no one was hurt more than Bill and Sally Hunter, who'd sold their furniture business to the Seales on credit. When the Seales disappeared during the night, they'd already sold off most of the store's inventory, and the bank was foreclosing on their house they'd used as security for the store's purchase. "They hurt us for a few hundred thousand dollars," Hunter said.

"They came to Hilton Head with a lot of money and a lot of dreams, but they left literally in the middle of the night, owing hundreds of thousands of dollars," Ellen Cole, a former business associate recalled.

Everyone wondered where the high-flying Seales had landed, especially those still owed money. No one knew at the time, but the Seales selected not some obscure lower-income town in middle America, but the resort community of Vail, Colorado, as their residential hideout—1,800 miles from friends and creditors.

Still wanting the good life, Art and Jackie Seale, with terrible credit and no jobs, managed to rent a half a million dollar townhouse that sat along the Vail Golf Club and White River National Forest. "I always thought [Jackie Seale] came from old money back east," recalled neighbor, Linda Myers. "That's how she acted, anyway." Others who came to know the Seales in Vail referred to them as the "ultimate yuppies."

They did eventually find employment in Colorado. Jackie worked as a secretary at a small business called Convention Designs and for a travel agency called Western Ski Specialties in Vail for $7.00 an hour while Art Seale worked at Merrill Lynch in Denver. But Jackie Seale was soon fired. "I let her go after a few months," Susan Brody said. "She was a very talkative person, particularly talkative, which sometimes got in the way of her work." Art Seale did little better. After six months, he quit his job. To shield themselves from creditors, the Seales hired a

Denver lawyer and filed for bankruptcy protection.

The stress of their failures was building at home, too. According to a Vail officer, police were summoned four times to the Seale townhouse. Their daughter attempted to run away three times and one of their children had been arrested for shoplifting, the officer recalled. There also had been a domestic disturbance call. An official with the Eagle County Bureau of Social Services confirmed that the agency had "been actively involved" with the Seale family, but declined to elaborate.

"They seemed to come here ready to begin a new life in the mountains," one neighbor said. "But after some very serious family problems here, they suddenly left."

After only two and a half years away from New Jersey chasing their dreams, Art and Jackie Seale loaded up their kids in their eight-year-old Mercedes with more than 160,000 miles on the odometer and returned to Hunterdon County, New Jersey, much worse off than when they'd left. With no money, no jobs, but plenty of creditors, they moved in with Art's retired parents in January 1990. Jackie's brother recalled that his family hadn't seen his sister and her husband for over two years. "My brother-in-law wanted no part of my sister's family," he said. "They went to Hilton Head and that was it."

But like a bad rash, they came creeping back. And two and a half years later, in June 1992, they were still there, living with Art Seale's parents, sleeping in the basement, without jobs. It seemed that they'd hit rock bottom, but their solution would take them even deeper down below.

* * *

It had been six weeks since Sid Reso was taken. Pat still waited and hoped. What else could she do? Wait, worry, and dwell on her missing husband. She continued to brood over things like: *Where is Sid? How is he? When will I see him again?* and at her weakest:

Is Sid dead? From the night at the Villa Restaurant to subsequent calls and letters followed by silence, each disappointment may have felt to Pat as if her husband had been kidnapped all over again. Kidnappers who'd appear and then disappear; there was no getting used to it. She couldn't reunite with her husband and she couldn't bury him. She just waited. Hers was a life in limbo.

Pat may have felt like a prisoner within her home at times, especially with the dwindling number of agents and detectives still milling about inside, and a pair of officers standing guard outside. Fatigue and the desire to avoid sorrowful looks may have curbed her desire to venture out. Still, friends took her to dine occasionally and sometimes even took short road trips about New Jersey and into Manhattan. When she did, she often was escorted by Exxon security or a county detective. Although her chances of being kidnapped were remote and would have been far from ordinary, very little about her husband's kidnapping had been ordinary so far.

Pat often stepped onto her wooden deck and into her backyard, away from the prying eyes of neighbors and reporters, though reporters rarely showed up anymore. She'd smile at the deer and occasionally call out to one bearing familiar markings. She'd also plant a few flowers in the back, flowers that weren't on a deer's menu, like daisies, lavender, and aster. Whether she realized it or not, the passing days were conditioning her for the receipt of any news, good or bad.

It was difficult living alone in New Jersey. She and Sid had moved there because of Sid's job; that was her only connection. Sid's relatives lived in New Orleans. Pat was also from The Big Easy, but her mother and father had died in 1968 and 1973, and Pat was their only child. Other than a handful of cousins, Sid's family was Pat's family.

She busied herself in the mornings with Bible reading, prayer, and meditation, and in the afternoons on phone calls with friends and relatives. Those she spoke with told her to remain positive and reinforced her hope that Sid would soon be home. She may have undergone a bit of "sympathy fatigue," where everyone repeatedly extended their kind words and optimism, sometimes so much so that it sounded as if they were simply humoring her. With weeks having passed, however, some supporters began to crack and suggested that perhaps she should accept the worst and make plans accordingly, just in case. Pat would have none of it.

An avid reader, Pat Reso tried to absorb herself in books, yet sometimes found herself reading the same sentence over and over, her focus always shifting back to Sid. She'd recently started reading the newly-released, *The Pelican Brief*, and also *French Silk* set in her hometown. They were a welcome distraction for her mind. She also entertained herself with her favorite television programs, like *Murphy Brown* and *Murder She Wrote*. Just as her thoughts veered too far from Sid and his predicament, however, her mind always snapped back to him.

And there were the ever-present thoughts of should'ves, could'ves, and would'ves. Perhaps she should've noticed the kidnappers lurking outside their home, she thought; after all, she stayed at home almost every day. If she'd been outside that morning and seen Sid taken, perhaps she could've called the police who would've caught the kidnappers before they'd gotten away. And perhaps she thought she should've hugged and kissed Sid longer, and spoken her last words more lovingly, the way someone speaks to someone who might never be seen again.

Everything Pat Reso may have felt was reasonable and normal. She endured a constant battle of physical and mental suffering that overwhelmed her: distress, confusion, stress, anxiety, lack of sleep, too much sleep, inability to eat, anger, sadness, ambivalence, and depression. Sometimes she may have thought she was going mad. Not knowing had to have been horrible. The fear of never knowing had to have been unbearable. She must have felt suspended in a state of pain and uncertainty. When her husband had first been kidnapped, she likely sprang like a cat when the phone rang anxious to hear any word of Sid's whereabouts. After six weeks, however, there may have been a strange comfort in not knowing, afraid that when the phone rang it would bring only bad news.

Pat's prayers remained constant and zealous. Her priest's words and visits from fellow church members continued to comfort her. Through it all, Pat's faith and devotion to her religion and church remained steadfast; she never doubted or challenged her God. Her faith sustained her unwavering hope that her husband was alive and would return to her soon.

That's what she wrote in her diary that night; but the words were coming harder. After forty-two days, she'd said about all she could say—what could she write tomorrow?

* * *

Few, if any, law enforcement agencies are as professional, methodical, and thorough as the Federal Bureau of Investigation. The United States also has NSA and CIA, and Great Britain has MI5 and MI6, but they are intelligence and counter-intelligence agencies. The FBI is both federal law enforcement and counter-intelligence. That is what makes the FBI what it is—a formidable deterrent force against domestic and foreign crime. The FBI literally leaves no information ungathered; and *everything* is written down.

The Bureau's job can be daunting. Operation SIDNAP was no different. Besides investigating the obvious, like potential eco-terrorists, disgruntled Exxon employees, and even local skydiving schools (because the first ransom note had demanded a piloted plane with jumping capabilities), the FBI also investigated the obscure.

One example in the FBI's 16,000-page SIDNAP file involved

the Bureau considering whether there might be some link between Sid Reso's terrorist-kidnappers and groups that had threatened to tamper with products of U.S. corporations unless large ransoms were received. From threats of poisoning baby food to injecting battery acid into men's cologne, agents sifted through stacks of paperwork searching for any connection. Although "Fernando of the Avengers" had threatened to poison Nabisco products five years earlier, which sounded much like "Fernando Pereira Brigade of the Warriors of the Rainbow," the Bureau found no connection between any product tampering extortionist group and Reso's kidnappers.

Agents pursued not only the legitimate leads, but also had to run down leads called in or mailed to FBI offices, to state and local police, and to Exxon that proved to be bogus. There were countless numbers of extortionists "piggybacking" on Sid Reso's kidnapping that demanded payment for his return. Those that appeared similar to the Reso case were investigated to determine if a link existed, and when it was learned they did not, the cases were treated as unrelated criminal acts of extortion.

Then there were the crank calls that weren't obviously fake. Many had believable stories. Others simply left cryptic messages, like an unknown female (not Jackie Seale) who telephoned the Exxon Research and Engineering Company switchboard in the Florham Park complex. She told the operator that Sid Reso was being held at Newark International Airport and hung up. Nothing more specific was said. An airport-wide search ensued. Lawmen searched all terminals and service areas, parking garages, and even parking lots of nearby airport hotels, paying particular attention to white vans. The search consumed two entire days for two special agents along with members of the Violent Crime Task Force that included a Hackensack police detective sergeant, a Bergen County sheriff's deputy, and a lieutenant with the Port Authority of New York and New Jersey. State police dogs, including Buffy, sniffed more than 15,000 vehicles. Nothing was found. It was simply another prank call and a waste of law enforcement's limited time and energy.

And there were calls and letters from the fanatical or deranged. The FBI's files were full of those. For example, the Bureau received a letter from one person who claimed that Sid Reso was taken because he was about to turn over evidence to authorities that linked Exxon to a scheme to obtain oil and hostages from Iran in exchange for money to help Oliver North and the Contras purchase weapons. The Iran-Contra debacle during the Reagan administration had been five years earlier.

Another example included a letter from a person who claimed students from a local high school and community college had gotten carried away by "youthful misguided environmental activist enthusiasm" and taken Reso.

More amusing, however, was a local seventy-year-old angler who notified the FBI that he'd been fishing with Sid Reso on Budd Lake the day before. According to the man called "eccentric" by those who knew him, he and Reso had discussed many things, including their pets and recent veterinarian bills. He said Reso was driving a blue-and-cream-colored GMC truck. The FBI sent an agent to check the story. It wasn't Reso.

One person claimed to be psychic and had "feelings" that "zeroed in on Hackettstown, New Jersey." He said that Sid Reso was being held in a brown, single-family house off New Jersey Route 46 on a street that began with the letter "H." Again, it was checked out. Nothing.

Not to be outdone, an unemployed clairvoyant in Los Angeles telephoned the Bureau on May 28 and reported receiving "premonitions" of Sid Reso's whereabouts. He was near water, the seer said, either in Lincoln Park or somewhere with Lincoln in the name. He visualized the number 354/40 or 354/20, and he had the sensation that Reso was very uncomfortable. A background check led agents to discover that, not surprisingly, their soothsayer suffered from mental illness and had made previous threats against President George H.W. Bush.

Another gentleman claiming to be a Reagan conservative said he was in communication with Sid Reso telepathically. He told an agent that Reso was now a "corporal in the spirit world" busy battling bad spirits in Jamestown, California. Though portions of television shows, such as *Petticoat Junction*, *Green Acres*, and *Little House on the Prairie* had been filmed in Jamestown, even the shows' harshest critics believed that the town was haunted only by memories of cheesy television scripts. Nevertheless, the Reaganite told the FBI agent that Reso was okay, but the spirits enjoyed his company so much that they didn't want him to "materialize back into a human." He also mentioned that he'd learned through his telepathy that the Warriors of the Rainbow were a group of leftist homosexuals from New York City. It seemed conservative politics may have interfered with his telepathic reception at times. This so-called lead was not checked out.

The FBI did dispatch an agent to the all-white-resident Somerset Valley Nursing Home in nearby Bound Brook, New Jersey, when a female caller claimed that the nursing home had become a Communist stronghold run by black females who were holding Reso.

One woman from New Jersey who claimed to possess psychic powers also later claimed to have assisted the FBI with Sid Reso's kidnapping. According to an article in *The Philadelphia Inquirer* seven years *after* the kidnapping, she claimed to have contacted the FBI and explained that she'd had a vision, like a color motion picture playing on a screen inside her head, where she saw a van, a woman jogging, a man in a dark closet, and fir trees. The same article, however, highlighted that she was offering a series of ten courses to help people tap into their psychic tuition or sixth sense.

The craziness filled hundreds of pages of FBI reports on Forms 302 as agents call them. Intermingled with those reports were others from citizens accusing their neighbors, family, in-laws, and bosses, and still others offering advice on how the FBI should conduct the investigation. The Bureau might have felt like throwing a net over the whole bunch.

Nonetheless, the relentless FBI continued its investigative efforts, no matter how genuine or how crazy the clues appeared, all the while continuing to investigate all other cases that fell within the jurisdiction of the Newark field office. That's one of the things that makes the FBI, the FBI. And although Sid Reso's kidnappers had evaded the FBI's dragnet for seven weeks, their time was running short.

Chapter 7

On the night of Wednesday, June 3, Art and Jackie Seale took their seats around the dinner table with their daughter and Art Seale's parents as they did almost every night. The television played in the den in open view of those filling their plates. Following a brief narrative of national news, Sid Reso's disappearance and the lack of clues opened the local telecast with an intensifying volume. As a retired deputy chief of police, it is likely that Mr. Seale had already discussed the case several times with his son, also a former police officer. They may have advanced theories and possibly even a profile of the kidnappers that very night.

"They're just a bunch of amateurs," Mr. Seale quipped. "I'll bet you those kidnappers are anything *but* environmental terrorists. These guys only want the money like most two-bit criminals. Just wait till they're caught. You'll see I'm right."

"I wouldn't be so sure about that, pop," Art replied, perhaps even enjoying being coy. "They haven't got caught yet. They sound like—"

"Food's getting cold," Jackie Seale interrupted, a bit frightened when hearing Mr. Seale's gloomy predictions.

After dinner, the husband and wife kidnappers retired to their basement bedroom. While stretching under their comforter with their bedside lamps aglow, the couple reviewed the ransom note Art Seale had typed that afternoon in the basement. They also discussed places to drop the note. Dropping a ransom note is tricky business. The time of day, presence of surveillance cameras, and the number of passersby have to be carefully considered. Early mornings in local parks seemed to work best for the Seales.

Before lunch that day, Art had driven into New York City and applied for a U.S. passport at the Rockefeller Center Passport Agency. His application listed his occupation as "consultant" and his destination as "business trip to the Bahamas." Jackie Seale did not apply for a passport; only Art would be traveling. The agency issued the passport while he waited (this was pre-9/11). With his crisp, dark blue passport book in his pocket, Art Seale then drove to a travel agency at the Phillipsburg Mall in Phillipsburg, New Jersey. He purchased roundtrip tickets to fly USAir from Newark to Miami, and then from Miami to Nassau on New Providence Island in the Bahamas. His flight would depart in just three days and return on June 10.

The passport and airline tickets had been pricey for a couple without jobs and no savings. Even so, they viewed it as part of the cost of doing business as kidnappers, just as buying gloves, ski masks, and duct tape had been. When they turned the lights off in their bedroom that night of June 3, they didn't mind that their bank account would soon be overdrawn again. They expected an enormous return on their investment—$18.5 million would fill many bank accounts.

The next morning, the Seales left their home and drove their Mercedes through Mendham and Bernardsville before entering I-287 heading northbound. Just south of Morristown, the couple exited into the Harding Township Rest Stop (now open only to truckers). Parking in the rear of the heavily-wooded rest area, Art Seale stepped out of the car and walked to the edge of the woods where several picnic tables stood. It was early and the picnic area in the rear of the rest stop was deserted. Most visitors occupied the restrooms at the main building or milled about out front smoking cigarettes. With no one nearby, Seale placed an envelope draped with gray duct tape beneath one of the picnic tables and strolled to his Mercedes parked at the far end of the rest stop as if enjoying the pleasant morning. He drove back onto I-287, soon exiting at Morristown where the kidnappers looked for a payphone in an area with little traffic. They spotted one; a new model. New, clean payphones were always preferably to the chipped and smelly old ones, though all required wiping the ear and mouth pieces before calling. Jackie exited the car wearing her baby blue Rubbermaid gloves and filled her mouth with washed, shiny nickels before inserting a wiped quarter into the coin slot. Her ritual was becoming almost routine, albeit a routine she surely detested.

"Hello. Morris County Parks Commission."

"You will find a ransom note about the Exxon president taped under a picnic table at Harding Township Rest Area."

"What? This is the Parks Commission. Hello?"

Jackie Seale hung up and hopped back into the car. Despite the impossibility that the call could be traced, Art Seale pulled away quickly. As they drove, the husband and wife kidnappers discussed her call. "Tell me exactly what you said, exactly how you said it." Annoyed by her husband's tone, she wrapped the saliva-coated nickels in tissue and placed them in a plastic bag. "I said exactly what you told me to say."

The Seales had written and dropped the latest ransom letter at the rest area because of a statement released by the Morris Country Prosecutor's Office the previous day. According to Prosecutor Mike Murphy, his office needed proof that Sid Reso was alive and in good health. That infuriated Art Seale. He felt he'd already given them enough proof, and how dare they make any demands of him. *He* was the kidnapper. *He* was in charge. So, Seale wrote the note to remind Exxon and the prosecutor's office who was running the show.

Their latest note demanded that Exxon place an ad in Saturday's *The New York Times* to signal that Exxon was ready to pay without conditions. So far, the kidnapping had been a stressful venture, but the kidnappers were once again becoming excited. It looked as if payment of the ransom was about to happen at last. Their ransom letter stated almost verbatim the same threats and blame. It seemingly gave Exxon one last chance to comply:

> If you decide to pay with no further conditions
> place the cattle ranch ad in the Saturday NY
> Times stating that you are ready to close.
> Remember . . . if you do not pay as instructed
> you are sentencing Reso and others to their
> deaths. Prepare Mrs. Reso for this . . .
>   Instructions will follow shortly.

The letter closed with a cryptic statement: "We are on a countdown towards an end that no one wants."

Saturday morning came and the Seales hurried to a local store on their way to Newark International Airport. Unlike many Hunterdon County couples shopping for six-packs of beer, cigarettes, charcoal briquettes, and pretzels on their way to a body of water, Art Seale grabbed a copy of *The New York Times* in the racks and hurried back to his Mercedes parked among the ordinary domestic cars and trucks. He quickly fanned the newspaper's pages to the classified ads, zeroing in on page 19, sections 356-357, FLORIDA REAL ESTATE. He began reading and then—

"What the hell?"

There were only ten ads in that section and the one Art Seale had directed Exxon to place wasn't among them. He scanned the section once again and then the section below, SOUTHERN REAL ESTATE, and then the section above, FARMS COUNTRY HOMES. It just wasn't there. He looked at all the real estate sections on two full pages: HOUSES NEW JERSEY, HOUSES CONNECTICUT, VACATION LEISURE HOMES, and on and on. Still nothing. He'd explicitly threatened to kill Sid Reso within twenty-four hours and to display his body in public if Exxon didn't place the ad signaling its willingness to pay the ransom without conditions. He'd instructed that the ad be placed that Saturday. He was the boss. He was in charge. Yet, glaring down at the black and white newspaper—no ad.

He became angry. Afraid, Jackie snapped. The two began

to argue, bouncing blame back and forth as though they'd just been arrested. He hadn't taped the note well enough beneath the picnic table and she'd called the wrong number or said the wrong thing. Regardless of the cause, Art Seale's flight for the Bahamas departed in two hours. His plan had been that once he saw the ad, he would fly to the Bahamas and arrange for a wire transfer of the ransom money to an overseas bank account in the name of a newly-formed Bahamian corporation. According to the FBI report, Art Seale had spoken with a Bahamian attorney about setting up the corporation. The attorney's brother-in-law apparently was the president of a bank that could receive the wire transfer. Without Exxon's signal to proceed, Seale wasn't sure what to do. He decided to drive on. He would call the cellular number from a payphone at the airport.

When they reached Newark International Airport, Art Seale pulled into an overflow parking lot and stopped at a payphone. On went the gloves and into the payphone dropped a wiped quarter. Hearing a dial tone, Seale punched in the Exxon cellular number manned by the FBI and the prosecutor's office. It was 11:45 a.m. The cellular phone rang once, then again, and again, and once more. No answer. Art Seale hung up. First, no ad and now no one answered the cellular phone.

"What in the hell is going on?"

"What's wrong now?" Jackie asked.

"I don't know," he replied. "Nobody answered."

Jackie Seale spiraled into a panic. She fired off one question after another, her voice rising with each one, questions that Art Seale couldn't answer. He yelled back and they began to argue again as they drove on to the USAir terminal. He parked at the curb and she scooted behind the wheel while he grabbed his bag from the back. Still angry, they nonetheless hugged and she wished him good luck. A few minutes later, he was aboard USAir flight number 461 on his way to Miami.

As Jackie drove home, the FBI trapped and traced the missed

call to Bus Stop 22, Remote Parking Lot F, near a FedEx building at Newark International Airport. An FBI agent had answered the cellular phone at the end of the fourth ring, but Art Seale had already ended the call. The FBI alerted airport security to respond immediately to the airport payphone, and dispatched agents to the remote parking lot. Only a red Chevy Blazer belonging to a Morganville, New Jersey, construction company was seen near the payphone. The FBI clipped the phone receiver from the payphone, received the coin box from Bell Atlantic Telephone Company, and investigated the construction company, all while Art Seale was 35,000 feet in the air eating from a bag of peanuts and sipping a soft drink.

By the time Art Seale landed in Miami, he'd lost his nerve to fly to the Bahamas since he hadn't heard from Exxon. Instead, at 4:44 p.m., he rented a 1992 white Chevrolet Corsica, Florida plate YXL73I, from Avis Car Rental inside the terminal. With three days to burn before his return flight departed, he decided to drive 500 miles to Hilton Head to visit his nineteen-year-old son, who was spending the summer there with friends. Seale stayed at the Hilton Head Marriott Resort Hotel and dined out with his son and a few friends to whom he didn't owe money. He spun tall tales of being in town to negotiate the purchase of a marina and moving back soon. "He wanted to return to Hilton Head for another go-round," one friend said, "wealthier than the day he left."

Each morning, he checked *The New York Times*. On Monday, June 8, he checked again. Still no ad. He couldn't stand it any longer. Falling apart, he took off in his rented Chevy Corsica and drove forty miles west, far enough away from Hilton Head, he believed, that he couldn't be traced back there. At 11:24 a.m., he turned off I-95 at Exit 102 and stopped at a Gate petroleum station just off the interstate on U.S. Highway 80 in Pooler, Georgia. He entered the Gate Food Post and located a payphone in a back corner away from foot traffic. He called the cellular phone.

"Hello? Hello?" Special Agent Carolyn Zimmer answered.

"Why no res-ponn-sse?" Art Seale asked in what Zimmer later described in her report as a "disjointed and eerie, disguised voice," like a high-pitched, ghostly voice that trailed off at the end of each sentence.

"Hello? Hello?"

"Why no res-sponn-ssse to note Thurr-s-da-a-ay?" Seale repeated in the ghostly voice.

"What note Thursday? What note? Can you tell me what note? Where was the note? Hello? Hello?"

Seale hung up and quickly drove away toward Hilton Head. The FBI trapped and traced the call to the payphone inside the Gate gas station's convenience store. Agents dispatched from the resident agency in Savannah, Georgia, ten miles away, arrived at the scene within minutes. They swiftly interviewed people inside the gas station and convenience store. As had been the case each time before, there wasn't any witness who saw someone make a call. One clerk described a white male in a maroon Ford pickup truck who'd asked for several quarters. Agents also interviewed desk clerks at surrounding motels to determine who had registered recently with out-of-state license plates from the northeastern United States, especially New Jersey, New York, Pennsylvania, and Connecticut. Credit cards used to pay for gas and rooms were checked out. One motel manager objected until an FBI agent mentioned "obstruction of justice;" the manager complied. Eventually, everyone was eliminated as a suspect. Agents cut the phone receiver cord at the Gates station and retrieved the coin box with the assistance of Southern Bell Telephone Company. The FBI's report listed its contents as thirty-five dollars in quarters, seventy-five cents in nickels, one dollar sixty cents in dimes, and two pennies. The Bureau was amassing quite a collection of coins and payphone paraphernalia.

Art Seale had escaped detection once again; but he'd made

a phone call from another state, an act referred to by federal prosecutors as "interstate travel in aid of extortion."

Back at the Hilton Head Marriott that night, Art telephoned Jackie and explained about the phone call he'd made from Pooler, Georgia, and how the person who answered the cellular phone sounded confused about the last note, as if perhaps Exxon had not received it. He told Jackie that maybe Exxon hadn't been playing rough after all; maybe the rest stop employee simply hadn't relayed their phone call. He wasn't sure.

After spending two more days lounging under the Hilton Head sun, most likely on his parents' credit card, Art Seale left early Wednesday morning and drove to the Miami airport where he dropped his rental car at 12:03 p.m. and caught USAir flight number 1974 to Newark an hour later. Jackie picked him up and they returned home.

Wasting little time, the kidnapping couple typed another ransom note, placed it in an envelope and the following day, Thursday, June 11, drove to the Morristown National Historical Park (the nation's first historic park) and taped the envelope to the back of the middle post holding up the First Maryland Brigade Camp sign. At 3:50 p.m., Jackie again stretched rubber gloves over her hands, filled her mouth with coins, and placed a call from a payphone at a pizza place parking lot on New Jersey Route 31 in Washington Township.

"Morristown National Historical Park Visitor Center."

"Listen very carefully. Call Exxon Security. Tell them info regarding the executive is at the Maryland Brigade site."

"What did you say?"

"Call Exxon Security. Tell them info regarding the executive is at the Maryland Brigade Site."

Unlike the person who'd received Jackie's phone call at the Harding Township Rest Stop a week earlier, the historical park's employee telephoned park rangers and the Morristown police at once. Park rangers drove directly to the First Maryland Brigade

Camp site.

When Jackie returned to the Mercedes, Art Seale insisted that she make another phone call and give the same message. He wanted to be absolutely sure there wouldn't be any mix-ups. Jackie didn't want to make another call and the two argued, as husband and wife kidnappers apparently are often prone to do. Twenty minutes later, at 4:10 p.m. that Thursday, Jackie donned her gloves once more, sucked in her nickels, and placed another call, this time to the Morris County Clerk's Office. She grew angrier as the recorded message announced several options for reaching different sections within the government office. By the time a human answered, she just didn't care anymore and blurted, "Listen, my name is Pat. I know where the Exxon executive is. I'll call back!" She clanked down the receiver, spit the nickels into her hand, and marched back to the car. "Okay, I did it. Satisfied?" The person receiving the nonsensical message notified the police and said she'd heard traffic noises in the background, though she couldn't provide any other information.

Meanwhile, Agent Kevin Kane and Detective Sergeant George Nunn arrived at the heavily-treed site of the First Maryland Brigade Camp inside the Jockey Hollow Encampment Area where the Continental Army had camped during the harsh winter of 1779-80. The park rangers had not removed the envelope taped to the post, instead securing the area for the FBI. Agent Kane removed the envelope and bagged it. The men also snapped three Polaroids of the middle sign post, the sign, and the area surrounding the sign. Once back at the command post, agents opened the envelope:

```
Mr. Lawrence Rawl:
. . . Do you expect us to believe that you have
received all of these messages except the two
dealing with Reso's tapes of current events .
```

. . You have now received 2 tapes and two phone
calls with directions in Reso's voice. That is
all that you will get. No further demands will
be met.

. . .

If you are fully ready to comply place the
Florida cattle ranch ad in the New York Times
beginning Saturday through next week. Indicate
that you are ready to close. We will contact
you with delivery instructions soon.

If you do not respond Reso will die next
Friday.

. . .

Warriors of the Rainbow

Art and Jackie Seale were falling apart. Though they had the
weekend to relax, by Sunday, June 14, the two were a mess. The
Seales's daughter and the elder Seales must have noticed Art
and Jackie's short tempers and odd behavior. As Art would later
say: "At this point in time, I was already under extreme stress,
and I basically lost it."

It's at times like these that a kidnapper can make serious
mistakes, and can be very dangerous. In that volatile state of
mind, Art Seale read the early edition of Saturday's *The New York
Times* that Friday night. The ad that the FBI had placed on Friday,
June 12, appeared on page 19. Art Seale initially was relieved to
see the ad, but after reading it, the FBI's wording rubbed some
serious salt in Seale's angry wound:

CENTRAL FL CATTLE RANCH,
160 Acres. 2 Previous tapes not received, current photo of property needed. Condition of property your responsibility. Upon receipt, ready to close.

To make matters worse, a headline on page B1 of The Metro Section caught Art Seale's attention: *The Mystery of a Missing Executive; Where Is Sidney Reso? No Demands, No Clues, No Idea.* According to the article, Lois Ferguson, spokesperson for the Morris County Prosecutor's Office, told reporters: "We don't have any concrete proof that he is in the hands of any group or individual. We have no photograph. No voice recording." Exxon did not want to pay without proof that Sid Reso was still alive. Authorities agreed.

Art Seale's blood pressure had to have risen almost as high as his ransom demand. After seven weeks and after sending his last note and making another phone call, Exxon's ad still imposed conditions on payment of the ransom, and the prosecutor's office still maintained they needed proof that Sid Reso was kidnapped. He may have felt like the Rodney Dangerfield of kidnappers. He'd had enough.

Anger and frustration can rise to a level where desperate kidnappers will cut off an ear or a finger and mail it to the family, as had been done in the case of J. Paul Getty III in 1973. Art Seale, on the other hand, called New Jersey Bell Telephone Information and obtained the home phone number for Exxon's spokesman, Jim Morakis. He then telephoned the Morakis residence in Edison, New Jersey, at 10:15 p.m. that Sunday night. Morakis was in Boston on business for Exxon, so Seale left a message. One of Jim Morakis's adult sons, Lee, just happened to stop by the house and played the answering machine in order to relay the messages to his father. One of the messages shook the young man.

"Morakis, listen carefully. It now appears that in order to establish our bona fides we will be forced to eliminate Reso. So that there is no confusion in the future when we seize the next Exxon employee, you will be given twenty-four hours to complete payment of the $18.5 million. If you do not complete payment, we will eliminate the next employee and seize another. Perhaps after three or four you will then understand that you and the FBI do not make the rules. You can still prevent an unnecessary tragedy. Exxon must make a public statement. Indicate that you unconditionally want Reso back. Warriors of the Rainbow."

Lee immediately telephoned his father in Boston. Jim Morakis told his son to leave the house immediately and take the mini-cassette from the answering machine with him. He telephoned the FBI at the command post who sent agents to meet Lee at a nearby gas station to retrieve the cassette tape. SWAT operators guarded the Morakis home for the rest of the week, shouldering their weapons outside the home in clear view of anxious neighbors.

The Bureau now understood that the kidnappers had been pushed far enough and that any further attempt to negotiate with the kidnappers would not be conducive to Sid Reso's well-being. By this time, however, most agents and detectives believed it no longer mattered—Reso was likely dead.

The next day, frustrated Morris County Prosecutor Murphy told reporters: "We haven't given up hope that there will be positive developments for Mr. Reso's return."

Things were anything but positive.

* * *

Pat Reso called a press conference in her living room, on Tuesday, June 16. Seated in an armless, upholstered chair near a fireplace, wearing a floral blouse and eyeglasses, with Billie Holiday's 1944 recording of "I'll Be Seeing You" playing faintly from speakers throughout the house, she faced more than a dozen reporters, all standing about with pens, pads, and recorders, waiting for her to begin.

"It has been seven weeks since my husband has disappeared," Pat said, reading from a prepared statement, emotionless and monotone. "I wish to make it clear that my family and I and the officials at Exxon *unconditionally* want my husband back. Since the time of his disappearance, Mother's Day has passed and our family has been greatly troubled. We desperately miss him and eagerly look forward to being reunited with him. It is my hope and prayer that my husband join us for Father's Day this Sunday. Sid, please, if you can hear me, know that I love you, miss you, and pray for you every day."

Pat raised her head and removed her glasses, placing them on a small table beside her chair. That was the end of the prepared statement that had been carefully crafted by Pat, with input from Exxon, the prosecutor's office, and the FBI, in a collaborative attempt to put the kidnappers at ease. Though the statement had been fewer than one hundred words and had taken her only thirty-eight seconds to say, the statement captured the constant pain, worry, frustration, and fatigue she'd experienced during the last forty-nine days.

Not taking any chances, Exxon released its own statement through its spokesman, Jim Morakis: "Exxon is fully dedicated to bring about Mr. Reso's safe return and to avoid any unnecessary tragedy."

Following the official press conference, Pat permitted reporters to remain and ask questions, though she, like Exxon and members of law enforcement, refused to address the reason for the conference or whether she'd heard from the people who held Sid. Reporters concentrated their questions on the personal impact that Sid's disappearance had on Pat and her family.

"How have you been spending your time since your husband disappeared?" one reporter asked.

"Well, I've had many quiet evenings, quiet days," Pat said. "Fortunately for me, I have wonderful friends and they've done everything they can to keep me occupied. I try to live as normally as I can. I know that it's essential to me and to Sid that life goes on, and I know that's the way he would want it . . . Friends stop by and we've taken a few day trips away from home, and have shared some lovely dinners. I also tend my garden."

Seated beneath a skylight next to the white-washed, brick fireplace, Pat still wore the blue ribbon pinned to her blouse that had been presented to her by Charlie Roxburgh as a reminder that Exxon employees were thinking of and praying for Sid and his safe return.

On the other side of the fireplace was a small bookcase holding well-worn biographies on presidents, generals, and other historical figures that Sid Reso enjoyed reading. Much of his interest in famous individuals stemmed from his desire to learn about their management techniques in hopes of discovering something he might bring to his own work.

"Do you think he's in good health?" another reporter asked. "Do you worry about his heart?"

"I think I'd be lying if I said I wasn't concerned about his health," Pat confessed. "I'm counting on the fact that wherever he is, he is being well-treated. That's all I have."

"Is he a tough guy?"

"He's very strong," she replied. "And he's got a great faith, and so do I. I just think without question he's coming home."

"So you do think you'll be reunited soon?"

"I believe that—really deep down in my heart—I believe that Sid is alive. There's fear, of course, fear of the unknown, but I can only say that when the fear comes, there's a sense of calm that overcomes that. There's a stillness inside of me that I am most appreciative of, and I don't doubt for a moment that it comes from prayer that's lifting us up constantly."

"You do seem to be handling all this pretty well. Better than many would." While the reporter was speaking, Pat reached for a glass of water she'd placed on the side table before the conference began. She sipped and then responded.

"Most people would say I'm in, quote, shock. I don't think I am. This is me. I can't pretend. So what you see is what I have been. Certainly there have been times, moments when anger or fear creeps in and tears come. But generally, I'm private. My journal has been a wonderful form of release for me." Pat then explained that she'd written in her diary twice each day, talking to Sid, telling him what she does and who she sees, and sharing details about the cards and letters that arrive almost daily.

When Pat called an end to the conference, a reporter requested Pat to make a closing remark. She obliged. "I just want to be able to see that he's well and tell him I love him. And also assure him that life will go on and our family will all come together again," she said. "I look forward to the day he walks through that door . . . I just want him back. I want him back real bad."

As hoped, the kidnappers heard the television and radio reports of Pat's conference. The Seales also read the statements made by Pat Reso and Jim Morakis in *The Star-Ledger* and *The New York Times*.

At last, the kidnappers felt that they could make plans for the ransom drop again. They entered Secure Storage twice that day. Preparations were almost complete.

* * *

Energized by the deferential messages from Pat Reso and Exxon, Art and Jackie commenced putting their plans to receive the ransom payment into action. On Monday, June 16, they typed a ransom note (their tenth) and drove along Route 24 between Mendham and Morristown. They dropped the envelope containing the ransom letter into the mailbox of the Morris County Sheriff's Labor Assistance Program (SLAP), a structured manual labor sentence program for low-risk offenders. The unidentified black mailbox stood leaning in isolation along rural Route 24/Mendham Road near Sunrise Lake.

At 11:45 p.m. that Monday, Art Seale telephoned the Exxon cellular number from a payphone in Morristown. Perhaps having grown a bit complacent by the passage of time without word from the kidnappers, the cellular line wasn't adequately supported by agents. The sole officer present was from the Morris County Prosecutor's Office. He called his superiors, Chief Detective Richard Riley and Deputy Chief of Investigation John Dempsey, who ordered back-up should the caller demand immediate action. They waited for another call.

Once again, the unanswered call angered Art Seale. Rather than calling the cellular number again, he dialed the two Exxon hotline numbers advertised in the newspapers in quick succession. The second call was answered by Detective Steve Foley of the Morris County Prosecutor's Office, whose principal job had been guarding the ransom money in the safe at the command post.

"Hello?"

"Go to Sheriff's Labor Assistance Program mailbox. 300 Route 24, Mendham. Note there." Once again, the voice sounded ghostly.

The call was recorded as were all calls made to Exxon's hotline numbers. A transcript also would be made and placed in the file.

Detectives Riley and Dempsey drove three miles west along New Jersey Route 24 to the location of the obscure mailbox. Riley later recalled opening the mailbox with a long stick in case the mailbox had been booby-trapped. He carefully retrieved the letter from inside. A forensics team arrived and processed the mailbox and driveway.

Back at the command post with FBI agents present, the envelope was opened. The letter read in part:

```
    . . . Preparations for delivery:
    1. Gather $18.5 million in used $100 bills.
    2. Equally divide the bills and place them
in 10 green colored Eddie Bauer laundry bags.
    3. Use Reso's white Subaru station wagon.
    4. Delivery people to be Mrs. Reso, one of
```

their daughters, and J. Morakis, the Exxon Spokesperson.

5. Be ready to leave from Reso's house.

6. To prevent a repeat of the first attempt — KEEP THE

PORTABLE PHONE WITH YOU.

Mrs. Reso is to act as the spokesperson for the group . . . We will ask her questions that only she will be able to answer. Any substitutions will have very serious consequences.

WARRIORS OF THE RAINBOW

Art Seale left the payphone in Morristown that night and drove directly to Secure Storage. Strangely, he attempted to enter the storage complex at eleven minutes after midnight, but since the facility closed at 9:00 p.m., as it always had (which he should have known), Seale's entry code was refused and the gates did not open. He returned to the storage facility at 10:20 on Tuesday morning. Later that day, back at home, he typed the ransom delivery instructions. It was finally time.

Part II
THE RANSOM DROP

Chapter 8

On Tuesday, June 17, Art and Jackie Seale busied themselves with last-minute kidnapping errands. Their mood was tense. It would turn out to be a very demanding day for the eco-terrorist impersonators. There were ransom delivery instructions to craft and type. It was decided that five notes should do the trick. Art typed away in the basement bedroom that morning as Jackie showered and primped after a morning run. The Seales also decided that nine, perhaps ten, payphone calls should be enough to carry out their plan, so Art jotted down notes for each call. He'd record them later to play over the payphones that night.

Jackie insisted and Art Seale agreed that they wouldn't carry guns, as they had on the morning of the kidnapping. They weren't expecting a night-long shootout or a week-long siege. Above all, they didn't want to get themselves killed.

They also checked their kidnapping provisions. Their existing inventory included more than a half roll of quarters, four boxes of rubber bands to wrap packages of money, and an unopened box of surgical gloves. Jackie's shiny nickels had been cleaned and bagged. There were a few items still on the kidnapper's shopping list, such as gasoline for the Mercedes, five large Rubbermaid bins with lids to hold some of the ransom, clear plastic sheeting, and another roll of duct tape to fasten ransom notes. And, of course, they'd need a rental car.

While the Seales carried out their secret arrangements, their sixteen-year-old daughter was out doing whatever teenagers do during the summer while Art's father puttered about the house and yard. Art's mother may have been volunteering that day at the Red Mill Museum Village twenty miles south in Clinton, as she often did. Perhaps she was enjoying a luncheon with friends at the Hunterdon Hills Garden Club where she was a member. Despite all the typing in their house and their son's many clandestine rendezvous with payphones and storage units, the voluminous FBI investigation report contains no evidence that either knew anything about the kidnapping. In all likelihood, their son and his wife spun plausible stories and excuses to cover their odd behavior, and as parents are often inclined to do, Mr. and Mrs. Seale wanted to believe their son.

Almost fifty miles away in Hillside, New Jersey, Jackie Seale's mother was spending her day watching television. The seventy-two-year-old retired nurse, Irene Grant Szarko, had been a widow since Jackie's father died eleven years earlier at the age of sixty-three. Jackie rarely visited her elderly mother. Her older brother, who was married with children, watched after their parent. And Jackie rarely, if ever, saw him either. According to Jackie's brother, "My brother-in-law wanted no part of my sister's family," he said. "It was closed company, just the two of them. No one really knew what was going on with them . . . It was all Arthur's show . . . And the Szarkos got sick of hearing Art's lies, stories, and dreams."

On the night of Monday, June 17, the elder Seales and the Szarkos were simply spending a comfortable evening at their homes. Within twenty-four hours, their lives would be turned upside down.

* * *

It was ransom day—again. Eighty-one degrees and sunny, a perfect day for a multi-million dollar ransom pickup. The last attempt had occurred forty-two days earlier at the Villa Restaurant. It ended in failure when Jackie Seale repeatedly punched in the wrong phone number before she and her husband finally gave up, blaming the FBI for botching the exchange. Seven weeks later, they were ready to try again. This time, they believed there'd be no mistakes. Art Seale had certainly had plenty of time to devise a masterful ransom drop. And now, on

Thursday morning, June 18, 1992, the time was drawing near to implement that plan. If they weren't successful, they'd be back at the Seale house pleading for more time to live there—or they'd be in jail with no more concerns about finding future accommodations. They had to get it right this time.

Art and Jackie arrived at Aries Rent-a-Car in Hackettstown around 11:30 that Thursday morning. The rental car office was only a mile from Secure Storage and five miles from the Seale home. It was a small office in the corner of an L-shaped metal building that housed many auto-related businesses with service bay doors. The owner, Elizabeth "Bette" Thomassen, a business woman actively involved in the community, leased Jackie a green 1992 Oldsmobile Ciera bearing license plate number HJR41U. Seale told Thomassen she'd return the car either that night or first thing the next morning. She paid the rental charge with her mother's credit card.

Like Art Seale's parents, the elderly Irene Szarko occasionally helped her daughter financially and permitted her to carry one of Mrs. Szarko's credit cards. After their bankruptcy, Art and Jackie had been unable to obtain credit cards, especially with their inability to maintain jobs. Mrs. Szarko could have never imagined, however, that her credit card rented the van that had been used to kidnap Sid Reso weeks earlier and now it was renting a car to be used to extort millions from Exxon.

The Seales parked the Oldsmobile at the ACME grocery in Washington Township while they ran errands in their washed and gassed Mercedes. The trunk of the Mercedes still contained loads of kidnapping paraphernalia, acting as the Seales's own "secure storage," a concealed repository for the trappings of their new trade. Their Jeep Cherokee's engine would no longer run and they couldn't afford to repair it. It sat in the backyard of the elder Seale's home.

With their shopping complete, Art retrieved the Oldsmobile and drove about Morris and Somerset counties placing notes in numerous locations. He also went to his mother-in-law's house and dropped the IBM typewriter in her trash bin for pickup later that day. It was never located by authorities.

At 2:55 p.m., Art placed his first call. It was a simple one.

"Exxon hotline?"

"Tell Morakis be ready."

That was it. The FBI traced the call to a payphone in the Cedar Mills area in Warren County, although no further trace information could be obtained.

Art and Jackie Seale placed four more calls, all within the next hour. Two were made to an Exxon reward hotline and two to the Exxon cellular number. One was traced to the Chicken Restaurant in Hillsborough, one to a payphone in Far Hills, another to Mendham Investment Company, and another couldn't be traced. Curiously, only one was answered before the Seales hung up:

"Hello?" Agent Carolyn Zimmer said.

"Be ready."

"Be ready? Be ready when? When do you want us to be ready? Can you tell me when you want us to be ready? Hello?"

The call ended.

Then at 4:09 p.m., Jackie Seale called the Exxon cellular number.

"Hello?" said another agent.

"Money ready?"

"The money is ready. If you'll please tell me where you want us to take it, we'll take it."

"Shortly."

"Shortly? You want us—hello? Can you talk to me? Hello?"

Jackie had hung up the phone. The call could not be traced.

It isn't clear what the Seales did between four and eight o'clock, though they may have simply returned home to eat dinner with their family before resuming their ransom pickup plans later that evening.

At 8:30 p.m., Art and Jackie met in their separate cars at King's Food Market in Mendham. The market's parking lot had been used earlier on May 1 when the kidnappers called the Exxon cellular number for the first time and directed listeners to the second ransom note at Lewis Morris County Park. Now Art stepped out of the rented car and joined his wife in the Mercedes. Their intention had been for him to record several messages that he'd play that night over payphones, but once again, the tape recorder wasn't working. The Seales entered King's Food Market to purchase batteries. Surveillance cameras recorded their entry at 8:41 p.m. and store receipts later showed their purchase was made eight minutes later. They returned to the Mercedes and Art Seale snapped in the batteries.

"Dammit!" The tape recorder still wouldn't work. Rather than drive to the Radio Shack store in Flemington where they'd purchased it, they decided to use their own disguised voices. Art returned to the rented Oldsmobile to begin the first round of phone calls. Jackie left in the Mercedes and parked at a lot in Lamington, twenty miles southwest of Morristown. She'd also make some calls from her location.

The FBI and Morris County Prosecutor's Office realized something big was up at last, or at least they hoped so. Six phone calls in a matter of an hour and fifteen minutes meant the kidnappers were up to something. It made sense. There'd been a flurry of messages just days before, ending with Pat Reso and Exxon declaring that they were "unconditionally" ready to pay the ransom. Charlie Roxburgh relayed the day's information to Pat personally. She grew anxious, yet enthusiastic. Sid might be coming home at last.

The FBI swiftly made preparations for another ransom drop. Agents drove Sid Reso's station wagon to a secret location where the exterior was sprayed with a chemical that would illuminate the car in darkness to agents wearing night vision goggles (the FBI logically presumed the drop would be that night). Firefly sensors also were attached to the roof of the car and its bumpers so that the car would, as Agent Walker recalled, "light up like a Christmas tree" when viewed from forward looking infrared (FLIR) equipment in aircraft. Agents with goggles would trail the car aboard a helicopter and a small airplane, including the FBI's special Nightstalker aircraft. Agents also removed the seat and the spare tire from the station wagon's rear compartment to conceal a shooter with an automatic weapon beneath bags of fake money. All interior lightbulbs in the car were removed.

Rather than placing the entire $18.5 million in ten Eddie Bauer bags as the kidnappers had instructed, agents packaged newspaper clippings with used $100 bills covering the ends in tight plastic bundles and stuffed them into the bags. Exxon now refused to hand over $18.5 million because the kidnappers had refused to prove Sid Reso was still alive. The FBI never planned on the kidnappers getting the money anyway. Several tracking devices were hidden in various packages of money and the linings of the bags. Agents planted additional devices in the car and in the cellular phone that would be used inside the car to communicate with the kidnappers. Listening devices were also planted.

The FBI assigned Special Agent Ed Petersen to pose as Jim Morakis again, and a young female agent, Theresa Reilly, to pose as Reso's twenty-eight-year-old daughter whom she resembled. Petersen and Reilly studied their subjects carefully to avoid being exposed as fakes. Both meticulously reviewed information about Morakis and the Reso's daughter and questioned both so that they could *become* the two. As Exxon spokesman Jim Morakis later recalled, "I have never been so impressed with any group of people as I was with those two FBI agents." Though the ransom note had also directed that Pat Reso come along and be the contact person, the FBI didn't designate anyone to play her role. The Bureau assigned the small-statured but sure-shot SWAT operator, Anthony "Tony" Backus, to secrete himself in the rear of the station wagon beneath the bags of phony money.

Agent Reilly would drive Sid's VW wagon while Petersen would be assigned to receive calls and retrieve notes. Neither had ever driven a manual transmission vehicle. Agent Reilly, from the Bronx, learned to drive a standard transmission from her boyfriend just before the ransom drop.

Helicopters and planes were fueled and pilots assigned. Aircraft have been used by the Bureau for decades. The first FBI "surveillance" plane, a Stinson Reliant high-wing monoplane took off in 1938 to observe the drop of extortion money from a moving train. The G-man pilot was instrumental in catching the Depression-era chiseler. Art Seale apparently did not know that a plan like his had been foiled way back in 1938 by a simple monoplane, now seen only at air shows with wing walkers.

Fifty-four years later, the FBI had improved upon the monoplane with its highly-sophisticated Nightstalker. The Cessna 182T surveillance aircraft with the ominous-sounding name and black fuselage was one of a fleet of fixed wing aircraft that served as the Bureau's eyes and ears in the sky. The planes, some propeller-driven and others jets with muffling to keep them quiet, contained zoom and infrared cameras and listening equipment. The surveillance planes are often used to observe criminal cells, yet also come in handy in kidnapping and extortion cases (now with the aid of drones). When the thermal imager spots people on the ground at night, they look like walking ghosts to those in the aircraft, and the ghost's voices come in loud and clear with the plane's audio surveillance equipment.

The FBI and Morris County law enforcement also employed a simple yet ingenious tactic that had been used in the Seagram heir's kidnapping case nearly twenty years earlier. Because almost all calls from the kidnappers had come from payphones in local counties, the FBI positioned personnel at numerous payphones in most of north-central New Jersey, basically within a fifteen-mile radius of the Reso home. They were divided into surveillance teams labeled T-50, T-51, and so on. An FBI agent was accompanied by a local detective or officer in each car. One hundred and ten teams of law enforcement were stationed a safe distance from payphones and watched for any notable activity. Others cruised down streets within their watch zone to observe phones since there weren't enough personnel to cover every single payphone in the area. (Unlike today, most commercial establishments in 1992 had payphones inside and outside).

By early afternoon, the FBI had completed its preparations in the event the kidnappers called that evening with ransom delivery instructions. Nonetheless, all of the preparations could have been in vain; the kidnappers might not call. They had called before and then disappeared for days and weeks.

At 9:07 p.m., Art Seale approached a payphone in Somerset County. It had begun.

* * *

"Leave now!" shouted Art in an excited and shrill voice from a Somerset County payphone.

"I, I can't hear you," Special Agent Carolyn Zimmer replied, having answered the Exxon cellular telephone.

"Leave now."

"Who is . . . what?"

"Leave now. Go to Tingley Road at Patriot's Path," Art Seale continued, still using a ghostly disguised voice.

"What road?"

"Tingley Road."

"Tingley?"

"Tingley Road."

"Spell it. Spell it."

"T-I-N-G-L-E-Y."

"Tingley Road?" Zimmer asked.

"Road at Patriot's—"

"At what?"

"Pa—Patriot's."

"At Pat—"

"Path."

"At, at what? Patriot's what?"

"Path."

Surely at this point in the call, Art Seale should have known that the person on the line was attempting to trace the call and keep him standing at the payphone, but Seale remained on the line.

"Go to Tingley Road at Patriot's Path, and what, and do what?" the female agent asked.

"Look on the ground. Envelope."

"Look, look on the ground?"

"Envelope."

"Look on the ground?" Zimmer asked again.

"Envelope."

"Where on the ground, can you tell me?"

"Envelope on the ground."

"Envelope on the ground. Where on the ground? In the front?"

If the call hadn't been ridiculous already, it certainly became so when the telephone operator interrupted and asked the caller (Art Seale) to insert additional coins.

"One minute," Art Seale actually said.

"I'm sorry, can you—hello? Hello?"

Art Seale either couldn't find his roll of quarters fast enough or he'd simply had enough of the charade. The operator terminated the call.

The FBI scrambled. The call was trapped and traced to a payphone at the Gladstone Train Station in Somerset County, a small community fifteen miles southwest of Morristown. No one had been assigned to watch that phone, so agents raced to the location. The caller had vanished. Agents secured and searched the scene as they had all the other payphones used by the kidnappers. Simultaneously, an agent grabbed the cellular phone at the FBI command post and rushed it to Agent Petersen, who was waiting at the Reso home.

Then Agents Petersen and Reilly, along with their shooter, Tony Backus, loaded into the VW station wagon with the bags of fake money. In addition to all of the listening devices concealed inside the car, Agents Reilly and Petersen wore hidden microphones should they become separated from the vehicle. Armed with an MP5 9-mm submachine gun, Backus lay in the empty spare tire compartment beneath ten green Eddie Bauer bags.

A helicopter hovered overhead to follow at a safe distance as the FBI Nightstalker took off from Morristown Municipal Airport. No flight plan was filed. The FBI simply demanded emergency clearance and took off from the busy airport. Besides the pilot, two agents sat within the fuselage of the propeller-powered Cessna, manning infrared cameras and hi-tech surveillance equipment. They would pick up the location of the VW wagon within minutes.

Agent Reilly pulled out of the Reso's driveway and drove south on Whitehead Road before turning west onto Mendham Road. The heavily-wooded Patriot's Path was only a tenth of a mile off the two-lane Tingley Road. The distance for the entire trip was fewer than three and a half miles, yet the "drop team" was already running behind the kidnappers' schedule.

Art Seale became flustered. At 9:23 p.m., just fifteen minutes after he'd ended his last call, he again called the cellular phone that was now in the hands of Agent Reilly as she drove the stick shift wagon. The call would be traced to another payphone in Gladstone that, again, was not one of the payphones under surveillance.

"Hello?" Agent Reilly answered.

"Where are you?" Seale asked, still speaking in an eerie

disguised voice.

"We're coming."

"Hurry."

"Okay. We're coming. We're coming," Agent Reilly did an excellent job sounding worried. The fear and tension were clear in her voice.

"Who are you?"

"I'm their daughter."

"Address in Houston?" Art Seale asked, testing the woman to see if she really was who she claimed to be. He possessed the 1985 Exxon executive directory that listed the Reso family's old Houston address.

"What?"

"Your address in Houston?"

"I don't live in Houston. I live in Washington, D.C.," Reilly said, speaking rapidly and sounding terrified.

"Mom and Dad lived in Houston," Art Seale said.

"I . . ." Agent Reilly didn't know what to say at that point. She had no idea what the Houston address had been. Agent Petersen grabbed the cellular phone.

"Eh . . . this is, this is Jim, umm, she's is pretty upset," Petersen said with a Jersey accent similar to that of Morakis. "We're, we're enroute. We got your directions and, and we're, we're en route right now. We're making the turn. Can you please repeat everything so it's clear to us, okay?"

"Tingley Road, Patriot's Path," Art Seale replied. He continued despite that Agent Reilly had failed to answer his identification question. Petersen's quick thinking had averted trouble and convinced Seale to continue.

"Okay, Tingley Road, Patriot's Park. We're, we're—"

"Patriot's Path."

"Patriot's Path. We're en route. Just bear with us because we're not used to doing this, we're a little nervous. But we're trying—"

Then the operator interrupted. "One minute has ended. Please signal when through."

"Envelope on the ground. Envelope on the ground," Art Seale repeated quickly and loudly, attempting to get in the last words before the operator terminated the call.

"Okay, the envelope is on the ground?"

"Follow directions."

"Okay, we, we're getting there as quickly as we can. Just bear with us and—"

The operator terminated the call—a call between an FBI agent and a kidnapper of one of the most important corporate executives in the country involving $18.5 million—over a quarter. It appeared that despite all the detailed preparations of the FBI, the Morris County Prosecutor's Office, and the kidnappers, none had spoken beforehand with the people who actually seemed to be controlling the night's exchanges: New Jersey Bell Telephone Company.

* * *

Pat stood in the kitchen with a cup of coffee in her hands. Just moments before, her house had been swirling with activity. Those who'd form the drop team reviewed various scenarios as other agents readied Sid's car while their walkie-talkies squawked incomprehensibly. She'd seen the agents leave in Sid's car. It was an eerie sight watching the Volkswagen back out of her garage like on the morning of the kidnapping. She wished the agents good luck and waved at them as they backed out, though she didn't think they'd seen her.

Incredibly, Pat had made dinner for the agents before they left. Agent Ed Petersen, who then had five children and now has twenty-four grandchildren, later recalled that Pat was worried about his safety that night. "That's the kind of person she was," Petersen said. "During that tense night when the safe return of her husband may have hung in the balance, she was worried about me because I'm the father of five children."

Within the first half hour, Pat began wondering if the agents had met up with the kidnappers. Sid may have already been turned over to them, but agents would have called her. Maybe they were just finishing up the exchange and hadn't had a chance to call. Just as quickly, thoughts may have flashed through her mind that there might be a problem. Maybe agents had drawn their guns and so had the kidnappers, possibly even putting a gun to Sid's head creating a standoff. It had been thirty minutes. Sid could be coming home within minutes or, Heaven forbid, they found him dead.

The drop team had arrived at Patriot's Path shortly after 9:30 p.m. Their car lights shone into the deep woods as Petersen and Reilly scanned the area through the windshield. They could see that no one was at the scene, though the woods were thick and dark. An ambush was a real possibility. Agent Petersen stepped out and searched for the note with the aid of a flashlight and the Volkswagen's headlights. Agent Reilly stayed in the station wagon and kept the command post advised of what was happening. She watched for any movement in the darkness and spoke to Backus who gripped his submachine gun in the rear of the car.

Petersen spotted the envelope on the ground just as the kidnapper had described. Wearing gloves, he picked up the envelope and returned to the car. It contained two letters. He quickly read them aloud using a flashlight.

Charlie Roxburgh, who was listening at the command post, telephoned Pat and explained that the first envelope had been retrieved and opened by Petersen. It contained two letters. Roxburgh told Pat that the first letter simply reiterated the terms of the ransom note discovered two days earlier. Pat surely had grown sick of receiving yet another meaningless ransom letter.

"What is the other one?" Pat asked.

"Directions to the next letter at the Ralston General Store."

"The next letter?"

Pat poured herself another cup of coffee. It was going to be a long night.

Chapter 9

Agents and detectives stood about the command post on the top floor of a Morris County government building in Morristown. All the chief officials were there—Mike Murphy, Gary Penrith, and Jere Doyle. U.S. Attorney Chertoff was on his way. The communication center was the busiest it had been in weeks. Phones were ringing, recorders were taping, and telephone company employees and other technical support personnel were manning the equipment. The entire room was lined and draped with wires. Because Agent Petersen was miked and operated a two-way radio using an encrypted frequency buffered by listening devices inside the VW station wagon, agents at the command post remained in constant communication with the drop team.

It was a tense night. A large map of the local area, jabbed with multi-colored pins and laced with strips of string and tape, hung on one wall like a diagrammatic tapestry. It exhibited the drop team's location and route as well as the origins of the kidnappers' calls in relation to the more than one hundred surveillance teams dispersed throughout the area. Those assigned to the command post were confident they'd soon catch the kidnappers in their dragnet, but like a fisherman reeling in the big one, everyone hoped the kidnappers didn't slip away before bringing them in.

As the night continued, Agent Petersen relayed information to the command post as Agent Reilly shifted the station wagon's manual transmission and worked its clutch and accelerator along the winding country roads. Both agents were focused and anxious to arrive at the next stop. The drive from the main entrance of Lewis Morris County Park to the Ralston General Store in Mendham was a fairly direct five mile-route west along New Jersey Route 24. Yet, the route was mostly rural with little room to pass, along a road encroached on by numerous blind driveways. It's not a patch of roadway to speed along safely, especially at night. Besides, the VW station wagon, equipped with its dawdling five-cylinder, 115-horsepower engine and snowflake wheels, wasn't going to set any land-speed records, even if Exxon's premium gasoline filled its tank. Even so, about fifteen minutes later, at 9:50 p.m., the drop team arrived.

Agent Reilly slowed the car as its headlights revealed a white sign on a wooden post, "Ralston General Store," a tiny museum beside the highway. She turned right and parked on Roxiticus Road. Petersen stepped out shining a flashlight. Twenty-feet from the highway sat the one-room, wood-shingled, whitewashed cabin adorned with a solitary rusty cast-iron planter and a large scraggly bush. The location was dark and the darkness was still. There was no passing traffic; not even a breeze. Again, the potential for an ambush troubled the agents. Petersen watchfully stepped onto the tiny museum's creaky wood-plank porch where he spotted a white envelope taped to the narrow gray door in plain sight. Wearing gloves, he carefully removed the envelope and duct tape, and returned to the station wagon. He read the letter aloud to the command post. It gave directions to the Williamson Building where the next note would be located.

With the content of the note relayed, the drop team wasted no time. Agent Reilly pulled out onto New Jersey Route 24 to head to the next stop four miles due west. Again, the agent drove the underpowered car along a level, though curvy, road that meandered through the countryside between the towns of Mendham and Chester. Agents Petersen and Reilly talked about what to expect at the next stop. They also spoke to Backus in the back, cramped and perspiring while gripping a submachine gun beneath heavy bags.

Between 9:51 and 9:55, Art Seale attempted three times to call the cellular phone inside the station wagon from a payphone in front of the Somerset Hills Elks Club on New Jersey Route 206 in Gladstone. Because of poor signal strength in the rural area, Seale's calls could not reach the cellular phone. He hadn't taken that into account. He cursed as he punched in the number on the payphone's touch-tone keypad. The ransom delivery was already behind schedule and now he couldn't reach Jim Morakis (Agent Petersen) in the Volkswagen. The FBI intercepted Seale's failed calls and even recorded what Seale heard on his end of the line. Each message was the same, though the message was cut shorter by Seale hanging up sooner on each call: "The Cellular One customer you have called is unavailable or has traveled outside the coverage area. Please try your call again later. Message number TB20." The recording infuriated Seale each time he heard it.

Frustrated, Seale slapped the payphone receiver down on the cradle and drove to Far Hills to join Jackie. Far Hills is a small town of about seven hundred residents fifteen miles southwest of Morristown. It was ten o'clock and things weren't going as planned. The husband and wife kidnappers parked their cars parallel to each other facing in opposite directions so they could discuss the night's problems through open driver side windows.

"These assholes are slow as Christmas," Art Seale said. "If they don't hurry up, they're gonna miss the train."

"Really?"

"It'll be close. I'll see if I can hurry 'em up. Go on to Chester. I'll be there in about five minutes."

"Okay."

The two drove away. Though the Seales didn't know that surveillance teams were posted at numerous payphones, Art Seale did know that they had to keep moving to avoid appearing suspicious. It would be easy to draw the attention of police on a late Thursday night in the small communities scattered about Somerset, Warren, and Morris counties.

The drop team drove the station wagon farther into the countryside. They glanced to the sides of the lonely road at wood-paneled homes with their porch lights on, some displaying American flags visible in the dim light. They also passed a sprinkling of churches and a small American Legion Post brandishing twin World War II artillery pieces out front. The agents looked, but didn't notice. They had more important things to think about than the landscape. The station wagon approached an intersection. They were in Chester.

At 10:07, Art Seale parked the rented Oldsmobile at a payphone on Peapack Road across the street from the Far Hills Fairgrounds nine miles from the Williamson Building. He rang the cellular phone.

"Hel . . . Hello?" Agent Petersen answered.

"Your location?" Seale asked, satisfied to speak only to Morakis (Agent Petersen). He never asked to speak to Pat Reso, whom the ransom notes had designated as the contact person. An FBI agent posing as Pat wasn't even in the car. Petersen was prepared to tell Seale if he asked that Pat was too upset to come along.

"We're, we're about four buildings away, I think," Petersen said as he looked about to determine their location with the aid of the command post. This was a time before cars and cell phones were commonly equipped with GPS navigation. "We're, we're, we're, I think we may have passed it, we're close though. We're right, eh, we just passed St. Lawrence. Are we close? St. Lawrence Catholic Church? Are—"

"Ch . . . Chester?" Seale asked.

"Yes, we're in Chester. We just passed the ga . . . gas station, the Amoco gas station. And we're passing St. Lawrence Church. Are we close?"

"Yes."

"Okay, how far up do we have to go?"

"On your right. Hurry! Hurry!" Art Seale shouted, losing his patience. The train would pull away from the Peapack Train Station any minute.

"Okay, we're hurrying. Just give us a chance," Agent Petersen said. "We're doing the best we can. This is new to us. We're trying the best we can."

Seale hung up. He had miscalculated how long it would take the drop team to drive to the location of each note, find it, read it, and move on to the next.

Agent Reilly turned left onto Main Street and passed St. Lawrence the Martyr Church on the right. Less than a half mile farther on the right sat the Williamson Building, a two-story orange brick building with long windows and shutters. The former Chester Public School had been renamed and renovated into office space. Now it served as a ransom note drop site. Reilly parked at the front and Petersen jumped out, hurrying toward a recently-trimmed shrub smelling like fresh evergreen. He had no problem spotting the envelope. It was lying on the ground to the left of the building's front doors beneath a columned portico.

Petersen returned to the station wagon with its engine running and headlights on. Once again, he read the letter so that the command post could hear. It directed the drop team to the Komline-Sanderson Corporation plant six miles away. The note instructed them to be there before ten o'clock and wait for a call at a phone booth.

Reilly took off driving south on the dark and isolated Route 206, a sparsely-populated stretch bounded with tall trees and cornfields. Though it may have seemed as if they'd been exiled to a far corner of the earth, they were not alone. Not only was the command post listening, but the FBI's Nightstalker flew overhead reporting every stop, turn, and conversation. Two dark-colored, unmarked sedans each carrying two agents acting as security teams also followed a safe distance behind.

The drop team didn't know it yet, but Art Seale was sending them to the Peapack Train Station to catch a train. Seale was very familiar with the New Jersey Transit commuter rail line, known as the Gladstone Line, which runs between Gladstone and Summit, Newark, and Hoboken. He'd often taken that train when commuting to New York City. The Gladstone Line commuter schedule showed that eastbound trains departed the Peapack Train Station at 10:07 p.m. and 12:11 a.m. on weeknights. It was already 10:10 p.m. and the drop team hadn't even made it to the Komline-Sanderson Corporation plant that sat beside the station.

Seale had specified in the Williamson Building ransom note that he'd intended for the drop team to arrive at the Komline-Sanderson plant no later than ten o'clock. He was beside himself when he met Jackie near the Chester Mall where the drop team had been moments earlier. The drop car was definitely going to miss the 10:07 train out of Peapack so the Seales had to decide whether to wait and direct those inside the station wagon to board the 12:11 train out of Peapack or call it quits for the night. Jackie Seale exited the Mercedes and entered the Oldsmobile to discuss what to do.

"They've missed the goddamn train!"

"Maybe there's still time," Jackie said calmly.

"No, Jackie," Art said in a condescending tone. "The train leaves at 10:07. I bet it's already left the station. And they're still driving. Shit!"

"What are we gonna do?"

That was the big question. An intense conversation between the husband and wife kidnappers ensued and it was decided — they weren't quitting. They'd simply have to stall the drop team for a couple hours. Art drove away to make a call that would begin doing just that.

Seale's original plan, the one that had begun an hour earlier and carried the Volkswagen and its occupants far out into the countryside, had been to phone Morakis when he reached Komline-Sanderson and instruct Pat Reso to cross the railroad tracks on foot and pick up a note tacked on the wall of the Peapack Train Station seventy-five yards away. The drop team never retrieved the note that night, which instructed Jim Morakis and Pat and her daughter to board the eastbound train with the money and the cellular phone. Seale intended to call the cellular phone from the Far Hills Train Station and instruct Morakis to force the conductor to stop the train at a secluded railroad crossing on Whitenack Road one hundred and seventy-five yards off New Jersey Route 202, between Far Hills and Bernardsville.

At that point, Seale would instruct Morakis to toss the ten bags of money off the train onto the side of Whitenack Road that ran east of the crossing. Morakis would then order the engineer to resume heading east toward Bernardsville immediately. When the train rolled out, Seale would drive up to the railroad crossing and load the ten bags of money weighing forty pounds each into the Oldsmobile. Then he'd meet up with Jackie at a Catholic church on Schooley's Mountain Road south of the rental car office in Hackettstown. They'd transfer the money into Rubbermaid containers and place them in the Mercedes's trunk and backseat before returning the Oldsmobile to the rental car lot. From there, they'd drive away in their Mercedes scot free. Then there'd be mansions, sailboats, sports cars, designer clothes, Europe . . . At least, that had been the plan.

* * *

Stakeouts can be brutally dull. Special Agent Carrie Brzezinski, of surveillance team T-112, had been assigned the duty of watching payphones near the intersection of New Jersey Routes 24 and 206 in Chester, which included those in the Chester Mall parking lot. She'd been sitting in her car since 1:45 that afternoon peering through binoculars and logging dozens of descriptions of individuals and their vehicles who used payphones within her surveillance area. For nine long hours none had proved notable.

At 10:40 p.m., an Oldsmobile pulled up and parked fewer than one hundred feet in front of her vehicle. She watched as a white man with blond hair beneath a blue baseball cap emerged from the driver's door and walked toward the payphone outside a store that had closed for the night. The agent could see him clearly. She straightened in her seat and stretched her neck when she observed him wearing a blue jacket and clear latex gloves, which was not the typical attire for a seventy degree evening in June. She continued to watch as the man began to place a telephone call.

Seconds later, Agent Petersen, standing in a phone booth at the Komline-Sanderson plant seven miles south of Chester Mall, grabbed the phone receiver on the first ring.

"Hello. This is Jim speaking," Petersen said, careful not to use his own name. The rusty and disheveled plant area was dimly-lit with lots of concrete, gravel, and equipment that created an eerie atmosphere for the FBI agent. The Peapack Train Station stood only yards away from him. Before he'd arrived, the 10:07 had pulled away from the station only minutes earlier.

"Take Route 206 south to Route 287 south, then take Route 78 east," Art Seale said in a disguised voice. "Contact will be made on cellular phone while traveling east on 78. If contact is not made, return to Komline phone booth."

Agent Petersen repeated the instructions and Seale ended the call.

While Seale was giving Petersen his improvised directions, Agent Brzezinski and the other surveillance teams received an alert from the command post over their radios that a "hot call" between the kidnapper and the drop team was in progress. As Agent Brzezinski listened to the alert, she watched her suspect hang up the telephone and return to the Oldsmobile, casually removing his gloves as he walked. Another alert came in from the command post that the call had just terminated.

"My heart told me," Brzezinski recalled later, "this is the kidnapper, this is the guy we've been waiting for, for fifty-plus days, waiting to stumble upon, waiting to identify. This is him and he's not going to get away." When the Oldsmobile began to pull out, she spotted a second person in the car. She couldn't make out whether the figure was a man or a woman. She could only see a shadow in the front passenger seat. As the Oldsmobile drove away and headed south on New Jersey Route 206, the agent followed long enough to record its license plate number, HJR41U, and then she lost him. Brzezinski picked up the microphone to her two-way radio and called the command post:

"This is T-112. Reporting UNMALE [unidentified male], white, heavyset, blond hair, forties, wearing gloves. Observed making call at Chester Mall payphone at 22:40 hours. Driving late model dark green Oldsmobile Cutlass Ciera four-door sedan, New Jersey plate number HJR41U, heading south on Route 206. UNSUB [unidentified subject] in passenger seat. Unable to identify. Contact lost. Advise."

Adrenaline had been pumping through the agents and detectives at the command post all night, but Agent Brzezinski's report lit them on fire. After seven weeks of long hours and tedious investigating with no significant clues as to the kidnappers' identities, they now had a man's description and a plate number. The feeling was overwhelming, but they didn't have time to celebrate. Straightaway, the command post notified all surveillance teams, including those patrolling the streets, to be on the lookout for the Oldsmobile and its blond male driver.

Agents also ran a vehicle registration check. Instantly, they learned that the Olds was registered to Aries Rent-a-Car, Inc. in Hackettstown, New Jersey. The rental company would have the driver's name and address on file. Unfortunately, the rental agency only listed a post office box as its address. "Get that rental car address. Wake up the whole town if you have to," Agent Walker directed.

With the command post in a frenzy trying to locate the Olds and chase down the identity of its driver, Art Seale puttered along New Jersey Route 206, completely unaware that he had been spotted by an FBI agent. He believed he'd successfully salvaged the night's plan. His last call to Petersen at the Komline-Sanderson plant had sent the drop team on a wild goose chase. He'd directed them south and then east in order to consume two hours before the 12:11 train left the Peapack station.

Seale believed the night's events were once again in his favor and he'd get the drop team on the 12:11 — with the money.

* * *

While the unknown suspect cruised around the area, Agent Walker pulled surveillance teams off Morris County and Warren County payphones and directed them to converge on Somerset County. He instructed the teams to patrol streets and roads in search of the green Oldsmobile with license plate number HJR41U and its blond male driver. They were told not to apprehend, but only to shadow from a safe distance. He also alerted the Nightstalker team as it zipped through the night sky unnoticed.

Back on Jonathan Smith Road, agents at Pat's home communicated with the command post and relayed some of what was happening to her throughout the evening. She was excited, but also frightened. Two and a half hours had passed since the drop team left her home and the kidnappers still had not turned Sid over. The FBI told her it expected to wrap the matter up that night, once and for all. That meant Pat could see Sid walk through the door at last, or maybe he'd have to go to the hospital and she'd meet him there; that would be wonderful, she thought. But Pat realized she could be called to identify Sid's body at the morgue; and that would be unbearable. She continued to wait.

Not far from Pat's home, Chief Detective Richard Riley, who was at the command post, called a friend who knew the location of Aries Rent-a-Car. It was in Hackettstown. Riley then telephoned the Hackettstown Police Department to obtain an emergency phone number for the owner, Bette Thomassen, who lived in nearby Roxbury. (Born on March 23, Thomassen had named her business "Aries" after the astrological sign.) Riley called and woke up Thomassen. "I'm sending a car over to pick you up," he told her. "We need you to unlock your business for us, ASAP." Riley didn't tell Thomassen the reason; just official business. Minutes later, Detective Lieutenant Chris Linne of the Morris County Prosecutor's Office pulled up in front of Thomassen's house and hustled her into his car.

"At eleven o'clock that night after I'd gone to sleep, I got a phone call from the city police," Bette Thomassen recalled. "When the cops picked me up with flashing lights and the sirens blasting, I thought, 'Oh, my God!' He drove me to my store so fast, I . . . Let me just say it was the fastest I've ever traveled on land."

Thomassen unlocked the rear door to her car rental office around midnight and she and Detective Linne entered. Linne handed her a piece of paper with the license plate number and a description of the Oldsmobile. Thomassen began searching her files.

The command post directed Special Agents Tom Cottone, John Turkington, Hoyt Peavy, and Joe McShane to join Linne at Aries Rent-a-Car to assist reviewing records and also to establish a staging area nearer to the latest sightings of the suspected kidnappers. Chief Detective Richard Riley wanted to send along another detective from the Morris County Prosecutor's Office, but was shorthanded. Detective Steve Foley, whose principal function had been to guard the ransom money at the command post, volunteered. Though he hadn't been involved in the investigation, he'd read all the files to pass the time and knew the Reso case backwards and forwards. This would be his first action in the field.

"Okay, here's my tablet," Thomassen told Detective Linne as the others raced toward her office. "I keep all my renters in here." Linne stood patiently as the woman thumbed through the ruled spiral tablet. Agent Linne hoped the driver hadn't been carrying a fake driver's license and given Thomassen a bogus name and address.

* * *

At 10:59 p.m., nineteen minutes after being observed by Agent Brzezinski, Art Seale parked the rented Oldsmobile at yet another payphone. This phone was at the Gladpack Sunoco gas station on Pottersville Road in Gladstone, between Chester and Far Hills. The Peapack train didn't leave for another hour. Seale knew he had to keep the drop team on the move until then. Wearing gloves, he punched in the cellular phone number.

"Hello, this is Jim. Hello?" Agent Petersen said.

"Go back. Go back to other phone."

"Go back to other phone?" Petersen asked, surprised.

"Hurry. Go back to other phone."

"Okay, we'll try and get off at the first exit. We're at exit 33 on Route 78 East." Petersen had no choice but to be patient and continue to play along, though the night's charade was becoming a bit ridiculous. The ransom drop team had been driving for more than two hours.

"Hurry back," Seale said.

"Oh, ah, hurry back? Hello, hello?"

Seale hung up the phone and returned to his car, once again removing his gloves as he walked. This time, he hadn't been observed. No surveillance team had been posted to watch the payphone at the two-pump gas station in tiny Gladstone.

The drop team turned off Interstate 78 at exit 33, crossed over the interstate, and then reentered the interstate heading back to the Komline-Sanderson plant, ten miles away. They'd be there in fifteen to twenty minutes. But because the Peapack train didn't leave for another hour, the drop team's tour of the backroads of Somerset County was far from over. The same went for the flight crew of the Nightstalker that constantly maintained visual contact with the chemically-luminescent station wagon with fireflies attached. The FBI security teams also continued trailing behind.

A few minutes later, at 11:11 p.m., Art and Jackie Seale met in separate cars at a phone booth outside the Somerset Hills Elks Club in Gladstone. The kidnappers stood beside the Mercedes discussing their plan. Performing her ritual of donning surgical gloves and placing nickels into her mouth, Jackie called the payphone at the Komline-Sanderson plant while her husband listened. No one answered. Petersen and the drop team were still on their way to the plant.

By chance, Special Agent William Crowley and Morris County Sergeant Darryl Neier, who'd been assigned to provide security for the drop team, were driving north on New Jersey Route 206 to intercept Agents Reilly and Petersen. As they passed the Elks Club, which sits along the highway in plain view, the lawmen spotted two parked cars and a man and a woman standing outside a telephone booth in the empty gravel parking lot. To avoid being seen, they drove a short distance and then turned around and headed back to the Elks Club.

As they did so, Art Seale called the cellular phone. It was 11:16 p.m.; fifty-five minutes before the next train departed the Peapack station.

"Jim speaking," Agent Petersen said.

"Your location?"

"We're, we're passing right now, we're on 206. We're passing Forbes Newspapers. We're, we're rushing as quickly as we can. Please be patient with us."

"Hurry."

"We're, we're trying as, as best as we can. Just crossed, we're, we're crossing the intersection now by the Texaco station. We're on 206 north and we're, we're going to be coming, ah, back and make the—"

Art Seale hung up. "Give them five minutes and call again," he told his Jackie. "They're almost there. I'm going on to Far Hills."

When Crowley and Neier returned to the Elks Club to check out the suspicious activity at the phone booth, they parked nearby and observed a blonde making a call, but the man and one of the cars had disappeared. Jackie Seale dialed the Komline-Sanderson phone booth and Agent Petersen answered. It was 11:21 p.m.; fifty minutes before the train left Peapack Station.

"Hello?"

"Go back to Route 206, make left on Route 202, make right on Whitenack Road," Jackie said in a disguised, highly agitated voice. "Leave money on east side of railroad cross—ing. No . . . wait! Go to Far Hills Train Station. Wait for instructions."

She hung up. Jackie had gotten ahead of herself. The instructions to the railroad crossing were meant for later. Things were getting confusing, even for the kidnappers.

After the call, Jackie emerged from the phone booth and walked toward her Mercedes. Crowley and Neier watched as she got into the car and drove away. She was headed to Our Lady of the Mountain Catholic Church on New Jersey Route 517 in Washington Township where she'd anxiously wait for her husband to show up with the ransom money. As she pulled onto the highway, the lawmen read the Mercedes's license plate. Crowley quickly radioed in Jackie Seale's description and the plate number. The command post sent out an alert to all surveillance teams. The FBI also wasted no time running a vehicle registration check on the Mercedes. The Seales did not know it then, but the noose was tightening.

In 1992, Gladstone had only a handful of streets and a population of maybe five hundred households scattered over six square miles. The tiny downtown had little more than a gas station, post office, grocery, and a few shops sandwiched between two city limit signs. With all the federal, state, and local law personnel cruising about at such a late hour on a weeknight, the vehicles on Gladstone's roadways may have belonged exclusively to law enforcement and kidnappers, apart from a town straggler or two. The entire area was now swarming with law enforcement—more than three hundred.

With the drop team back on the road, Art Seale confidently arrived at the Far Hills Train Station, pulling into the parking lot with his car lights off. He stepped out of the Olds and walked around the station for about three minutes. Surveillance team T-98 was already parked there, waiting and watching. The agent reported what he observed to the command post at 11:27 p.m. At last, the command post had regained visual contact of its misplaced suspect. T-98 described Seale as a "white male, blond hair, potbelly, 230 to 250 pounds, wearing dark framed glasses, white denim jeans, and blue short-sleeve shirt." (Police descriptions can be brutally honest.) Seale didn't make a phone call. Instead, he continued walking around as if looking for something. He reentered his car and pulled out of the station headed west on New Jersey Route 202 toward Whitenack Road with his headlights off. The time for the drop team to board the train was drawing nearer, just forty-five minutes longer.

As Seale pulled onto the highway, the drop team passed by the Far Hills Train Station on its way to the Whitenack Road railroad crossing. The drop team and Seale were now separated by a mile of roadway. Agents Petersen and Reilly may even have been able to see Seale's tail lights. The drop team eventually reached the railroad crossing and waited there for further instructions. After ten or fifteen minutes without further contact, Agent Reilly turned around and drove to the Far Hills Train Station and waited.

Around 11:30, Art Seale continued on to Bernardsville, where surveillance team T-96 spotted the green Oldsmobile traveling west on two-lane Lyons Road out of Basking Ridge with its headlights still off. Undetected, the agents followed Seale along a circuitous route through Bernards Township as part of Seale's stall for time. Before long, he headed back in the direction of Far Hills near where the Whitenack Road railroad crossing was located.

As Seale passed Lyons Mall and continued southwest along Lyons Road, he suddenly found himself approaching a police roadblock with lights flashing.

"Damn!" He hit his brakes and made an immediate U-turn, speeding off east toward South Finley Avenue. The quick and unexpected maneuver caused T-96 to lose their suspect. Though Seale thought the roadblock was meant for him, it was not. Local police were simply rerouting traffic because of a car accident.

Spooked by the unrelated roadblock, Art Seale drove out into the countryside hiding from what he expected would be an imminent police chase. There was none. At 12:30 a.m., nineteen minutes *after* the train he'd wanted to put the drop team aboard pulled out of Peapack Train Station, Seale pulled into the parking lot of the Catholic church where his wife waited.

When Jackie saw the Oldsmobile pulling in, she hopped out of the Mercedes and trotted to the car's trunk, eager to transfer $18.5 million into the Mercedes. Only the Seales know what was said when Art arrived without the money, but it couldn't have been a pretty scene. After spending six months planning and implementing a kidnapping, taking care of a sick and wounded hostage in a storage unit, and running about five counties placing countless calls and littering the countryside with ransom notes—the night was a bust.

To make matters worse, as Jackie stood with her husband behind the trunk of their Mercedes a Washington Township police officer on routine patrol saw the two loitering. He may have been the only officer who hadn't heard about the big three-county stakeout going on in his backyard. With police gear jingling from his belt as he approached, the Seales's hearts skipped a beat. "You're trespassing on church property. Leave now before I take you in." The officer believed that the Seales were partaking in a romantic rendezvous on sanctified asphalt. The Seales explained they were having a marital spat and the two skedaddled. Art drove away first in the Oldsmobile followed by Jackie in the Mercedes.

With their nerves in shreds and the 12:11 train out of Peapack far down the line, the Seales had no choice but to scrap their plans for the night. First, the blunder at the Villa Restaurant seven weeks earlier and now tonight's fiasco. They'd just have to try again. Exhausted, the brooding kidnappers headed for Hackettstown—to drop off the Oldsmobile at Aries Rent-a-Car.

Part III

THE CAPTURE

Chapter 10

"Here it is," Bette Thomassen said, lifting her eyes from the spiral notepad. The time was around 12:30 a.m. Detective Chris Linne leaned over to look as Thomassen swiveled the ruled notepad around so he could have a better view of her notations. Adorned with colorful rings and bracelets, her hands jingled as she flipped the page.

"The '92 Oldsmobile Ciera you asked about, it's a new car. I rented it to Irene Seale, Box 238A, Washington, New Jersey, yesterday the 18th, at 11:30 a.m.," Thomassen said, pointing at the page with painted nails. "I can't believe she's in trouble. She was somebody I positively would have invited to dinner. You wouldn't think twice."

Studying the records, Linne ignored Thomassen's remarks. "Mind if I smoke?" he asked.

"No . . . Oh, and see right here," Thomassen said, excited to be part of an FBI investigation, "she put it on the Visa card of Irene Szarko, S-Z-A-R-K-O. I remember she said that's her mother. See, here's the credit card number."

Bette Thomassen's records completed the puzzle. Just minutes earlier, agents had initiated a vehicle registration check on the white Mercedes spotted by Agent Crowley and Sergeant Neier at the Somerset Hills Elks Club. The car was registered jointly to: "Arthur D. Seale and Irene J. Seale, Box 238A, 201 Musconetcong River Road, Lebanon Township, New Jersey 07882." There was no question in agents' minds these two were the kidnappers. Now all they had to do was find and arrest them. The kidnappers would then tell authorities where to find Sid Reso and the whole ugly mess would be over at last.

While Detective Linne stood in the back of Bette Thomassen's office reviewing records, a car pulled into the lot from the side entrance. It was a dark green 1992 Oldsmobile Cutlass Ciera, license number HJR41U. It was Art Seale. He was returning the Olds to the rental agency.

Yet unnoticed, Art dilly-dallied in the rental car for a minute or so before stepping out into the parking lot. Jackie pulled into the lot in her Mercedes two minutes later to give her husband a lift home.

Seconds later, four FBI agents and Detective Foley arrived at the rental agency to meet up with Detective Linne and Bette Thomassen. They pulled in the front entrance. The lawmen approached the front door of Aries Rent-a-Car, but it was locked and the office appeared dark. They knew Linne and Thomassen had to be around somewhere; they'd been told they'd be waiting there. Detective Foley saw a man standing along the side of the building in the dark, almost as if trying to hide. Foley walked toward Art Seale, not yet aware of Seale's identity. Foley spotted a blond woman standing around the corner.

"Are you the owner?" Foley asked Art Seale.

"No, I'm just returning a rental car," Seale replied. Art then turned and coolly walked to the green Olds Cutlass. He motioned for Jackie to get back in the Mercedes. Both started their engines and Art began backing out of the side parking lot.

Foley realized that the green Olds matched the description given by Agent Brzezinski and called out to the others, "It's the Oldsmobile! It's them!" Agent Tom Cottone jumped in his car and blocked the side entrance, preventing the Seales from leaving.

"Freeze! Out of the car! Out of the car! Hands behind your head!" Foley shouted with his gun drawn as he pecked on the driver side window of the Oldsmobile. When Art Seale stepped out, he was met by Foley and Agents Cottone and Peavy. Agents Turkington and McShane gave Jackie Seale a similar welcome several feet away. The Seales did as they were told and stepped out raising their hands.

"Against the cars!"

The Seales leaned forward with their feet spread apart and their hands on the roofs of their cars. Because the license plate number matched that seen by Agent Brzezinski, and because Art Seale matched the description of the payphone caller she'd seen, agents believed they had probable cause for an arrest. To be sure, Foley called Morris County Prosecutor Mike Murphy at the command post. Murphy didn't hesitate. "Take them down," the county prosecutor instructed.

The Seales were summarily frisked. Then they felt and heard what has to be one of the most disheartening sounds for a criminal: the click of handcuffs. The jig was up at last.

"You have the right to remain silent," began Detective Anthony Soranno, reading Miranda rights to the Seales separately. "Anything you say can and will be used against you in a court of law. You have the right to have an attorney present. If you cannot afford an attorney, one will be appointed for you. Do you understand these rights? Acknowledge by saying 'yes.'"

The Seales seemed visibly smaller, as if they'd wilted during the reading of their Miranda rights. Both nodded and mumbled something that sounded like yes.

By this time, Detective Linne stepped out of Thomassen's office surprised at the commotion in the parking lot. Though the agents and detectives earnestly carried out their duties, several of them grinned like the proverbial cat that ate the canary. They couldn't believe their good fortune. Seven weeks with nothing and to have both kidnappers drive up and practically shake hands with them was almost beyond belief. It was as Thomassen later remarked: "Everything was so coincidental."

With the Seales cuffed, agents brought Bette Thomassen out to identify the two. A more official identification would take place later at the jails. She said Jackie Seale was the woman who'd rented her cars. Detectives asked Thomassen for permission to search the Oldsmobile driven by Art. She agreed. Detective Foley then asked Jackie Seale if they could search the Mercedes.

She replied, "Go ahead. Help yourself." Opening the doors and trunk and shining flashlights inside, they didn't find Sid Reso, but they did see plenty of incriminating evidence.

Disappointed that Sid Reso wasn't in either of the cars, agents attempted to question Art and Jackie Seale about Reso's whereabouts. A comprehensive interview would be conducted at the jail. When asked what they were doing there, Art claimed that he and Jackie had been out for dinner in Bernardsville with friends. When asked what restaurant, Art Seale couldn't name it right away. Jackie didn't say a word. She let her husband do the talking as he'd instructed her should they ever be apprehended. Art provided agents with names of friends who supposedly dined with them, but when federal agents later asked the individuals if that was true, all of them emphatically denied it. Seale also showed agents his old police identification card and began talking about his days with the Hillside Police Department in an attempt to bond with fellow law enforcement. It didn't work.

Special Agent Tom Cottone grew impatient with Art Seale's diversions. "You know, we've been looking for Sidney Reso. He's been missing," Cottone said, standing directly in front of Seale.

"Oh, yeah, I heard about that," Seale coolly replied.

"Well, let me tell you something," Cottone said angrily. "He's not missing. He's been kidnapped and you did it. Now where is he?"

Art Seale paused and said, "I don't know what you're talking about." He continued his denials for several minutes.

A frustrated Cottone sternly ordered, "Get them out of here." At that point, officers escorted the Seales to separate cars and placed them in the backseats. Loaded with agents, detectives, and prisoners, the cars pulled out of the parking lot. Art would be taken to the Morris Township Police Department and Jackie would be detained at the Morris County Prosecutor's Office. Art twisted in the backseat to catch a glimpse of his wife as they pulled away. It was too dark. He later said of his arrest: "In some ways [I felt] a sense of relief that it was over, that the problems were no longer mine, that I couldn't be responsible for them anymore . . ."

Even after everything, Art Seale could think of only himself.

* * *

Exxon International vice president Charlie Roxburgh arrived at the Reso home. He had the unpleasant task of telling Pat what had happened at the rental agency. Rather than simply call, he wanted to tell her in person. Pat had been a nervous wreck all night, waiting. When Roxburgh arrived, he led Pat to the living room while answering her questions about Sid and attempting to calm her fear that he might be dead. After sitting, he explained that Art and Jackie Seale, a local married couple, had been arrested and that a search of their automobiles had not produced any clues to Sid's whereabouts. Worse, he told Pat that the kidnappers weren't talking. Pat's reaction was later described by an agent in a manner that preserved her dignity: "Obviously, she was upset."

A neighbor spotted the congregating cars and television crews outside the Reso home the next morning. "I saw all the cars and I thought maybe they had found him, that maybe he was safe at home and everyone was happy," Doris Bonanno said. "But a reporter told me that a couple had been charged with his kidnapping, and he was still missing."

Hope wasn't gone, but it was rapidly disintegrating. Mike Murphy and Agents Walker and Chapman reminded Pat that absolutely no one in law enforcement had given up. If anything, they were going to work even harder. They pointed out that just because the two kidnappers were in jail, it didn't necessarily mean that Sid was dead or in captivity alone. It was possible that another kidnapper was taking care of him. After all, Agent Brzezinski had seen another person in the Oldsmobile with Art

Seale at the Chester Mall.

That was only one of the leads that the FBI and the prosecutor's office were investigating. A review of the Seales's phone records revealed conversations between Seale and another man on the day of the kidnapping and again on other key days during Reso's disappearance.

The county prosecutor and agents explained to Pat that the FBI had just obtained a warrant to search the home of Art Seale's parents. They told her that everyone involved hoped that a search of the Seale's home would either produce Sid or provide a clue to where he might be. What's more, they told Pat that the FBI was adding even more resources to the investigation. Agents arrived from all over the northeastern United States to help find her husband. The case now surpassed the kidnapping and murder case of CEO Adolph Coors III in 1960 to become the third largest FBI kidnapping investigation in U.S. history behind Lindbergh's baby and Patty Hearst.

Pat respectfully listened as she always did and then retired to her bedroom to write in her diary — and to pray.

* * *

Agents with the Behavioral Science Unit had been correct. They'd been so precise in formulating the criminal profile of Sid Reso's kidnappers that it was creepy. If not for the fact that they were highly-respected special agents, they might have been suspects themselves. The FBI had heard from countless psychics, clairvoyants, mediums, telepathists, mystics, metaphysical conduits, parapsychologists, sorcerers, witches, or whatever they wanted to be called, but in the end, it was the FBI's Behavioral Science Unit in Quantico, Virginia, that possessed the crystal ball.

The Unit's report had concluded that there were only two kidnappers, both locals; they were a couple, probably married;

they most likely had two kids and a golden retriever; they were middle-aged Caucasians, most likely suburbanite yuppies; they were in dire financial straits; the husband was narcissistic; and most likely, the husband had prior law enforcement experience, and may have even worked for Exxon.

After the Seales's arrest, the Unit's criminal investigative analysis report was compared with the arrest report: Art and Jackie Seale were parents of teenagers, owner of Brandy, a golden retriever, both forty-five years old, both Caucasian, lived in outlying Hunterdon County, drove a Mercedes, wore designer-brand clothes, and were socially conscious. Art Seale had served with the Hillsdale police force where he was reprimanded and suspended numerous times for his aggression. He'd worked with Exxon security for ten years before he was terminated. And the Seales were flat broke. They'd filed bankruptcy three years earlier. For the last two and a half years, they'd slept in the basement of Mr. and Mrs. Seale's home.

Though the FBI's profile of the kidnappers was spot on and had helped with the investigation, it had not led authorities to the Seales; they had performed that little trick themselves. And so far, the Unit's crystal ball had not led authorities to Sid Reso.

* * *

Having obtained Bette Thomassen's consent earlier, agents commenced searching the Oldsmobile while awaiting a warrant to thoroughly search the Mercedes. Inside the trunk, agents found four large, blue, unused, Rubbermaid containers with covers, a rock about the size of a football, and a clear plastic sheet.

Around two o'clock that morning, agents finally received the search warrant for the Mercedes. Though it had taken some time, the search didn't disappoint. Inside the trunk of the Mercedes, agents discovered a Rubbermaid container, five designer carry bags, four boxes of rubber bands, two clear plastic sheets, two pairs of rubber gloves, two pairs of leather gloves, some clothing, a set of stolen license plates, a roll of quarters, and a briefcase. When agents opened the unlocked briefcase, they found a 1985 Exxon personnel directory, a New Jersey Transit train schedule, Arthur Seale's passport, a Hilton Head Marriott Resort & Spa hotel receipt dated June 9, 1992, in the name of Arthur Seale, scissors, and three .38 caliber cartridges.

Following the cursory searches at the rental agency, the two cars were towed to the Morris County Sheriff's Office for further processing. Agents vacuumed the vehicles for hair and fibers, swabbed mysterious stains, retrieved debris from the ashtrays and the trunks, and removed worn and soiled floor mats.

Besides careful searches of the vehicles, agents also conducted a more detailed examination of Aries Rent-a-Car records to ascertain what vehicles had been rented by the Seales and when the vehicles had been rented and returned. They also wanted to know anything else the rental agency's owner could tell them about her dealings with the Seales.

"She told me she owned a crafts business and needed a van to attend fairs," Bette Thomassen told federal agents. "She said she also wanted to sell arts and crafts out of the van. She . . . didn't want any names on the side."

Two agents recorded Thomassen's comments on paper. Since the Seales weren't talking to law enforcement, agents were trying to piece together when the Seales initiated their kidnapping plans and, among other things, whether anyone else was working with them.

"The first time she rented from me," Thomassen explained, "was on April twelfth during lunch according to my records. She said it worked out beautifully . . . Oh, that was the '91 Chevy van. I can show it to you if you want to see it. It's parked over on the side. The plate number is XV17HC. She brought it back the next day one mile shy of a hundred miles showing on the odometer.

It was clean when she brought it back, too, I remember."

"Did Irene Seale have anyone with her?" the agent asked, using Seale's first name, not yet knowing she used "Jackie."

"No, it was always just her."

"Okay, what about the next time?"

"Well, she came back on the twenty-third of April, and she rented the very exact same van," Thomassen said, looking at her notebook. "That time, she returned it again the next day and this time the odometer read exactly one hundred miles driven."

The FBI later learned that both times the Chevy van had been leased, the Seales drove to Sid Reso's neighborhood to kidnap him, but didn't go through with it. The same was true when the Seales rented a white Dodge cargo van on March 31 from Thrifty Rental in Bridgewater, another white Dodge cargo van from Thrifty Rental in North Plainfield on April 5, and a different white Dodge cargo van from the same North Plainfield agency on April 16. Each Thrifty rental had been driven approximately one hundred fifty miles and each time had been used with the intention of kidnapping Reso. Each van was returned by the Seales after observing the limousine pick up Reso from his home, or after he didn't show because he was out of town or he left for work later in the morning.

"Then on April 27," Bette Thomassen continued, "she rented a '91 Dodge van from me. Its plate number was XV88DK and she kept this one a couple days. She brought it back on the thirtieth. According to this, the odometer registered 107 miles more than when she took it."

"The next to last time she came in, on May 3rd, I didn't have any vans in inventory. I remember I talked her into renting a car instead. She ended up taking a red '91 Chevy Lumina. It's a good-looking car. More burgundy than red. It's a pretty big four-door sedan with a nice-sized trunk. She brought it back two days later as clean as a pin and with a full tank of gas . . . And the last one you know about already. The dark green

'92 Olds Cutlass Ciera. They rented it yesterday morning like I said before. That's all there is," Thomassen said. "You can look yourself, if you want."

As agents wrapped up things with Bette Thomassen, the Seales had arrived at the Morris Township Police Department and Morris County Prosecutor's Office for processing. Neither of them had said a word on the way. They simply weren't talking. "It would behoove them to take us to him if he's alive," one lawman said. "But they haven't."

Agents at the command post believed their silence meant one of two things: there was an accomplice out there holding Sid Reso who would soon use Reso's life to trade for the Seales's release and the ransom, or Reso was dead.

"This should be a cause for celebrating," Morris County Prosecutor Mike Murphy told reporters, "but it isn't because we still haven't achieved our goal—the safe return of Sid Reso."

* * *

Earlier that morning, June 19, all variety of law enforcement vehicles converged near the house of Art Seale's parents. Many believed that armed compatriots could be holding Sid Reso inside. Agents and SWAT operators had been briefed on the situation. Given the go ahead, the point man rushed the house followed by several others with their guns raised. No one knew what to expect. Agents and SWAT operators trained in rescuing kidnap victims and defusing hostage situations storm a house quickly and snake their way from room to room subduing anyone who poses a threat. If Reso was inside, SWAT tactics provided the best chance of getting him out alive. So everyone outside waited.

Seconds passed and there'd been no sound of shots; only commands shouted from inside could be heard. A message soon came over the radio to the command post that the house had been secured and its occupants were in custody—an elderly couple, a teenage girl, and a golden retriever. There was no sign of Reso.

At 7:00 a.m., with a warrant in hand, FBI agents and Morris County detectives commenced searching the interior of the house and the grounds. It would be a hot day, nearly ninety degrees, so most wore jeans and t-shirts bearing "FBI" or other law enforcement insignias. Hunterdon County deputies and local police officers set up barricades and ran crime scene tape around the property's perimeter to control traffic and curious neighbors while investigators did their jobs.

As their house was being searched, Art Seale's parents consented to being questioned. They weren't allowed to visit their son yet. Jackie Seale's mother also was interviewed by federal agents and county detectives. She also couldn't visit her daughter. All were terribly upset. Art Seale's younger sister and mother of three, who'd won the Miss UNICO (Union County) beauty pageant in high school, also had to have been distraught and humiliated. So was Seale's eighty-nine-year-old grandmother, who lived in Hillside. "This has got to be terrible for the family," said Angela Bento, who had purchased the Szarko family liquor store with her husband.

Agents and detectives interviewed neighbors and relatives. News reporters soon arrived and interviewed them also, as they always do when someone commits a crime.

"Nicer neighbors you couldn't ask for," Edie Martin said, who'd lived next door to Art Seale's parents for fourteen years. "If we needed them, they would be there."

Not one person in the neighborhood had anything bad to say about the elder Seales. Those same neighbors, however, said they only knew the younger Seales when they saw the couple at the grocery or post office. "They do a lot of exercise, walking on the road," Edie Martin added. Most referred to Art and Jackie Seale as "quiet" people who "kept to themselves."

Barry and Min Markowitz, former neighbors of Art and

Jackie Seale before they moved to Hilton Head, described them as "a very normal young family, trying to make it." Even former Hilton Head neighbors who weren't owed money spoke highly of the younger Seales. "They were lovely people. For them to do it doesn't seem in character," Diane Rochelle said. "Jackie baked cookies to give to neighbors every Christmas."

Jack Cunning, who lived around the corner from the Seales at Sea Pines in Hilton Head, was extraordinarily compassionate toward them: "If you had invested your life savings and lost it all, and lost your house in the process, it would obviously be very emotionally devastating. And that's what happened to them here."

Perhaps Jeri Maxwell, who ran a tailor shop in Changewater, New Jersey, summed it up best: "I'd say people are very surprised. But then again, what do we really know about the people living next door?"

While reporters continued running down stories from those who knew the Seales, the slow, tedious process of searching vehicles and the Seale property continued. New Jersey State Patrolman Steve Makuka arrived with Buffy, the cadaver dog. He led her around the lot and river bank before taking the German shepherd throughout the house and into the crawl space, but nothing was discovered. Agents also sifted through a barrel and fire pit near the river bank. They found pieces of charred lumber and plywood and several screws and nails, but no bones, teeth, eyeglasses, belt buckle, or even shoelace eyelets that might indicate the cremation of a body. A little later, a scuba diver arrived to scan the bottom of the Musconetcong River behind the Seale home. His assignment was not only to search underwater for a body weighted down or pinned beneath stones, but anything unnatural that might have been tossed into the water in an attempt to conceal evidence.

Inside the house, agents and detectives searched from the attic to the crawlspace and in between. Anywhere that a criminal could secrete evidence was searched. The locations were too numerous to list, but examples included mattresses, air vents, drain pipes, cereal boxes, coffee cans, and behind toilets and ceiling tiles. The dismantling and reassembly of the house lasted all day and into the next.

Agents and detectives tagged and bagged several items that they carried out in boxes to awaiting police vans, including twelve firearms, boxes of various calibers of ammunition, rolls of duct tape, a shovel, a pick ax, a hatchet, and handcuffs. Other items included clothing, a hypodermic needle, the golden retriever's hairbrush, Jackie Seale's hairbrush, plastic sheets, a sleeping bag, gloves, a bedspread, envelopes, paper, handwriting exemplars, the real estate section of *The New York Times* for June 18, carpet samples from every room, and several other items. All would have to be analyzed in the FBI Laboratory so that a report of their significance could be produced and disseminated.

Among the most significant items seized were Eddie Bauer sports bags; telephone directories with Exxon executives' names and addresses circled; newspaper and magazine clippings relating to Exxon and the kidnapping case; a book on money laundering; information on Swiss, Pakistan, and Cayman bank accounts; a passport application and passport; books entitled *Pakistan* and *The Secret Money Market*; and a .45-caliber pistol that likely was the weapon used to shoot Sid Reso in the arm.

Just after 12:30 p.m., an agent made a colossal discovery. While fanning through papers located in Art and Jackie Seale's nightstand drawers in the basement, the agent found a written contract between Art Seale and Secure Storage. He also located a key to a storage unit labeled "619" in the drawer. "This could be it!" the agent said to the others. Law enforcement had raced to the Seale residence that morning believing Sid Reso was being held there, but he wasn't. They now believed this piece of evidence would lead them to Reso at last.

Word spread quickly among the searchers. The excitement

grew. The command post telephoned Secure Storage and alerted the manager that SWAT and other law enforcement were en route and to close the facility to customers immediately. The storage facility was only eight and a half miles away.

Unmarked cars with wig-wag lights escorted by a patrol car with its siren blaring and red lights flashing sped their way along the narrow Musconetcong River Road. They turned north on New Jersey Route 57, a two-lane rural highway flanked by cornfields and rolling hills. The Musconetcong River flowed alongside. Emergency responders and an ambulance also converged on the Hackettstown storage complex hoping to find a bound and exhausted, and perhaps an abused and unwell, Sid Reso.

At 1:00 p.m., the intimidating motorcade arrived at Secure Storage. The manager let them through the gate. Everyone was electrified with the hope, no, the expectation, of finding Sid Reso inside the storage unit. It only made sense. Agents had checked apartments, motels, condos, and anything else that had recently been connected to utilities and phone service; but they hadn't checked storage facilities, even though law enforcement was aware that criminals often used storage space for illegal activities, such as storing drugs, guns, explosives, stolen goods, and ill-gotten cash. Though they'd never heard of holding a kidnapping victim hostage in a storage unit, it was certainly possible, especially since the Secure Storage contract was dated February 22. That date was only two months before the kidnapping and only one month before the Seales had rented the first cargo van.

"I was elated," Chief Detective Riley recalled thinking at that time. "I was convinced beyond any reasonable doubt that Sid Reso was inside."

A mass of law enforcement and paramedics gathered outside unit 619 in the rain as an agent unlocked the door. He reached down and grabbed the handle to raise it. The door rattled as it rolled up, just as Sid Reso had heard it rattle several times. It was already eighty-eight degrees. A wave of hot air slapped agents and detectives in their faces. They strained to look inside the dim space, some with guns drawn, but dared not step forward and contaminate a possible crime scene.

"A lot of us had talked about having heroic dreams in which we broke down a door and found Reso alive, tied to a chair or something," Agent Petersen recalled.

Instead, they were stunned and disappointed by what they saw—golf clubs, snow skis, a garden hose, galoshes, and more than fifty boxes full of household stuff. The typical kind of junk that people place in storage units to free up space at home. There were no signs of anything criminal or perverse nor were there any signs that Sid Reso had ever been held hostage inside. A forensics team would process the site to make sure.

Afterward, agents received news that the scuba diver searching the Musconetcong River behind the Seale house had discovered some rusted metal objects scattered on the river bed—three hinges and three sets of latches and padlocks. No one knew exactly what to make of the find, though it carried a nefarious overtone. Burnt pieces of lumber and plywood, and rusted hinges, latches, padlocks—all discarded—no longer in use. Worse, an agent also discovered a zipper attached to burned cloth fragments. That find sparked chills among the investigators. No one told Pat—not yet.

Chapter 11

Less than an hour after agents and detectives arrived at Secure Storage in Hackettstown, Art and Jackie Seale arrived at the United States District Court for the District of New Jersey, part of a downtown government complex in Newark called Federal Square. They arrived in separate black unmarked cars provided by the United States Marshals Service, the oldest federal law enforcement agency in the country. The Seales were now technically in the custody of the U.S. Attorney General and U.S. marshals.

City and county courts are typically spilling over on Saturdays, holding bail hearings for those arrested the night before on charges of DUI, drunken assault, or domestic violence. Federal courts are different. Any time someone is a criminal defendant in a federal district court, it usually means they are in serious trouble; hence the phrase: "Don't make a federal case out of it." The Seales were about to find that out.

Before the court went into session, two very large U.S. deputy marshals escorted each of the Seales into the courtroom. The marshals looked formidable in their dark suits, adorned with side-arms and the classic five-pointed star within a circle like the badge worn by Wyatt Earp a century earlier. The courtroom also looked intimidating, with its wood-paneled walls, wooden podiums, tables, railings, and pews, with a handful of dark leather-upholstered wooden chairs lined in front. Besides lawyers and defendants sitting past the bar, several reporters filled the gallery. They had arrived early to observe the kidnappers during the proceedings. The reporters would describe the notorious defendants' prison garb, expressions, and words in their newspapers and on television later that day and the next.

Still tanned and blond, the Seales shuffled across the well of the courtroom in dark blue prison jumpsuits monogramed with

MTPD in cursive script on the right chest. The manacles on their hands and feet were linked by a short length of chain that rattled as they hobbled along taking short steps. Two court-appointed attorneys, conservatively dressed and coiffed, waited for each of their clients at the defendants' table with legal pads and glasses of water. Chester Keller with the Federal Public Defender's Office represented Art Seale, and Sallyanne Floria with the firm of Floria & Callori of Verona, New Jersey, represented Jackie Seale. Before the judge stepped into the court, Art leaned forward to glance at Jackie seated on the other side of the table separated by their lawyers. Jackie also leaned forward to see her husband of twenty-five years. She mouthed, "I love you."

All sat quietly until the bailiff loudly announced the arrival of U.S. Magistrate D. Gordon Haneke. Everyone stood until the bespectacled judge wearing his black robes seated himself in a high-backed, black leather chair beneath a gold-colored seal hanging on the wood-veneered wall. He banged the gavel to commence the arraignment of the prisoners.

That Saturday's legal proceeding would last only fifteen minutes. It was a preliminary probable cause hearing. There'd be much more complicated legal wrangling to come, not only in federal court, but in state court.

The prosecutor's complaint, attested to by Special Agent Richard Smith, charged the Seales with specific crimes even though Sid Reso had not yet been located. Magistrate Haneke read the four criminal counts charged in the complaint against each defendant: kidnapping, conspiracy to commit kidnapping, extortion, and conspiracy to commit extortion, which carried sentences up to life in prison. Those were the federal charges. The Seales also would face arraignment later in state court for charges filed by the Morris County Prosecutor's Office. Those charges would be in addition to the federal charges and would carry their own sentences to run concurrently or consecutively with the federal sentences.

When the judge asked Art Seale if he understood the charges against him, an emotionless Seale replied firmly, "Yes, Your Honor." He similarly answered when asked if he understood the penalties the charges carried, his right to an attorney, and the right to a jury trial. When asked how he pleaded, Art Seale replied, "Not guilty."

The judge repeated his statements and questions to Jackie Seale. She echoed her husband's earlier answers, though her voice quivered several times as her eyes filled with tears.

The judge next considered whether bond should be granted. There was no way Magistrate Haneke was going to let the Seales out for the weekend. "Bail denied," he ruled. He scheduled a more comprehensive and adversarial bond hearing for Monday.

With the brief proceeding over, the Seales shuffled out of the courtroom in their shackles escorted by U.S. deputy marshals. They'd be held in separate jails until the Monday hearing: Art Seale in the Passaic County Jail fifteen miles away and Jackie Seale in the Union County Jail eight miles away.

The U.S. Attorney's Office, the FBI, and the Morris County Prosecutor's Office issued a joint statement to the press that announced the arrests of Arthur D. Seale and Irene J. Seale for kidnapping and extortion. The statement noted that they could face a maximum sentence of life in prison and more than $1 million in fines. It emphasized that authorities were still searching for Sid Reso and provided two Exxon hotline phone numbers for anyone with information about the case.

Our criminal justice system can seem peculiar at times. Its foundation is to protect the rights of the accused and make clear that criminal defendants are innocent until proven guilty. There are procedures that must be strictly followed to accomplish those lofty goals, which can make for an extremely complicated system. Often, victims would prefer more simplicity. It's likely Pat and the Reso family wished that the judge had deviated from criminal procedure just long enough to have asked: "Where the hell is Sidney Reso?"

The following day was Father's Day . . .

* * *

Michael Chertoff, the United States Attorney for the District of New Jersey, handled very few criminal cases personally. The Reso case was only his third major case since he was appointed to the position two years earlier by President George H.W. Bush. That didn't mean he wasn't qualified; quite the contrary. Educated at Harvard College and Harvard Law School before clerking for U.S. Supreme Court Justice Brennan, Chertoff had worked as a young assistant prosecutor in New York. Just as impressive, he was hired in 1980 by Rudy Giuliani, who was then the United States Attorney for the Southern District of New York. Chertoff handled cases ranging from political corruption and organized crime to corporate fraud and terrorism. Chertoff was not someone a criminal defendant would want personally prosecuting his case.

Michael Critchley, a well-respected local defense lawyer, said of Chertoff at that time: "Chertoff's record speaks for itself . . . He is not someone who loses cases. You have to be at the top of your game to beat him; he doesn't lose."

Much of Chertoff's success in the courtroom derived from his endless preparation and hard work. He was renowned for his brilliance and his fierce doggedness at cross-examination.

On Monday, June 22, Chertoff stood inside the federal courthouse in Newark waiting as U.S. marshals once again transported Art and Jackie Seale to appear before the federal judge. This time, reporters were waiting with cameras, microphones, and tape recorders. When the official vehicles arrived with the Seales inside, reporters rushed the cars and snapped photos through the windows. Two U.S. marshals locked arms with Art Seale as did two others with Jackie, pushing their way along the sidewalk through the mass of reporters and audio/video equipment, making their way up the front steps of the granite courthouse. The words, "FEDERAL BUILDING UNITED STATES COURTHOUSE," hung overhead as the Seales entered.

Wearing a dark blue prison jumpsuit, Jackie Seale covered her face with cuffed hands as two marshals led her inside. Art Seale, on the other hand, looked directly at reporters in his orange prison jumpsuit and most likely wanted to speak to them, but had been advised against it by his court-appointed attorney.

It seemed that a weekend of contemplation inside a seven-foot by eight-foot jail cell and advice from her lawyer had already affected Jackie. Unlike Saturday morning when she mouthed "I love you" to her husband, she didn't even look at him on Monday, which had to have bothered Art Seale immensely for both matrimonial and prosecutorial reasons.

The bond hearing before U.S. Magistrate Donald Haneke on Monday lasted forty-five minutes. The two defense attorneys, Keller and Floria, presented arguments for the granting of bail while Chertoff argued against it. Art Seale's attorney argued that his client should be permitted to live under house arrest with his parents and daughter, subject to ankle monitors and other electronic monitoring devices. Mr. Seale had offered to mortgage his home to raise bail for his son "if it wasn't too high." Jackie's attorney advised the judge that the Szarko family was attempting to raise bail money, too. Chertoff responded by saying that authorities would have to transform the Seale home into a "mini-Leavenworth" to prevent the Seales from escaping.

Chertoff reminded the judge that the Seales had threatened the lives of other Exxon executives. He also shared with the court written information seized by agents that indicated the Seales had planned to hide the ransom in foreign banks and then possibly flee to Pakistan, a nation that had no extradition treaty with the United States. All the evidence pointed toward a high risk of flight from the country.

After hearing several procedural matters and additional arguments on both sides, Judge Haneke denied bail. "It's not even close," he remarked.

Three days later on Thursday, a federal grand jury in Newark indicted Art and Jackie Seale on six counts each of kidnapping, conspiracy to commit kidnapping, extortion, conspiracy to commit extortion, using the mail to transmit ransom demands, and interstate travel in aid of extortion. The eight-page indictment included a statement that surprised everyone: "The defendants did knowingly, willfully, and unlawfully conspire and agree with each other *and others* to . . . kidnap . . . and hold for ransom Sidney J. Reso . . ." This was the first that anyone had heard anything about "others" being involved.

U.S. Attorney Chertoff and Special Agent-in-Charge Gary Penrith stopped outside the federal courthouse to speak with reporters for just a moment. Reporters wanted to know about the "others" referenced in the indictment. Chertoff said, "Our primary objective is to find Mr. Reso and return him safe and sound to his family." Penrith echoed the U.S. Attorney's statement and added that more agents had been assigned to the case and would "do everything possible to get Mr. Reso back." When pressed for additional comment, Chertoff said that he was reluctant to divulge further details because Sidney Reso's life "may hang in the balance."

* * *

Pat remained at home suffering through the hours and days following the arrests of the Seales. It had been a tortuous week for Pat. She was a smart woman. She knew it didn't look good, but what else could she do? She couldn't give up hope. She telephoned her children to comfort them and she, in turn, was comforted by them. Other than attending Mass, she didn't speak with anyone outside the authorities, her close-knit family, and her friends. Calls from reporters were answered by others with "no comment," except for one simple statement released by Pat the day after the arrests: "I still hope for my husband's safe return."

A security expert told reporters, "Personally, I find it ominous that they haven't found Mr. Reso yet." Privately, some agents and detectives expressed the same concern since so far there was no hard evidence to show that Sid Reso was still alive. Many believed that if the Seales had Reso hidden somewhere, they would have already offered his safe return as part of a plea deal. "We fear they don't have their ace in the hole," one said.

Rev. Peter Schuenzel of Resurrection parish in Randolph, New Jersey, where the Resos attended church told reporters he would end each Mass with prayers for Sid Reso and his family. "To have no news," he added, "is the most frustrating part."

"Frustrating" was putting it mildly. Sid Reso had vanished fifty-two days earlier and his kidnappers still weren't talking.

Pat Reso received a telephone call from the director of the FBI, William Sessions, who assured her that the Bureau was doing everything possible to find her husband, despite the arrests of the two suspects. He reiterated that he had committed "all resources" of the FBI. A truly appreciative Pat thanked the director for his call and for the Bureau's monumental efforts.

"We desperately want that Hollywood ending," one lawman said. "We want that third somebody to be out there somewhere, caring for Sidney Reso. But right now, it's hard to be upbeat."

* * *

Many agents and county detectives believed that a third person could be holding Sid Reso. The indictment filed by Chertoff had indicated, and he had confirmed to reporters, that other suspects could be involved and at large because an FBI agent spotted a second occupant in Art Seale's rented Oldsmobile at the Chester

Mall on the night of his arrest. Though it could have been Jackie Seale, she had been spotted by another agent in her Mercedes just half an hour later. Agents also had uncovered a strong suspect while examining Art Seale's phone records. Seale had telephoned a man twice on the day of the kidnapping, including just four hours after he'd grabbed Reso and tossed him into the van. And the man had telephoned Art Seale twice that same day. Seale also had called the man the following day and again on the day of the proposed ransom pickup at the Villa Restaurant. The FBI desperately wanted to find this man. They thought if they located him, they might locate Sid.

While hunting down the mystery man, the FBI and detectives also followed up on a mountain of information that agents and detectives had collected after the Seale arrests. "Anywhere [the Seales have] been or where we believe they've been, we're interviewing people," Murphy said. "Of course, we are proceeding on the assumption that Mr. Reso is still alive," Bill Tonkin added.

The FBI collected and analyzed all store receipts, car rental receipts, telephone records, financial records, and travel receipts. Agents examined everything trying to piece together Art and Jackie Seale's day-to-day activities and acquaintances in order to find evidence of their crime and where Sid Reso might be held and who might be holding him.

Officials also were checking tips received on two separate hotlines that might lead authorities to Reso. The only problem was there was an extensive and growing list of eyewitness sightings of the Seales for the seven weeks after the abduction. Hundreds, in fact, and all had to be checked out.

Many of the callers claimed to be holding Reso or to know something about his whereabouts in an attempt to extort money from Exxon. Chertoff told reporters that investigators were busy trying to determine if the calls were made from people "who have genuine control of Mr. Reso or who are trying to commit a fraud or hoax." And, of course, there were the nuts.

Agents interviewed anyone that the Seales had come in contact with in recent years. Former employers, friends, and family living in New Jersey, Colorado, and South Carolina were questioned, including Art and Jackie Seale's son who was still in Hilton Head. "We have no indication at this time that any other family members are involved in the Reso kidnapping," noted FBI spokesman Bill Tonkin to avoid any aspersions on the family.

Not only were officials searching, but they were "praying [to] find a third party," one lawman said. "If we don't find another suspect in the kidnapping, the odds of finding Reso alive are slim."

But Bill Tonkin made it very clear: "We are searching for Mr. Reso—alive. We are not searching for a corpse."

Chapter 12

Among the hundreds of people interviewed by agents and detectives, it turned out that none was more important than Irene Szarko. Granted, she didn't know who the third kidnapper might be nor did she have any evidence to offer. She was as shocked as anyone to learn about the crime. She did, however, possess one key attribute that no other person on the planet could claim—she was Jackie Seale's mother.

On Sunday afternoon, two days after the arrests, Agent Ed Petersen and Detective Brian Doig sat down to interview Mrs. Szarko. She'd already been questioned about her daughter's complicity in Sid Reso's kidnapping, but that wasn't why Petersen and Doig were there. They knew Jackie Seale was the weaker link. They hoped to convince Mrs. Szarko to persuade her daughter to cooperate with authorities.

"It was all Artie's fault," Irene Szarko said. "He's the one who got my Jackie into this mess." Mrs. Szarko said that she didn't care for her daughter's husband. None of the Szarkos did.

Petersen explained to Irene Szarko that law enforcement was working against the clock to find Sid Reso. Time was running out. He reminded her that Sid could be out there dying, and that if authorities didn't reach him soon, he *would* die. Not only that, Petersen emphasized that Pat Reso and her children had been crazed with worry for over seven weeks now, even more so after the arrests yielded no word of Reso's whereabouts.

Detective Doig asked if she could imagine how Pat Reso felt. The father of Pat's children might be dying because *her* daughter wouldn't tell police where to find him. He stressed to Mrs. Szarko that she could save Sid Reso by persuading her daughter to cooperate with authorities. And if Reso was already dead, she could provide some much-needed closure for the Reso family. It was in her hands.

Mrs. Szarko gazed at Petersen and Doig for a moment and then said, "I did not raise my daughter to be a kidnapper or a murderer . . . I'm an old woman who just wants to see my daughter." She explained that she'd waited for five hours to visit her daughter the day before and that she'd experienced severe pain from varicose veins while waiting. Despite her pleas, the jailers hadn't allowed her inside. "If you can get me in to see my Jackie, I'll do my best to get her to tell you what she knows."

Petersen didn't blink before replying, "I promise I will get you in. I'll call the warden right now."

The interview was over and the lawmen were optimistic the mother could influence her daughter. Petersen called Joseph Fitzgerald, Assistant Director of the Union County Jail, to explain the situation. The interim warden told Petersen, "You tell her to ask for me, specifically, and I'll make sure she sees her daughter."

On Monday morning, a weeping Irene Szarko sat at a table across from her daughter in the Union County Jail and did what mothers do when their child has been bad—tell her daughter that now is the time to do the right thing, which in this case meant telling what she knew even if it meant incriminating her husband. Jackie's lawyer, Sallyanne Floria, also consulted with her. Jackie needed time to mull it over. While Jackie sat in her cell thinking, Pat and her children agonized. The relentless torment of the Reso family still continued.

* * *

Jackie Seale found herself in a fix. She had not gotten her share of the $18.5 million ransom and all that it would buy her, like big houses, fancy cars, island holidays, expensive clothes, cosmetic surgeries, personal trainers . . . and that was disappointing. Worse, jail was fading her tan.

Agents and detectives continued to struggle in persuading

Jackie to reveal Sid Reso's condition and whereabouts. They were not only frustrated with her refusal to talk, but flummoxed by her aloofness, vanity, and sometimes downright quirky behavior. When agents questioned her about the case, she would stray off topic and talk to them about trivial things like busying herself with cleaning her cell and her desire to teach aerobics in jail. Aerobics? A mother of two teenagers who'd just been arrested and jailed on federal kidnapping and extortion charges where her victim was still missing was focused on teaching aerobics to convicts?

Fortunately for Jackie, she was represented by a lawyer who was concentrating on the legal ramifications of what she had done. Though Sallyanne Floria had been appointed by the court, she was a solid lawyer. She'd graduated from Seton Hall University and had been practicing law for fourteen years, including some time at the Essex County Prosecutor's Office. The thirty-nine-year-old attorney worked at a small law firm with her husband, Anthony Callori, in Verona, New Jersey—hence the firm's name: Floria & Callori. Just months earlier, however, on Halloween 1991, Mrs. Floria's husband died, leaving her with a young son to support and legal cases to handle alone.

As if she didn't have enough on her mind, now Floria had to devise a legal strategy to keep her client out of prison for life, or worse, from receiving the death penalty if she'd participated in murdering Sid Reso. The approach that made the most sense was to amass as much leverage as possible on her client's behalf in order to cut the best plea deal possible. One way to do that was to claim that Jackie Seale suffered from "battered woman syndrome," meaning that she did not act of her own volition, but had been forced to participate in the crime by her husband. Though that strategy might carry some weight with one or more jurors should Jackie face trial, Floria must have realized that it would be an uphill battle convincing U.S. Attorney Chertoff and Morris County Prosecutor Murphy to accept the defense as the impetus for a plea deal. Not because there is anything inherently wrong with the legal defense, but because in Jackie's case, Floria must have suspected that prosecutors simply would not believe there was sufficient evidence for it. In fact, the FBI was already reviewing police reports from New Jersey, South Carolina, and Colorado, and interviewing friends and relatives to determine the veracity of Seale's battered woman defense.

But prosecutors were more interested at the moment with whether Sid Reso was dead or alive than with Jackie Seale's past matrimonial hardships. That meant Jackie was one of only two people who could tell prosecutors what they wanted to hear, and Floria understood that was worth a great deal.

There was an old law on the books in New Jersey, however, that could make it more difficult to craft a plea deal. Obviously, prosecutors would expect Jackie Seale to testify against her husband as part of any agreement. Yet according to a New Jersey evidentiary rule in 1992, a criminal defendant could veto his wife's decision to testify against him. It was an archaic law that originated centuries earlier when a wife had no separate legal existence, but was basically a possession of her husband. The antiquated law wouldn't affect the proceedings in federal court, but could create a problem for prosecutors in state court.

The Morris County Prosecutor's Office set out to change the law, *posthaste*. Mike Murphy spoke with William Gormley, a senator in the New Jersey Legislature. Gormley agreed to "move expeditiously" and sponsor a bill that would permit a person to voluntarily testify against their spouse without the spouse's consent. Other states had adopted similar laws. Some legislators more conservative than Gormley said the old law protected the institution of marriage. Gormley pointed out, "If a spouse is willing to testify against an accused in a criminal proceeding, it would appear there isn't much of a marriage to protect." The only question for Gormley was whether the state legislature could enact the new law before the Seales's state trials began.

With Irene Szarko and the New Jersey Legislature focused on helping Jackie Seale flip on her husband, Sallyanne Florio set out to probe the prosecution's interest in a plea deal for her client. But first, she'd have to convince her client to accept a deal that called for her to testify against her husband—a husband who'd been the dominant person in her life for twenty-five years. Everyone waited on Jackie Seale's decision.

* * *

Even though the Seales were behind bars, agents and detectives didn't let up. They worked the case hard, continuously gathering evidence and trying to find Sid Reso. They were professionals, but as sometimes occurs, many had become emotionally tied to the case. They desperately wanted to find Reso, if for no other reason than to bring him home to Pat and her children, whom they'd gotten to know and like.

All evidence had been sent to the FBI Laboratory in Washington, D.C. The laboratory had boxes, bags, and shelves full of items that had to be tested and analyzed using all manner of basic and complex methods, like mass spectrometry, ballistics, chemistry, biology, biometrics, mineralogy, and even DNA testing. In 1992, forensic DNA analysis was in its infancy. The FBI Laboratory had recently become the first public crime lab in the U.S. to perform DNA analysis. It also had just launched a small national DNA database.

Agents in the lab collectively logged thousands of hours on the SIDNAP case. They examined hairs and fibers under microscopes, scanned and compared fingerprints, matched tread marks to tires on rental vans and cars, compared envelopes and papers taken from the Seale home with ransom notes, examined paint and polymer samples, compared fragments from torn duct tape with rolls found in the Mercedes and the Seale home, and so on. And if the lab technicians didn't have enough to do, Penrith and Murphy sent additional men and dogs to Mr. and Mrs. Seale's property to search for more evidence.

While the lab was busy, field agents continued searching for a third kidnapper who might be holding Reso. Just days before the arrests, the FBI had begun investigating a security officer at Exxon's Florham Park location. The man had made some peculiar comments about Reso's disappearance that drew the attention of coworkers. He was interviewed and agents discovered that the security officer had a drinking problem, was divorced, was in financial difficulty and had misused funds. He boasted of having been a Maryland State Patrolman and a sergeant in the U.S. Army Special Forces when neither was true, though he had been in the Maryland National Guard. FBI notes described him as a "bullshitter." He raised enough suspicion that agents administered a polygraph test, but the results were inconclusive. He would be investigated until August when he would be dropped as an additional suspect. The FBI concluded that, yes indeed, he was a bullshitter, but he was a harmless one.

And then there was a little administrative matter to take care of—returning $18.5 million in $100 bills to Exxon. At 3:15 p.m. on June 19, merely thirteen hours after the arrests of the Seales, the FBI handed over the money. The agent asked the Exxon representative to sign a receipt: "I hereby acknowledge receipt of EIGHTEEN MILLION, FIVE HUNDRED THOUSAND DOLLARS ($18,500,000) in U.S. currency in three locked footlockers from the Federal Bureau of Investigation." Even though the FBI was still looking for a third kidnapper who might have stashed Sid Reso away somewhere, the Bureau didn't believe it needed the money any longer.

* * *

The FBI had hunted down the mystery man . . . and like the Seales, he wasn't talking; at least not without an attorney present.

He also refused to take a polygraph test. An agent sat down with the man and his attorney in the lawyer's office and discussed the man's background and his affiliation with the Seales.

The unemployed forty-two-year-old divorced man lived in Spring Lake, New Jersey, and though his house was for sale, he told agents that he wasn't planning to leave the state or the country. He said he'd known Art Seale since they'd met as neighbors years earlier. He described their relationship as merely "distant friends," who spoke on the phone occasionally about business and their plans for the future. He did admit that he'd spent one New Year's Eve with the Seales on their sailboat in the Bahamas while they were living in Hilton Head. He described Art Seale as "family-oriented" and "high strung" with "lots of problems."

The agent's questions grew more difficult.

"Can you account for your whereabouts during the period from April 29, 1992, through May 5, 1992?"

"No, not specifically, but I was probably home in Spring Lake."

"Do you recall telephone calls between you and either Art or Irene Seale during the same period, April 29, 1992, through May 5, 1992?"

"No, I don't recall them at all. If I did get or make those calls, they would have been between me and Art Seale and not Jackie. That's what she goes by, not Irene."

The agent pressed for a more absolute answer, but the man said he just couldn't remember.

"Did you see Art or Irene Seale, between Easter and Memorial Day of this year?"

"No, I didn't."

"Do you have any business involvement with Art or Irene Seale through limited partnerships or otherwise?"

The man's lawyer leaned over and whispered something. "No, I haven't and I don't plan to," the man answered.

"Have you ever provided any financial support to Art and Irene Seale?"

"No."

"Have you had a romantic relationship with Irene Seale at any time?" the agent asked. Jackie had sent the man a letter after her incarceration in the Union County Jail.

After a brief objection by the lawyer, the man replied, "Absolutely not."

"During your telephone conversations, did Art Seale mention that he was planning on moving out of his parents' home to South Carolina or Florida and opening a marina there?"

"Yes, we talked about his financial difficulties and his plans to move south. I think he first mentioned it around Christmas last year, 1991. He said he planned to open a marina business somewhere in Florida or Hilton Head." The mystery man also told the agent he'd never had any intention to invest in the marina nor had he had any contact with marinas in the southeastern United States. He said he knew Art Seale had recently visited Hilton Head, but learned about the trip only after Seale had returned.

The man also denied any conversation with Art Seale about storage areas and said he'd never been to a storage unit rented by Seale. Agents later learned that Art Seale first thought of using a storage unit while he and Jackie were driving back home after visiting the man.

After a few more questions, the man admitted to the agent that, yes, he had discussed the Reso kidnapping with Art Seale. He made it clear, however, that they discussed it only after he'd read about it in the newspaper. He added that he recalled nothing unusual about their conversation. He also denied any knowledge of the Reso neighborhood, environmental groups, or Warriors of the Rainbow.

"Do you have any personal knowledge of, or did you have any involvement in, the kidnapping of Sidney J. Reso?"

"No, none whatsoever."

That concluded the interview. Though a couple things seemed odd to the agent, and though the FBI would have liked to have administered a polygraph test, nothing in the man's answers or in his financial records or otherwise implicated him in the kidnapping.

"We wanted to . . . restart our lives . . . and purchase a business," Art Seale said later to agents. "An associate of mine and I had started looking for a business that we could obtain using owner financing for most of the purchase price . . . We had several brokers looking for such opportunities for us." He was referring to the mystery man as his business associate, a statement that conflicted with that given by the man to the FBI. But Seale concluded by saying, "That person had no knowledge of our plot and no involvement in it." Because the FBI could not prove otherwise, it had to continue its search for a third kidnapper.

* * *

Agent Petersen had been very busy. Besides his usual duties, he'd impersonated Exxon's Jim Morakis for four hours as part of the drop team, he'd interviewed Irene Szarko and persuaded her to speak with her daughter, and now he was sitting down with Jackie Seale in the Union County Jail to interview her. Along with Detective Sergeant Brian Doig, Petersen asked Jackie a few preliminary questions. She cried and kept telling the men she couldn't answer their questions without first speaking to her husband. Then perhaps she remembered the conversation she'd recently had with her mother, who'd surely repeated what she'd said to Agent Petersen: "I didn't raise my daughter to be a kidnapper or a murderer," because Jackie Seale softened during the interview. Much of that softening had to do with Detective Doig's demeanor. Jackie always seemed more relaxed and willing to talk when Doig was present.

"The family is going through an agonizing time not knowing whether their loved one is dead or alive," Petersen said to Jackie as Doig looked on. "If you were me, would you be looking for someone dead or alive?" Jackie dropped her head. Petersen reached across the table and gently raised her chin. "Dead or alive?" he asked.

Devoid of emotion, Jackie Seale looked directly at Peterson and answered his question: "Probably dead."

Chapter 13

Following the indictments of the Seales in federal court on Thursday, June 25, six days after their arrests, Sallyanne Floria made an appointment to meet with federal and state prosecutors Chertoff and Murphy in a conference room at Chertoff's office. Special Agent Gail Chapman also was there. When they met, she presented the prosecutors with a "hypothetical situation" in which one of her clients would tell the two prosecutors everything she knew about the Sid Reso disappearance and his present location in exchange for a plea deal.

Eventually, the conversation moved beyond the hypothetical. The lawyers agreed that in exchange for Jackie Seale's complete cooperation, truthfulness, and testimony against her husband, and provided they had not intentionally murdered Sid Reso, Chertoff would drop all federal charges, except extortion and conspiracy to commit extortion. Murphy agreed that he would drop all state charges, except kidnapping. They would recommend to the judge that the court accept the plea deal, and most lenient of all, they'd request a sentence not to exceed twenty years in prison, with the federal and state sentences to run concurrently rather than consecutively. With good behavior, Jackie Seale could be out of prison in seventeen years. She'd be sixty-three years old; a senior citizen, yet a young one.

Mike Chertoff and the U.S. Attorney's Office had been involved with the Reso case from the first day of Sid Reso's disappearance. Chertoff had not only been in continual contact with investigators, he had spoken with Pat and her children several times. It was not the typical case for the tough federal prosecutor. "This one got to him," Penrith later recalled. "The way Reso died just got him steamed . . . I'm telling you, Mike did not want to make a deal with [Jackie] Seale."

Chertoff met with Pat Reso to discuss his options with her.

Being a staunch Catholic, Pat said that if Sid was dead, "her life would not be complete" without giving her husband a Christian burial. Chertoff felt he had no choice. He also knew, he later recalled, that Art Seale was the one who'd planned and led the kidnapping. Even more, twenty years in prison was a significant sentence for Jackie Seale. Murphy agreed. They'd do the deal.

On Friday, June 26, one week after the arrests, Chertoff dictated a letter to Floria setting out the terms of the plea agreement, with an addendum by Murphy, which was signed by Floria and Jackie Seale. The agreement would be submitted to Judge Garrett E. Brown Jr., who would preside over Jackie's arraignment in the U.S. District Court in Trenton, New Jersey, on the following Tuesday.

But first, the moment had come for Jackie to tell prosecutors what she knew. It was time to know what happened to Sidney Reso.

* * *

Inside a conference room at the Parsippany Hilton Hotel near the Union County Jail in Elizabeth, New Jersey, the attorneys met to listen to Jackie Seale tell her story. Those sitting around the table included Jackie Seale's attorney, Sallyanne Floria, and federal and state prosecutors Chertoff and Murphy, and Agent Chapman, who'd been assembling exhibits of the evidence for the Seales's upcoming trials. They met for nearly three hours.

Their first question for Jackie concerned Sid Reso's well-being and where he could be found. She told them. Maintaining his composure, Chertoff asked Jackie Seale to explain step-by-step exactly, from the planning to the night of the arrests, how she and Art Seale had kidnapped and held Sid Reso.

Agent Chapman took notes as Jackie spoke. When transcribed, Seale's story would exceed three hundred paragraphs. Prosecutors often interrupted her for further explanation or clarification. She told them how they'd planned the kidnapping in December, prepared for it, and carried it out. Later during the meeting, Seale told them about that first ransom day, on Sunday, May 3, at the Villa Restaurant in Summit, five days after Sid Reso's kidnapping.

"We woke up Sunday morning and went out to rent a car. First, I called Aries Rent-a-Car in Hackettstown, and I remember I was forwarded to the owner's home. Her name is Bette Thomassen. I told her I needed to rent a van that morning. She told me she didn't have one. I told her that was okay, I'd just be carrying people and other stuff. All I needed was a car with a big trunk."

"So, around 10:30, we drove over to the rental place and picked up a car. It was a red Chevrolet. We left there and headed over to the storage building. I remember on the way over thinking that this was finally going to happen, that it was going to work. Other than his gun going off and . . . well, you know . . . almost everything else had gone just as Artie planned."

Chertoff interrupted and asked a question. He then asked Jackie to continue.

"Around eleven o'clock, I guess it was, me and Artie pulled up at the storage place. Our space was 619. Artie opened the door and we went in. It was always dark in there especially with our sunglasses on. We put on our masks and gloves and Artie turned on his flashlight and shut the door."

The FBI would determine that when the Seales entered the storage unit that morning, it had been twenty-one hours since they'd last attended to Sid Reso. While it was possible the gate had been left open or the Seales had followed another vehicle entering the gate, the gate records on Secure Storage computers showed the Seales had visited only once in forty hours and thirty-six minutes.

"I went over to the back corner of the shed and started getting some water and bandages ready and then I heard Artie yell, 'He's had a heart attack!' I turned around and Artie was leaning into the box and pressing down on Mr. Reso's chest like he was giving him CPR. When I went over, I saw Mr. Reso's face. It looked very gray."

Murphy later recalled how Jackie Seale described Sid Reso's death without any emotion. "She was just matter of fact."

"How did you know it was a heart attack?" one of the prosecutors asked. "You said Art told you, 'He's had a heart attack.'"

"Well, we didn't really know for sure. But we knew he had heart problems. That's just what we thought, I guess."

"Okay, after you saw Mr. Reso looking gray, then what did you both do?"

"Artie kept up CPR for maybe another minute and then quit. I remember we were quiet at first and then Artie got pretty mad. We were scared. We didn't know what to do . . . I remember Artie closed the lid and locked it and then we went outside and sat in the car."

Jackie told prosecutors that she and Art remained in the Mercedes until they decided how to proceed.

"Our first reaction was to do nothing," Art later recalled. "We waited for many days . . ."

On that day, however, the Seales left Secure Storage and drove to a Jamesway discount store near their home to purchase plastic sheets, rope, disinfectant, and cleaning materials. They then went home to pick up a chainsaw and the Jeep Cherokee. Oddly, Art Seale made a seventeen-minute telephone call to his friend, the mystery man. Then Art and Jackie Seale returned to the storage unit.

At 12:34 p.m., Art entered the gate at Secure Storage in the Jeep. Jackie entered four minutes later in the Mercedes. They removed Sid Reso's dead body from the wooden box that he'd been in since he last knew freedom at the end of his driveway. He'd finally made it out. They placed his body on plastic sheeting stretched across a portion of the brown concrete floor. Wearing gloves, both Seales worked to remove Reso's clothing, leaving only his soiled undershorts. It was difficult, and the smell was absolutely horrible. The stringent odor of desiccated urine, feces, and sweat, now mingled with the smell of death, oozed from Reso's dead body and percolated inside the hot and unventilated storage space. Art Seale lifted the door a foot or so and Jackie sprayed deodorizer. She was not a happy kidnapper. Still wearing gloves, they wiped Reso's body with disinfectant. They hoped the disinfectant would reduce the stench of oncoming decomposition. The Seales wrapped the plastic around Reso's body and tied ropes over the sheeting, making a tight bundle.

Art Seale then lowered the unit's door and cranked the chainsaw. The raucous growling of the saw ricocheted off the metal walls and ceiling and its gas and oil fumes quickly consumed the small space.

"Artie!" Jackie Seale yelled, placing both hands over her ears and coughing.

He didn't hear her as he revved the chainsaw and lowered the blade to cut the heavy box into sections. She could not have been pleased with how her husband's sure-fire kidnapping scheme had evolved.

While Art Seale loaded the cut-up wood into the Jeep, Jackie gathered Sid Reso's dirty clothes and the pillows, sleeping bag, and blankets that had been inside the wooden box, and stuffed them into garbage bags. With Reso's wrapped body lying on the concrete floor, the Seales then mopped and wiped down the storage unit with disinfectant, bleach, and water. When finished, Art tossed the garbage bags into the back of the Jeep and the Seales left in their separate vehicles. The sanitized storage space contained only Reso's gray, stiffening body wrapped in clear plastic outstretched on the concrete floor. Unit 619 had become a temporary morgue.

After Art and Jackie Seale returned home from leaving Sid Reso's body in storage, Jackie helped her mother-in-law prepare dinner. While the two women chopped vegetables and set the table, Art stood beside a fire he'd started along the bank of the Musconetcong River. When the flames had grown stronger, he tossed in the cut-up wood, Reso's filthy clothing, the soiled bedding, and garbage removed from the storage unit. As red cinders floated into the night sky, it wasn't long before the bonfire consumed all evidence of Reso's confinement. Seale later returned to the burned out fire and scooped up the cooled ashes and remnants of what had burned, including charred wood, hinges, padlocks, and screws, and tossed everything into the river.

After dinner, Art and Jackie gave their excuses to Art's parents and drove away in the Mercedes. The couple stopped at a nearby parking lot and Art entered the Chevrolet Lumina they'd rented that morning. In separate cars, they continued to Summit to drop the ransom note at the Villa Restaurant in preparation for the ransom pickup planned that night. At no time did the Seales discuss abandoning their plan because of Sid Reso's death. As Jackie coolly pointed out during the meeting with prosecutors, "Well, we'd already rented the car. Our plan was in motion." Art later said, "We thought, he was already dead, we went this far, was there anything to be gained if we did not go through with it." Jackie also told prosecutors that Art had actually wanted to kidnap another Exxon executive, but she adamantly refused. Art Seale later denied his wife's accusation.

That evening, the Seales buzzed about Summit dropping notes and making phone calls only for Jackie to misdial the number of the Villa Restaurant payphone, failing in their efforts to obtain the money that night. All the while, Sid Reso remained in the storage space bound in clear plastic and rope, lying on a concrete floor in his soiled underwear. It would be his fifth and final night in the storage unit.

* * *

All those inside the hotel room were horror-struck and revolted by Jackie Seale's admissions, including her attorney most likely, who'd already been told the disgusting story by her client. Heads in the room dropped or shook or both as sighs cut through the thick air. Chertoff and Murphy had been repulsed since the onset of the meeting when Jackie Seale answered their opening question: "Where is Sidney Reso?" They'd refrained from expressing their true feelings in order to keep Jackie talking. More than an hour had passed since that initial key question. Jackie had since begun telling prosecutors about the day after the failed Villa Restaurant ransom call and what they did with Sid Reso's body.

"On Monday morning [May 4 at 7:48; five days after the kidnapping], me and Artie went back to the storage place. Artie backed the rental car to the door and opened it. We saw the body still on the floor in the middle of the shed. I remember I was relieved to smell only ammonia and bleach. We picked him up in the plastic and carried him out and put him in the trunk. He was already stiff. Artie had to bend the legs a little bit to get 'im in." Again, Jackie Seale revealed her grisly story without any signs of emotion or remorse.

She told those present that she and Art traveled south on the Garden State Parkway that runs parallel to the Jersey coast. Along the way, they discussed various ways to dispose of Reso's body. They thought about burning it and then talked about weighting it down into one of the many ponds or lakes in Ocean County, before deciding the best option was to bury him inside the Pine Barrens.

Comprising more than one million acres, almost one quarter of the entire state of New Jersey, the Pine Barrens, also called the Pinelands, is a heavily-forested and sandy stretch of coastal plain in southern New Jersey. Most of it has been set aside as federal and state lands free from development. It also is home to the legendary Jersey Devil that hops around like a horned, cloven-hooved kangaroo. Legend says it can swoop down like a gigantic bat with a forked tail terrifying those far and nigh with it's blood-curdling screams. Though not advertised as such, the Pine Barrens' unique terrain and folklore make the area ideal for burying a human body, and Art Seale understood that. He was familiar with the area from his days at Admiral Farragut Academy preparatory school twenty-five miles north in Pine Beach.

Art and Jackie Seale pulled off the Garden State Parkway on Exit 58 at the southeastern point of Burlington County and purchased a pick and shovel before heading down a two-lane road named, appropriately, Poorman's Parkway. Turning left on Otis Bog Road, the Seales drove a few miles into Bass River State Forest and turned off on one of the many rarely used, sand-packed roads that lead deep into the dense woods. It wasn't long before Art Seale spotted the entry to a path that appeared to weave into an inhospitable area overgrown with brush and scraggly trees. A discarded and rusted air conditioner a few feet from the road uniquely marked the entrance. Art Seale parked and popped the rental car's trunk.

"This is a good place."

The Seales lifted Sid Reso's body out of the trunk and laid him beside the sandy road. Reso's stiffened body retained the curled shape it had cast inside the car's trunk. The Seales then dragged the body into the scraggly woods. It was easier than they'd expected. Seale was a big man, around 225 pounds, while Reso's body weighed about 150 pounds, twenty pounds less than it had on the day he was kidnapped. The plastic also allowed the Seales to slide the body more easily along the path's sand and grass surface. After dragging the body almost 200 feet into the dark interior of the woods, Art Seale noticed a small clearing among several trees and shrubs. This was the spot.

Seale instructed his wife to go back to the car and drive around to kill time while he buried the body. A parked car might seem suspicious to a passing park ranger. Seale told her to use the large rusted air conditioner as a landmark when she returned. "Don't get lost."

Seale retrieved the pick and shovel he'd left at the roadside and started digging. It was hot and muggy and Seale wasn't in the best condition. He dug a shallow hole in the sandy earth, about six feet long, but only two feet deep. Wiping sweat and swatting away mosquitoes and ticks, he untied the ropes securing the plastic and rolled Sid Reso's curled body into the shallow hole. He covered him with loose sand and dirt, and then scattered twigs and leaves over the surface to camouflage the grave. Seale would later say in a dubious letter to judges before his sentencing, "I stood there several minutes, kneeled, and prayed." Coated with sweaty sand and dirt, Seale walked back to the road carrying his tools and waited for Jackie.

The prosecutors and officers in the meeting were not only sickened by what they were hearing, but also probably dismayed. The New Jersey prosecutors would have expected that kind of coldblooded behavior from mob hitmen they'd prosecuted in the past, but not from a suburban married couple with children and a dog.

According to Jackie Seale, she picked up her husband beside the road shortly afterward. She'd simply been driving back and forth while Art buried Reso's body. They drove back to Washington Township and cleaned the rental car before returning it. It had been a 250-mile round trip and taken them more than five hours. They were exhausted as they sat down at the dinner table that evening with Art's parents and their daughter.

Art's mother may have asked: "How was your day?"

* * *

Sid's secretary, Barbara Cruikshank, sat at her desk on Friday at Exxon International's Florham Park offices looking forward to the weekend. René Dahan, who was handling most of Sid Reso's duties, and Walter Schroth, the head of human resources, passed by her desk and stepped into her boss's office. They closed the door. Ms. Cruikshank thought that was strange because no one had gone into Sid's office and shut the door since Sid did it himself the day before his disappearance. He typically ate his lunch at his desk and closed the door to read the newspaper or to take a quick nap.

In a moment, the door opened. Schroth called out, "Barbara," and motioned for her to step into Reso's office. When she did, Schroth closed the door behind her. She had been with Exxon thirty-three years. Was this a Friday firing?

"Barbara, we've got some bad news about Sid," Schroth said. "The female kidnapper told authorities today that Sid is dead and they buried his body."

As Ms. Cruikshank delicately recalled later, "It was not a good morning."

* * *

About 8:00 a.m. on Saturday morning, June 27, a task force of federal and state investigators representing seven different agencies, along with Buffy, the trained cadaver dog, and Jackie Seale, their kidnapper-turned-tour guide, traveled south from the Union County Jail. They drove one hundred miles along the Garden State Parkway to Bass River State Forest where the Seales had buried Sid Reso's body almost eight weeks earlier.

The convoy had alerted park officials as a courtesy that they would soon be entering their park in a big way. Park rangers met them as they arrived and followed along behind the lead vehicle that now carried Jackie Seale and her attorney. Just inside the park, Seale recognized road marker 64 and then the sandy Munion Field Road she'd taken with her husband. They hadn't traveled much farther before she recognized a rusted air conditioner near the entry to a path. The caravan stopped. Sergeant Doig rolled down a dusty window so Jackie could get a better look. She thought this was the spot. Agents Chapman and Petersen stepped from the vehicle and opened Jackie's door. She climbed out and looked around to be sure. It was almost ten o'clock.

The other members of the group stepped out of their vehicles to stretch from the long drive when they heard an officer shout, "She says this is it!" Jackie Seale was told to wait while everyone grabbed their gear. She then led the group of roughly forty men and women, along with the cadaver dog and its handler, down the narrow sand and grass pathway. About 200 feet into the forest, Jackie pointed to an area where she believed Reso had been buried. Sergeant Doig noticed a spot in which the vegetation appeared different, newer, than that surrounding it. "The soil was uprooted," Doig recalled later.

The handler guided Buffy to the spot covered with little growth. The six-year-old German shepherd had searched for Sid Reso on Jonathan Smith Road the day he first disappeared, then at the Newark International Airport, and again at the Seale house. When she reached the peculiar spot, Buffy immediately gave an "alert" by lying down, an indication of a decomposing human body at that location. It had taken her sixty days, but Buffy had at last found Sid Reso.

The forensics team lead by Special Agent Bruce Hall commenced the tedious job of gathering evidence around the unmarked gravesite. An agent with a camera snapped photos, another brushed and hand-vacuumed suspicious spots, another searched for footprints to take casts, and others took measurements of the site and diagrammed and documented the area. All were important tasks that had to be completed before the first grain of sand was removed from the suspected gravesite.

Though the Ocean County Medical Examiner was present, agents determined that the probable burial spot lay a few yards inside adjoining Burlington County. So, Burlington County

Medical Examiner, Dr. Dante Ragasa, was called as was the Burlington County Sheriff. It was 12:20 p.m. After Dr. Ragasa arrived, he telephoned the New Jersey Medical Examiner, Dr. Robert Goode, who made the long journey from Newark while everyone waited. He arrived at 3:46 p.m.

When ready, a team of agents in jeans, t-shirts, and gloves began the slow and meticulous process of removing debris and inches of dirt. Others continued to document and photograph their progress. Agents established an outside perimeter of eleven feet square. They began digging a trench in a rectangular shape in the area of the disturbed soil measuring eight feet long by three and a half feet wide. Little by little the trench was excavated around the body. The soil was sandy and roots crisscrossed the dig area, many showing signs of having been cut previously.

The outline of a body gradually began to form between the area of the undisturbed soil and the disturbed soil. The heel of a foot and the fingers of a clenched left hand bearing a wedding band eerily emerged from the soil. While agents methodically removed more sand and dirt as sequential photographs were snapped, it became clear to everyone that Sid Reso had been buried face down wearing only his undershorts. Those present became angry. Fortunately for Jackie Seale, she was no longer at the site. She'd been escorted earlier to the Ocean County Prosecutor's Office in Toms River, New Jersey, where she was held until the recovery of Reso's body concluded.

Eventually, the forensics team completed the exhumation of Sid Reso's body. Those about to lift him from the shallow grave paused momentarily. It had been fifty-six days since anyone had seen Reso's face. The team carefully wrapped the decomposing body in a yellow body pouch, which was zipped and padlocked. Four men then grasped the bag's straps and, like unkempt pallbearers, slowly carried Reso's remains to a coroner's van parked near the path's entrance.

The forensic team members removed their gloves beside their

vehicles, many covered in ticks and mosquito bites anxious to get some relief from the heat. They drank water while Penrith found something stronger in his car. Everyone then packed up their gear and set off north along the Garden State Turnpike. They arrived back at their respective departments around eight o'clock that night. It had been a twelve-hour operation.

"It was one of the worst places I've ever been," Penrith said. "You wouldn't walk accidentally into that area. You wouldn't camp in that area. You wouldn't hunt in that area."

Penrith had just described the reasons why the Seales had buried Sid Reso there.

* * *

The FBI released a statement at 9:30 p.m. following the exhumation of Sid Reso's body:

After more than eight weeks since his disappearance from his residence in Morristown, New Jersey, on April 29, 1992, the remains of a corpse believed to be that of Sidney J. Reso, President of Exxon Company, International were recovered today by law enforcement officials in the Pine Barrens in Southern New Jersey. Positive identification is not expected until tomorrow, June 28. No further details are available this evening. The FBI, along with the United States Attorney's Office, the Morris County Prosecutor's Office, and the Morris Township Police Department, will hold a press conference on Sunday, June 28, at 11:00 a.m. in the Essex Room at the Gateway Hilton Hotel on Raymond Plaza in Newark, New Jersey, at which time additional details regarding today's developments will be provided.

As the FBI's press release had stated, a press conference was held Sunday morning before a mass of reporters inside the hotel. When authorities spoke to journalists that Sunday, the medical examiner had not yet completed his autopsy. Penrith told reporters that Sid Reso apparently had been dead for most of the time he was missing. "So there was nothing the family or law enforcement could have done to prevent this final criminal act . . . this unbelievably despicable crime," he said.

Because Reso died during the commission of a felony, Morris County Prosecutor Murphy told reporters that he intended to charge one or both of the Seales with felony murder that could carry a sentence of life imprisonment.

News reports had speculated that weekend that Reso may have died of natural causes, maybe a heart attack. A reporter brought up that possibility at the news conference, which angered U.S. Attorney Chertoff. "Nobody can say that a man who dies in captivity—having been abducted from his family and having been held against his will—died of natural causes. I cannot imagine causes that are less natural than the causes that apply in this case."

When asked if the investigation was over, Special Agent-in-Charge Penrith replied: "We have no knowledge of [additional suspects], but we're going to ensure that if there is anybody else involved in this matter, we're going to find out about it." Murphy agreed, "We have not ruled out the possibility of a third person being involved."

The mystery man had been cleared by the FBI as had Sid Reso's drivers. In addition, the shadowy figure that Agent Brzezinski had spotted in the car with Art Seale on the night of the payphone surveillance turned out to simply be Jackie. There were no other real suspects.

* * *

While the press conference was underway, New Jersey Medical Examiner, Robert Goode M.D., conducted an autopsy of Sid

Reso's body. It lasted from 8:00 a.m. until 8:10 p.m. Several observers were present during the autopsy: Tom Cottone and Bruce Hall with the FBI; Mark Prach and Jim Gannon with the Morris County Prosecutor's Office; and Frank Tomaino and Marius Lombardi with the New Jersey State Medical Examiner's Office. Cesar Rosario and Jeannette Aguilar assisted Dr. Goode.

Dr. Goode, who was known for his attention to detail, x-rayed Sid Reso's entire body while it was still inside the body pouch in the same position that it had been when exhumed from the shallow grave. Then Dr. Goode and his team withdrew Reso's body from the pouch and removed the sandy soil and debris from the body and retained them for examination. Reso's boxer shorts were removed and his body rinsed.

After an external examination of the entire body for wounds, Special Agent Jackie Bell fingerprinted Sid Reso's hands and compared them to his known prints. Dr. Ira Titunik, a consulting orthodontologist from New York City, examined Reso's teeth and compared them with his dental records. There was no question the body was that of Sidney Reso.

With the identification complete, an internal examination began with collection of tissue and organ specimens. No food particles were found inside the stomach. No feces were found in the intestines.

Additional x-rays of the abdomen were made that revealed three fragments of chipped teeth and a small leaden fragment identified as a partial dental restoration. No one knew how they got there. Jackie Seale wasn't aware of them. Some theorized that Art Seale had belted Sid Reso in the mouth with a pistol barrel and then taped his mouth shut. Most believed, however, that Reso had done it himself, either while banging his head against the lid of the box or while clenching at the moment of his death. Other than possibly Art Seale, no one will ever know for certain.

Dr. Goode conducted several other tests, including toxicology that revealed nothing suspicious. Reso's body revealed no wounds to the top or back of the head, nose, neck, back, or anywhere else, except the perforating gunshot wounds on his left forearm, contusions of both wrists from the handcuffs, and his fractured teeth.

It was impossible for Dr. Goode and his assistants to determine the exact cause of death. It "was a challenging task" due to decomposition of the body. When the autopsy was completed that night, Dr. Goode wrote on the death certificate, "Multiple traumatic injuries: gunshot wound left arm, blunt trauma to hands and face, under investigation." The death certificate was later amended to state "Cause of Death: Violence, Nonaccidental. Manner of Death: Homicide."

Most agreed that Sid Reso had likely died from a combination of systemic infection resulting from the gunshot wound, dehydration, and asphyxiation. Though it was possible Reso had died from a heart attack caused by the stress of the other factors, his personal physician told Dr. Goode that Sid Reso "had fully recovered clinically from his previous heart attack and that there was no residual functional deficit to his daily actions." Dr. Goode's opinion as to the cause of death was that Reso "died as a result of the combined effects of multiple forms of external violence and the manner of death is homicide."

For the time of death, Goode wrote, "Found 6-27-92" and "Found ≈ Noon." If Jackie Seale's story was truthful, Sid Reso actually died on the afternoon or evening of May 2 or the morning of May 3. But officially, the date was June 27; that was when law enforcement verified Reso's death. The medical examiner signed the certificate that Sunday, June 28. It was official, and the newspapers, radio, and television announced it—Exxon International President Sidney J. Reso was dead.

* * *

Special Agent Tom Cottone drove to the Reso home on Sunday,

the day after Sid Reso's body had been exhumed from the Pine Barrens. Pat had already been told about Jackie Seale's admission that had included Sid's death. Charlie Roxburgh also had told Pat the night before of the discovery of Sid's body. Despite there having been several indications of Sid's probable death for days if not weeks, Pat obviously was very upset when she received the news. Always strong and dutiful, she began planning Sid's funeral in New Orleans.

When Cottone arrived that Sunday, he parked behind a handful of unmarked cars and squad cars in the Reso driveway near the garage. A police officer assigned to stand guard at the end of the driveway had let him pass. Another patrolman kept watch near the garage. As Cottone walked along the sidewalk to the front door, he dreaded his unfathomable task. He was an excellent agent who worked violent crime cases on the street and could pilot fixed wing aircraft when needed, but this was something different. Members of law enforcement almost always say that informing family members of a person's death is the most difficult part of their jobs. But Charlie Roxburgh had already told Pat. Cottone had something more to do, perhaps just as difficult. He handed Pat the wedding ring that she'd slipped on Sid's finger almost thirty-seven years earlier. An indescribable moment. Then Cottone left. His gesture not only exemplified his character, but also the level of sensitivity that had developed between law enforcement and the Reso family.

Pat surely wrote to Sid in her diary that night that she had his wedding ring. Her words were private. She would continue to write to her husband each day for some time even though she knew he was dead. She believed he would read her entries from Heaven.

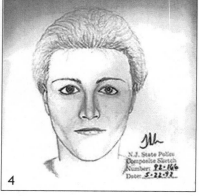

Missing person flyer

Picture 1 Sid Reso—family man. Picture 2 Reso's VW wagon at the end of his driveway where he was kidnapped. Picture 3 Missing person flyer. Picture 4 Police sketch of blond jogger that turned out to be Jackie Seale. Picture 5 Secure Storage facility outside of Hackettstown, New Jersey. Picture 6 Secure Storage unit 619 where Sid Reso died in captivity.

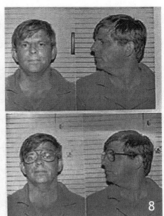

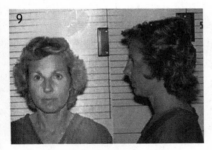

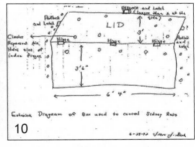

Picture 7 Art and Jackie Seale shopping for batteries on the night of their arrests. Picture 8 Art Seale mugshots. Picture 9 Jackie Seale mugshots. Picture 10 Jackie Seale's drawing of the wooden box where Sid Reso died. Picture 11 Soil-covered contour of Sid Reso's body in shallow grave. Picture 12 Press conference with Michael Murphy, Michael Chertoff, and Gary Penrith.

Chapter 14

Wearing a blue blazer, red-trimmed white blouse, and white pleated skirt, and still tanned, Jackie Seale appeared before Judge Garrett E. Brown Jr. in the U.S. District Court of New Jersey in Trenton, on Tuesday, June 30, Case No. 92-372. Her lawyer and U.S. Attorney Chertoff were present, along with members of law enforcement and reporters. Several people lined the walls of the overcrowded gallery.

The bailiff removed Jackie Seale's handcuffs as she took the witness stand and swore to tell the truth. As part of her arraignment, the judge questioned Jackie to make certain that she understood the charges and the consequences of the plea agreement she signed on the advice of her legal counsel.

"If I accept your plea," Judge Brown said, "you will be a convicted felon by virtue of your own statements. Do you understand that?"

"Yes," Jackie answered impassively.

"Now, you're pleading guilty because you're, in fact, guilty, and for no other reason. Is that correct?"

"Yes," she said with a nod.

The judge, described as well-prepared and demanding, but courteous, then asked U.S. Attorney Chertoff to examine Seale to determine if there was a factual basis for the guilty plea. It was a procedural requirement.

"On April 29th, 1992, did you and Arthur D. Seale, your husband, abduct Sidney J. Reso, the president of Exxon Company, International, from outside his home in Morris Township, New Jersey?" Chertoff asked.

"Yes."

"Did you and Arthur D. Seale then take Mr. Reso to a public storage facility and hold him there against his will?"

"Yes."

"On or about May 3rd, 1992, did you discover that Mr. Reso had died in the storage unit while still in captivity?"

"Yes." Her answer to this question was in a lower voice than the others.

"Beginning on April 30, 1992, and continuing till June 18, 1992, did you and Arthur D. Seale deliver a number of ransom letters demanding millions of dollars in ransom in exchange for the release of Mr. Reso?"

"Yes."

After a few other questions and procedural matters, the judge approved the plea deal contingent on Jackie Seale telling the truth and testifying on behalf of the prosecution at her husband's trial. Her sentencing would not be for seven months, on January 23, 1993. Until then, she'd remain in the Union County Jail— perhaps teaching aerobics.

When the thirty-five minute proceeding was over, federal marshals hustled Jackie Seale out of the courthouse and through a mob of reporters and camera crews waiting outside. Seale's lawyer stopped long enough to tell reporters, "By the time of the trial [of Art Seale], everyone will see that Jackie Seale is a very nice person who was abused and manipulated by her husband. But for the fact of his control, she would have never been involved in criminal activity." When reporters asked Chertoff if he thought Jackie Seale was a "very nice person," he curtly replied, "No!"

Many in the court and waiting outside were not pleased with the plea deal that prosecutors made with Jackie Seale. They didn't understand that although prosecutors believed they could convict the Seales without a *corpus delicti*, it wasn't certain. Perhaps the best they could do was to convict the Seales of conspiracy to commit extortion. Morris County Prosecutor Murphy responded to the criticism by disclosing the principal reason for the plea bargain: "There is no possibility we would have ever recovered Mr. Reso's remains, and the recovery of his remains was extremely important to the Reso family . . . We consulted with Pat Reso before accepting the plea agreement and she gave it her blessing."

One hour after Jackie Seale's appearance in court, Art Seale arrived at the same court in an orange prison jumpsuit. He was accompanied by his lawyer, Chester Keller. As the judge read each of the six counts set out in the federal indictment to him—kidnapping, conspiracy to commit kidnapping, extortion, conspiracy to commit extortion, using the mails to transmit ransom demands, and interstate travel in aid of extortion—Art Seale answered in a firm and clear voice each time, "Not guilty." In eight minutes, the judge was done with him. Flanked by U.S. marshals, Seale walked out of the courthouse to a government vehicle that would transport him back to Passaic County Jail. Just before the federal marshal shut the car door, Art Seale heard a reporter shout, "What do you think of your wife?" He yelled back, "I love her."

* * *

The following day, Pat Reso and her four adult children attended Sid's wake at Lake Lawn Funeral Home in their hometown of New Orleans. An estimated one thousand mourners streamed by Sid Reso's coffin for three hours. The funeral service was held the next day, Thursday, July 1, at 1:30, in the century-old Gothic-style Holy Name of Jesus Roman Catholic Church on the campus of Loyola University. Three Exxon executives, Harry Longwell Jr., J.H. Peery, and Charlie Roxburgh joined Sid's brothers, Robert and Warren Reso, as pallbearers. The five men bore Sid's coffin into the church ahead of his widow, four children, mother, and sister, all dressed in black. Pat also wore dark sunglasses, a string of white pearls, and her husband's wedding band on a gold chain around her neck.

Thousands of family and friends filled the church, including more than one hundred and fifty current and retired Exxon employees. "He was one of the nicest men God ever made," said one Exxon employee. Many of those in attendance had not seen Sid since the 1950s. Pat sat stoically on the front pew through the hour-long funeral Mass presided over by Archbishop Philip Hannon while her four children quietly wept beside her.

The Rev. Sean Duggan praised Sid Reso for "thoroughly leading a Christian life" and "trying to leave the world a better place than when he entered it." For those grappling with how such a terrible thing could happen to such a good person, Archbishop Hannon pointed out, "Yes, Sid Reso suffered a brutal, vicious death. But we must remember that Christ also suffered a similar death and that the thing that gives it all meaning is the final resurrection."

Following Mass, about twenty police officers on motorcycles and several others in patrol cars escorted a mile-long funeral procession to Lake Lawn Metairie Cemetery, sitting alongside the noisy I-10 just north of New Orleans. There, Sid Reso was buried on the hot and humid July day. This time, he was buried in a suit and within a coffin, accompanied by eulogies and prayers from those who loved him.

After fifty-seven years, Sid had returned home. It was something he'd expected, only it had happened a couple decades too soon. When he flew to his hometown in January to accept an honor bestowed on him by his high school, he could never have imagined he'd be the victim of a hideous crime and return six months later in a coffin.

"Life is something you do," Reso once said, "not something that happens to you." He had done much. He had achieved a top position at one of the top corporations in the world, and he and Pat had raised five children and created a wonderful life around them. The end of his life, however, came about because of something the Seales had done to him.

"It seems really unfair that such a good and decent person

who's never hurt anyone . . ." Pat said, not completing her thought. "I really believe in the horror in all this, there's a purpose. I have to believe that."

A week later at 3 p.m. on July 8, more than one thousand Exxon executives and employees as well as law enforcement officials joined Pat Reso and her children at a private outdoor memorial service. The service was held under a massive tent filled with orchids and purple and black crepe on Exxon's Florham Park property where Sid Reso had worked for six years. All those attending were handed a white rose as they entered the tent. The doors of Exxon's headquarters also were draped in purple and black and flags flew at half-staff. Guards allowed in only those invited and signs at the gate said, "No Cameras Please." The New Jersey Legislature even held a moment of silence.

The Rev. William Naughton of the Resurrection Parish, the Resos' church in New Jersey, presided over the ceremony, which included song, prayer, liturgy readings, and eulogies by Exxon executives Larry Rawl and Charlie Roxburgh. "Sid had made an invaluable contribution to Exxon during his thirty-five year career," Exxon CEO Rawl said. "He was one of the finest men I have known who combined outstanding professional competence and humanity and warmth."

Following the memorials, and after some time to reflect, Pat released a statement to the press on July 16 that read:

From the moment Sid was taken on April 29, our lives changed. Not for a minute could we have imagined the outcome of his disappearance. Together, with many of you who knew him and many who knew of him, we prayed for his safe return . . . The outpouring of love was overwhelming. Never did we dream that so many felt as deeply about Sid as we did. Friends and relatives, Exxon employees and law enforcement officials, the public and the media, all were there for us. The encouragement, faith, and love helped us more than I can ever say. On behalf of my family, I thank all of you . . . It is proof that good does exist in the face of darkness. Please continue to keep Sid in your prayers. He was a good man, father, and husband. We miss him and your words, prayers, friendship, and support have comforted the Reso family and will continue to comfort us in the days to come.

God bless all of you.

* * *

Shackled at the ankles and wrists, Art Seale grimaced as he shuffled into the Morris County Courthouse sandwiched between two stern-faced U.S. marshals. Like each time he'd entered before, the spectators, media, and law enforcement officials that packed the gallery watched his every movement and expression. The Seales were the hottest courtroom ticket around.

The state of New Jersey assigned Peter V. Toscano, Assistant Deputy of the Public Defender's Office, to represent Seale before the state court judge. That meant Seale now had two free lawyers: Keller in federal court and Toscano in state court. Toscano had been appointed scarcely minutes before the proceeding had begun. He'd not even seen the complaint setting out the charges against his client. The judge provided him with a copy as the 1:30 p.m. hearing got underway.

Chief Detective Richard Riley had signed the complaint charging Art Seale with kidnapping, conspiracy to commit kidnapping, extortion, and conspiracy to commit extortion. It was supplemented by a complaint signed by Sergeant George Nunn charging felony murder, aggravated assault, and possession of a dangerous weapon to commit a criminal act. Felony murder does not require a showing of intent to kill; it applies simply when the victim dies during the commission of a felony offense, such as kidnapping. If convicted, Seale could receive a sentence of thirty years to life imprisonment, in addition to any sentences for the other charges. A grand jury also could upgrade the felony murder charge to capital murder, in which case Seale would face the death penalty, if convicted. Morris County Prosecutor Murphy, however, did not have the evidence to support first or second degree murder. Jackie Seale had told the prosecutors that she and her husband didn't intend to kill Sid Reso. So far, all the evidence corroborated her story. FBI Special Agent-in-Charge Penrith believed Jackie Seale when he told reporters, "I don't think they intended for him to die." Penrith added, however, that: "There is not anyone alive today who would want to go through what Mr. Reso went through in dying. He suffered for a considerable period of time."

Dressed in a blue suit and a white shirt open at the collar, Art Seale sat calmly and politely before Judge Stephen E. Smith Jr. He answered the judge's questions about whether he understood his rights and the charges against him. When finished, Seale's state-appointed attorney, Toscano, said, "We reviewed a copy of the charges, and . . . enter a plea of not guilty to all charges."

The next issue addressed during the proceeding was that of bail. After some discussion, the judge declared, "Bail will be set at $5 million. Cash, no ten percent, no property." Unlike federal court in which the judge had denied bail, the New Jersey Constitution at that time required courts to fix bail at some amount based on all the circumstances presented to the judge, except in capital cases when it could be denied.

Bail permits a defendant to engage a bail agent to post a bond. Much like a secured I.O.U., the agent promises to pay the court the entire amount of bail if the defendant doesn't show up for his required court appearances. Knowing that Seale didn't have access to $5 million cash and having prohibited him from paying ten percent for a surety to supply bond, the state judge had effectively denied bail just as the federal judge had done.

Following the brief hearing, federal marshals escorted Art

Seale from the courtroom. Despite his wife's admissions and her agreement to testify against him, Seale told a reporter who'd asked if he had anything to say to his family, "Just that I love them all."

Three hours earlier, at 10:30 a.m., Jackie Seale appeared before the same judge in her first state court proceeding. Though she'd already cut a deal with the Morris County Prosecutor, she had to be arraigned, a procedural formality, just as she had earlier in federal court. The proceeding lasted a mere five minutes. Bail was set at $1 million cash, lower than her husband's because she'd cooperated with prosecutors and didn't pose a significant flight risk. It was irrelevant anyway; Jackie Seale couldn't raise that much cash.

Wearing handcuffs and the same blue blazer, red-trimmed white blouse, and white pleated skirt she'd worn at her June 30 federal court hearing, Jackie Seale was led out of the courtroom by federal marshals and down the front steps. She kept her eyes down as she walked, never looking up at the large crowd of reporters and spectators, who heckled her as she made her way to the government sedan. It was a small, but vocal crowd. Though not as bad as the old Western shouts to "string 'im up," it still wasn't pleasant. Several in the crowd were Morris County employees on their morning breaks hoping to catch a glimpse of the Seales.

"I think they both should go to jail for life. They killed someone," said Denise Wilmot of the human services office. "We're here to see justice," said John Nigro. "To me, they deserve life. What they did was the cruelest thing I can think of."

The prosecutors were still on the defensive over the deal cut with Jackie Seale. The day before, *The Star-Ledger* published an article stating that an "unidentified" federal official suggested that the plea bargain could result in Jackie being out of prison in fewer than fifteen years. Chertoff took exception. "Whoever made these statements was speaking without knowledge or authority. No responsible law enforcement official has endorsed these statements or predictions."

But probation clerk, Gloria Cifrese, agreed with the unidentified official. She wasn't happy at all with Mrs. Seale's plea bargain. "To take this man and stick him in a box—that's murder! There should be a very severe punishment," she said. "The Bible tells you an eye for an eye, a tooth for a tooth," said another. Kim Teates of Morris Plains said what few did, but many may have thought: "She should die."

* * *

On July 17, in the Morris County Surrogate's Court of New Jersey, Pat and Sid's cousin, Jerome Reso Jr., sat in court with Marc Stern, a Newark estate attorney with the same law firm that was handling a civil suit for wrongful death that had been filed by the Resos against the Seales. Sid Reso's last will and testament signed by him five years earlier was being offered for probate. Sid's cousin, an attorney, and Pat were named in the will to be the co-executors of Sid Reso's sizeable estate. Also present was Richard Bishop, a vice president of U.S. Trust Company of New York that would serve with Pat as the co-trustees of a trust created for her benefit under the will.

Pat had been married to Sid for thirty-six years, seven weeks, and twenty days. Then, within a span of only another twenty days, she had been notified of the discovery of her husband's body, attended his funeral in New Orleans and his memorial service in Florham Park, prepared her house for sale to move to another state, and attended the probate of her deceased husband's last will and testament. Like a knee that jerks when it's struck, Pat had to have been functioning involuntarily, almost instinctively. After all, she had been struck as hard as any wife and mother could, almost more than a human can endure. But there she stood in probate court before the judge accepting the responsibility to be an executor of Sid's estate. She would have preferred to remain his wife.

* * *

Like rats popping their heads out long enough to make brief appearances in court, the Seales would scurry back to their holes in county jail following each hearing. Separate jails confined the married couple until their sentencings.

Art Seale was incarcerated at the Passaic County Jail in Paterson, fifteen miles north of Newark. Because of his notoriety, the jail assigned him to the protective custody unit that at that time housed twenty-four inmates. They were isolated from the general population, but could mingle with each other. A guard watched them twenty-four hours a day. One indirect benefit of protective custody was that it allowed Seale to avoid the overcrowded conditions at the jail.

Built in 1957, the yellow brick, four-story jail was meant to house 455 prisoners, but was well-known for imprisoning almost four times that number. Prisoners are "packed like sardines" in "horrendous conditions," one newspaper reported. According to *The Record*, a Hackensack newspaper, Passaic County Jail was the most overcrowded county jail in the entire United States that year.

Besides his lawyers, Art Seale's parents visited him in protective custody, but not his children. Seale's son, who was on summer vacation from Norwich University in Vermont, was still in Hilton Head. Seale's sixteen-year-old daughter, who'd just finished her sophomore year at Voorhees High School, had hitchhiked to Hilton Head following her parents' arrests. Another source reported she'd had a breakdown and had been admitted to a hospital. Whatever the case, the Seale children had also become victims of their parents' crime.

Twenty miles south, Jackie sat in her cell at the Union County

Jail in Elizabeth. It was almost as if she was doing time at her hometown of Hillside. If not for the city limit signs, it would be difficult to tell where Hillside ends and Elizabeth begins. She was staying in the "new jail," an angular, thirteen-story modern structure built just three years earlier. It sits across a narrow street from the "old jail," an eight-story, old-fashioned blockhouse with iron bars built in 1925. The two are connected by a skybridge.

Like most New Jersey jails at that time, the Union County Jail experienced mismanagement and overcrowding, with reports of an inmate population as high as 1,500 in a jail designed for fewer than 1,000. Bad, but not near as bad as the conditions at the Passaic County Jail during the same time.

Jackie Seale's mother and other family members visited her occasionally, but like Art Seale, she also hadn't seen her children. She did receive visits from her attorney, and from authorities when they had additional questions to ask about the case as part of her plea deal.

The Seales may not have had a busy social calendar, but Art did have someone special who wanted to pay him a visit. Only this potential visitor caused authorities some concern. "We have received some letters," said Bruce Gebhardt, Assistant Special Agent-in-Charge of the FBI's Newark office. The letters were threats to break Art Seale out of jail. It could have been a hoax, but authorities still wondered if the Seales had one or more accomplices who'd not only assisted them with the kidnapping, but now wanted to bust Art Seale out. In response to the threats, the Passaic County Sheriff's Office issued an alert to all guards and other personnel advising them to take special precautions concerning visitors. "It has come to our attention that certain unnamed outside agents may attempt to free Arthur D. Seale from federal custody." Everyone knew who "Arthur D. Seale" was—he was the most famous inmate at the jail that summer.

"The U.S. Marshals and the Passaic County Sheriff are

prepared to deal with any attempt to break Seale out of jail,"
Gebhardt said.

Breaking someone out of jail is extremely difficult, but
not impossible. The fact that Seale was held in the protective
custody unit under round-the-clock observation, however, made
it nearly impossible for him to escape.

A few days later, on Friday, July 31, U.S. marshals moved
Seale to the Somerset County Jail in Somerville. The transfer
wasn't due to concerns over security, but because Seale had to
appear in federal court in Trenton on Monday. His previous
federal court appearances had been in Newark.

Monday came, and so did Art Seale to court, once again
shackled around the ankles though this time his hands were
cuffed behind his back. Dressed in a charcoal gray suit, light blue
shirt, and blue and red paisley tie, federal marshals seated Seale
at the defendant's table where he waited for his attorney and
Judge Brown. Those in the gallery were surprised, and perhaps
a bit gratified, to see Art Seale quietly weeping as he waited. It
was his first public display of emotion.

Once the judge entered and seated himself behind the bench,
he directed that Seale's handcuffs be removed and that he be
administered the oath. Seale sat in the witness stand to the
judge's left. Eventually, Judge Brown asked, "Mr. Seale, do you
plan to hire a private attorney?"

"No, Your Honor," answered Seale, though not as loudly and
firmly as he'd answered in previous court appearances. "When I
was arrested, my entire assets were about $200 in the bank." That
meant he was stuck with his public defender, Chester Keller,
and Keller was stuck with him.

Following more questions, Keller then entered a plea of
not guilty to the revised federal indictment on behalf of Seale.
Because the Seales had not carried Sid Reso across the New
Jersey state line, U.S. Attorney Chertoff had to drop the federal
charges of kidnapping and conspiracy to commit kidnapping,

though the charges of extortion and conspiracy to commit extortion remained unchanged. Kidnapping would continue to be charged in the state indictment.

With his part over, marshals escorted Seale out of court and transported him back to the Passaic County Jail. His public defender remained and argued for a change of venue. He asserted that news leaks by law enforcement agencies and extensive pretrial publicity were "inflammatory and sensational" and thus made it impossible for Seale to get a fair trial in New Jersey. He gave as one example the article that appeared in *The Star-Ledger* entitled, "Reso's Tomb of Pain," which described in detail the coffin-like box and Reso's suffering inside it. The judge ruled without much difficulty that Seale's federal trial would stay in New Jersey, which was scheduled to begin in five weeks on September 10 in Trenton.

The public defender also argued that searches of the rented Oldsmobile and the Mercedes on the night of his client's arrest were conducted without probable cause and therefore were unconstitutional. Hence, all evidence seized from the cars could not be used at trial. The judge again denied the attorney's motion.

Art Seale wasn't having much luck in court, though not for lack of his attorney trying. Worse, his wife was going to testify against him in federal court. Still worse, the New Jersey Legislature had just voted that same day to repeal the spousal immunity rule that would have prevented Jackie from testifying against him in state court. His defenses were dropping fast. Though a jury might find him not guilty, he'd have a better chance with the mysterious "outside agents" breaking him out of jail. It was looking very grim for the yuppie kidnapper and he knew it. That's why he'd wept in court for the first time. The futility of his legal defense and, perhaps more broadly, of his life was beginning to sink in, and so was the despair.

* * *

Sitting in the living room of her beautiful home that no longer felt beautiful, Pat Reso spoke with a female reporter from *The Star-Ledger*. It was the same room she'd talked with reporters numerous times about her missing husband. And it was the same room she'd pleaded for her husband's safe return in front of a television camera. It had been almost three weeks since Sid's body had been discovered and the passage of time had changed many things. Gone was the hope of reuniting with her husband. Substituted in its place was the hope of healing, forgiveness, and the strength to build a new life.

The reporter asked if Pat was any different now that the search for her husband was over.

"I'm stronger. I'm sadder. I'm certainly different," Pat said, sitting in the same high-backed chair when interviewed weeks before. The blue-ribbon on her lapel had been replaced with Sid's wedding ring hanging from a gold chain around her neck. "I know that I have to learn to make my own life new again. Oh, I'm definitely different."

She told the reporter that surprisingly, she wasn't angry. "Anger eats up an awful lot of energy," she said, "energy that could be used to help someone. And Sid wouldn't want it that way, either . . . I've received letters from people expressing anger toward them for what they did to Sid, but I ask them to let it go . . . I'm leaving it to God and the courts to judge them for their crimes . . . I don't know whether I'm just not feeling, or what. But I have never expressed anger at them and it doesn't seem to be within my control. It's like I'm in another place watching . . ."

When asked how that was possible when the Seales put her husband and her through so much suffering, Pat said, "I think the deed is hideous, but I deep down really feel badly that anybody feels that they have to hurt anyone else. There's a reason for it. We don't know the reason. So I can't judge those people. And that is a relief. I mean, I can't imagine living with any kind of burden like they have."

The reporter asked Pat if she'd been keeping up with the Seales's court appearances. "I've actually lost track of when or if a trial is scheduled. I take that as a good sign. I haven't been consumed at all with it," she said. Pat next explained that she'd been busy tending to family and legal matters, and packing to move to Houston, Texas, the following week. Having lived in Houston with Sid, she still had friends there, and her middle daughter lived there.

Outwardly, Pat seemed in control of her emotions, and more concerned about the future than the past. She was asked about moving away by herself, without her husband.

"There are a lot of times I get afraid, because Sid was very much a caretaker. It's tough to think about doing it all on your own. But at the same time, I know I'm not alone because I have so many friends and Exxon has been so wonderful . . . But it is hard. It's hard to think about being alone."

Pat then shared some memories from earlier in the year before her husband had been kidnapped. "We'd spent so much time together, traveling, like to the opening of Euro-Disneyland in Paris just a couple weeks before he disappeared. That was so much fun. Just the weekend before he disappeared, we'd spent the weekend in New York City seeing some Broadway plays and dining at some of our favorite restaurants. Everything we did toward the end was really nice . . . It's almost as if those times together happened in order to help me get through what was to come."

Pat sipped some water and straightened the hem of her skirt. "We just always thought he would come home, even 'til the very end," Pat continued. "Everybody was praying that he'd safely come home and then it occurred to me when he was not going to be, that he *had* gone safely home. He's in a better place than we are, and watching the whole affair."

"No, I haven't allowed myself to think about those five days," she said, referring to Sid's time in the coffin-like box. "It's not something that I'm determined not to deal with. It's just the way my mind works. It reminds me a lot of when my son died," talking about her older son's death five years earlier. "It was like four months when I finally said to Sid, 'Everybody knew that he was dead but me.' And that's, I'm sure, what's going to happen again. But by that time, I hope to be settled somewhere, with friends around when it sinks in."

Without her faith, Pat said she couldn't imagine how she would have been getting through the days since her husband's death. Her children, too, had experienced rough days, but being together for the funeral and memorial had helped them all. The letters and Mass cards from people all across the country who had been profoundly affected by Sid's kidnapping and death, along with donations to a fund the family had established at LSU, also provided Pat and her children with much comfort. Pat responded to each note.

"I keep wondering," Pat said, "why this tragedy so much, because things happen all the time that are so horrible. Why this has had such an impact. I don't know. I feel that gives it some sort of purpose . . . I always do believe that there's good that comes out of evil. Always. Without question it's showing up so loud and clear right now. You just have to look at the mail. People are good," she said, resolute in her belief. "We only hear about the bad ones. The good far outnumber the evil."

The reporter closed the interview by asking Pat if she still wrote to her husband in her diary now that she knew he was deceased. Pat replied, "Yes, I write him twice daily."

Pat had written only one entry in her diary before her husband's kidnapping, and she'd written it when she first purchased the journal several years earlier. That single entry was prophetic: *The old woman I shall become shall be quite different from the woman I am now. A new 'I' is beginning.*

Since the morning that Sid disappeared, she'd filled almost all the diary's pages. But when she wrote the previous entries, she believed she was one-half of a couple who'd been married for more than thirty-six years. Now, her husband was dead. She was no longer Mrs. Sidney J. Reso. She was his widow.

A new "I" was beginning—in Houston, Texas.

Chapter 15

The summer of 1992 in northcentral New Jersey was filled with art and music festivals, a state fair, barbecue cook-offs, seafood festivals, outdoor concerts, farm and horse festivals, and much more fun for many New Jerseyans. But the Resos would not be participating. Sid was buried in New Orleans and Pat was moving to Houston. The Seales also would not be joining in. Art and Jackie were in jail awaiting trial and sentencing. Art Seale's parents and Jackie's mother were hardly in the mood.

Jackie was spending her summer quietly in Union County Jail, searching for activities to keep her occupied. Like many in jail, she had to cope with feelings of loneliness and shame while trying to find something to do besides stare at a blank wall or watch television. Art Seale, on the other hand, occupied himself with grander notions. Jail had done little to temper his big ideas. He'd decided he would become rich and famous with best-selling books, blockbuster Hollywood movies, and a hit television series. Though he'd failed to swindle millions out of Exxon, he believed he'd found a way to salvage his extortion plan, despite of, or perhaps because of, the tortuous way in which Sid Reso had died at his hands.

He hired Rudy Westmoreland, a civil attorney from a small personal injury and commercial litigation firm in Egg Harbor Township (West Atlantic City). Westmoreland to retain Sterling Lord Literistic, Inc., a respected literary agency in Manhattan that had successfully represented several true-crime authors.

"We've had lots of offers from so-called movie producers," Westmoreland said. Seale "is strongly motivated" to tell his side of the story and show that "he is not a monster," the lawyer told reporters. Westmoreland entertained offers for Seale to appear on television news magazine programs like *60 Minutes*, *Primetime Live*, *Dateline*, *20/20*, *Inside Edition*, *Hard Copy*, and *48*

Hours. Seale also sought a book deal. The *Bergen Record* reported: "CELEBRITY KILLER: TV, book plans emerge . . ."

It was unclear who was enjoying the attention more, Art Seale or his small-firm attorney, Westmoreland. While O'Neill handled the real legal work, Westmoreland handled the press and those seeking Art Seale's story like Don Hewitt, Barbara Walters, Diane Sawyer, and Stone Phillips. "The phone would ring and Diane Sawyer would say, 'How you doing, Rudy?' And I said, 'Diane, only call me when I'm sitting down because you turn my legs to jelly.'"

The preposterousness of the situation was not lost on Art Buchwald, whose satirical article appeared in the *Los Angeles Times* entitled, "It's a Crime, but Killers Need Agents." The article pretended that the Seales were represented by a Hollywood agent recommended by serial-killer Son of Sam. The fictitious agent pondered whether Farrah Fawcett could portray Jackie Seale and asked his secretary, "Has Barbara Walters checked in?" The article closed by noting that criminals needed agents because: "With all the con men and sharpies in Hollywood, a murderer would be a fool to try to make his own deal."

But Pat Reso wasn't laughing. She was riled by the prospect of her husband's killer trying to whitewash his ghastly deeds for an audience and, worse, making money doing it.

Prosecutors were angry, too. Chertoff pledged to prevent Seale from profiting from his crime, vowing to seize any "blood money" and use it as restitution for the Reso family. "He has no more right to profit from selling his story than from collecting the $18.5 million that he and his wife demanded as ransom for Mr. Reso."

Chertoff and Murphy had a potential problem. The year before, the U.S. Supreme Court ruled that New York's "Son of Sam law" was unconstitutional because it violated the criminal's First Amendment right to free speech. Named after serial killer David Berkowitz, known as Son of Sam, the law intended to prevent criminals from exploiting their crimes for money (New York's law has since been revised).

Prosecutors Chertoff and Murphy believed they could sidestep the Supreme Court decision and stop Seale from selling his story through the imposition of millions in criminal fines, if the fines held up on appeal. Seale could still sell his story, but without the money, prosecutors believed that Seale's enthusiasm would disappear faster than his freedom had.

Pat Reso didn't have to rely on prosecutors to hamper Art Seale's efforts; she could do it herself. As Westmoreland told reporters, "I think we can expect a wrongful death suit by the Reso family." He was right. Pat and her children had filed a civil lawsuit against Art and Jackie Seale, requesting compensatory and punitive damages and injunctive relief for killing Sid Reso in hopes of quelling any movie, television, and book deals.

Only time would tell if the criminal fines and the civil lawsuit would have any effect on Seale's attempts to "tell his story."

* * *

Eight weeks after Sid Reso's body was discovered in a shallow hole in the insect-infested Pine Barrens, Exxon Corporation announced that René Dahan would replace Sid Reso as President of Exxon International. Dahan was born in Morocco and educated at Casablanca and Bordeaux, France. Still gun-shy over the abduction of their former president, Exxon officials refused to release any photos of Dahan to the press or disclose where he resided.

Dahan had worked almost thirty years for Exxon and had been an executive vice president of Exxon International when Reso was kidnapped. His office had been down the hall from Reso's. With his experience in refining, Exxon had assigned him to handle the downstream operations of Exxon International during Reso's absence.

Stock and oil analysts described Dahan as a "talented, sharp guy" with a "broadly diversified background." Another said, "He's got a lot of refining background, as well as exploration and production. So he looks like he's been pretty well groomed."

As one source told *The Star-Ledger*, "Exxon has a deep bench, so if you lose somebody, you have someone to fill in." Multinational corporations, unlike those who run them, never miss a beat. Just like that, Sidney Reso was gone and René Dahan was promoted; office furnishings were moved, and décor was changed. A Dutch national from Morocco had replaced an American from New Orleans. He had big shoes to fill.

* * *

The trial of Art Seale in U.S. District Court was two days away. The court had wasted little time putting Seale's trial on the docket; only eighty-three days had passed since the Seales had been arrested. Chertoff and Murphy were a pair of prosecutorial heavyweights and had uniquely joined forces across jurisdictional lines. Morris County Prosecutor Mike Murphy was named as a special U.S. prosecutor to assist U.S. Attorney Mike Chertoff in the federal trial, and Chertoff would assist Murphy in the state trial. The high-ranking prosecutors teamed up primarily because their offices had worked so cohesively during the investigation of Reso's kidnapping. They'd also be prosecuting the most notorious kidnapping case in New Jersey since twenty-month-old Charles Lindbergh Jr. had been kidnapped and killed sixty years earlier. Assistant U.S. Attorney Victor Ashrafi, Chief of the U.S. Attorney's Criminal Division, would be the third member of the federal prosecution team.

The trial was expected to last twelve days and would pit the thirty-eight-year-old federal public defender, Chester Keller, against Chertoff and Murphy. Murphy said, "This is probably the most visible criminal case in the country this year." Keller must have been nervous and excited to be involved in a case that had garnered so much news coverage across the country. When asked by a reporter, Keller admitted that it would be his first notable trial and laughed, joking that before this case, he'd "wallowed in anonymity."

Not only would Jackie Seale testify against her husband, which would be the trial's marquee event, but Pat Reso also was expected to testify. Prosecutors planned to call Pat as their first witness, not only to showcase the foremost living victim of Art Seale's kidnapping scheme, but to explain how she had discovered her deceased husband's abandoned car at the end of the driveway.

U.S. District Judge Brown's criminal docket had been cleared to make room for the trial. Jurors had been summoned by the court to undergo jury selection. The attorneys' pretrial discovery and motions had been completed. All seemed ready for a sensational trial until Art Seale's attorney contacted Chertoff—Seale would plead guilty. There'd be no federal trial; no judicial floorshow for taxpayers and the press. Instead, Seale simply would appear before Judge Brown to plead guilty to federal charges of extortion and conspiracy to commit extortion.

As Murphy recalled, Art Seale spoke to the prosecutors to discuss the plea as if he was one of their contemporaries working on a business deal rather than a kidnapper who'd tortured and killed another human being.

"What Arthur Seale did today was to unconditionally surrender on these charges," Chertoff boasted to reporters. "And I have to say I was a little disappointed it didn't go to trial . . . It's just so frustrating because the Reso family is so classy, and Art Seale is such a lowlife. I would have given my eyeteeth to have fifteen minutes with this guy on the stand, to show him up for who he is."

On the day that the trial would have begun, a handcuffed and manacled Seale entered court with federal marshals wearing the same dark blue pinstripe suit, though sporting a new blue shirt and gray tie. He joined a crowded defendant's table where criminal attorneys Chester Keller and Joseph O'Neill waited with Westmoreland.

At the beginning of the proceeding, U.S. Attorney Chertoff made it explicit that the hearing was to accept Seale's plea of guilty, not to accept a plea agreement. "I want to make it abundantly clear on the record. There's no agreement. The government has made no promises to the defendant, no commitments, and no conditions with respect to this. There has been no bargaining of any kind about the defendant's desire to plead guilty. In addition . . . it is the government's intention to seek the maximum possible penalties that are imposed by law . . ."

With the ground rules clarified by Chertoff, the judge got started. Unlike when Jackie Seale had told her story in detail to prosecutors inside a Parsippany hotel room, Art Seale would be permitted to answer only those specific questions posed to him by Judge Brown, who would be guiding Seale through the elements of his guilty plea.

After having his handcuffs removed to be sworn in by the bailiff, Seale sat in the witness box and scooted sideways to face the judge. Pat Reso and her children lined the front pew of the gallery and rarely removed their eyes from Seale as he spoke during the seventy-two minute hearing. He never looked their way.

"Now, the indictment asserts that you and your wife made plans and preparations for the kidnapping of Sidney J. Reso . . . . Among other things, you conducted covert surveillance. Did you do that?" Judge Brown asked, having to satisfy himself that "each and every aspect of [the guilty plea] is knowing, voluntary, with full understanding and has a complete factual basis."

"Yes, sir," Seale replied. "Jackie actually went there more often. She would jog by, try to determine Mr. Reso's schedule. I went there several times and used a house that was under construction and tried to observe the times that he would come or leave in the morning."

"It says also that you built a wooden box. Did you do that?"

"Yes, sir, *we both* built the wooden box."

Seale could not simply reply "yes" or "no," and for someone who said he loved his wife, he constantly reminded the judge of his wife's participation in the crime while casting his participation in the best light possible.

"Paragraph 4 . . . says defendant Arthur D. Seale abducted Sidney J. Reso at gunpoint from in front of his home. Did you do that?"

Seale once again felt compelled to elaborate.

"Jackie had rented a van, and we were sitting in the van up the street from the Reso home. We observed the garage door go up. At that time, I said, 'No, don't do this.' I was extremely nervous, but Jackie appeared calm. We pulled up in front of Mr. Reso, when he had gotten out of his car to pick up his newspaper. I got out of the van through the side door, yelled at Mr. Reso, grabbed him by the collar, and pulled him into the van. Jackie was sitting behind the driver's seat of the vehicle. When Mr. Reso got into the van, I got in behind him. He went to turn. The gun went off, and he received a wound in his left forearm. At that point in time, we were trying to handcuff Mr. Reso. Jackie immediately sped away from the scene. I then placed Mr. Reso inside this box that we had built and moved to the passenger seat."

The use of "we" seemed to pervade Seale's statements. And "he received a wound" sounded less offensive than "I shot him."

After other questions about how Reso had been restrained, the judge asked, "It further says . . . 'Sidney J. Reso died inside the wooden box.' Is that true?"

"No, sir," Seale replied. "He did not die inside the wooden box. He died outside the box. We had gone there that Sunday morning, and he was alive. We took him out of the box. Jackie gave him some water. I was sitting behind him holding him up.

He had obviously deteriorated over the course of the evening before. He actually died in my arms that morning, and we attempted to revive him without success."

That answer angered Pat. It also incensed Chertoff and Murphy. Jackie Seale had told prosecutors that Sid Reso was already dead when they arrived that morning. He'd died in the coffin-like box either the evening before or earlier that morning. And unlike her husband, Jackie had no reason to lie. Instead, she had every reason to tell the truth. Her plea deal depended on it.

The judge asked several other questions concerning the phone calls, the drafting and placement of ransom notes, the tape recordings, the interstate call from Pooler, Georgia, the research of foreign bank accounts, and the threats made against other Exxon officials. Following additional questions and procedural matters, the judge accepted the guilty plea. He then banged his gavel and announced, "The court stands in recess." It was done. Art Seale had pleaded guilty to federal charges. Only sentencing awaited him, and the state trial for kidnapping and felony murder that was scheduled for a week later.

As the hearing concluded, Pat and her children were quickly escorted out of the courtroom. She later appeared with prosecutors at a press conference. A wave of cameras and reporters with microphones and tape recorders crowded in front of a podium, behind which stood Pat Reso, Chertoff, Murphy, Assistant U.S. Attorney Victor Ashrafi, and Jere Doyle. They allowed Pat to make a brief statement first.

"My husband rests in peace. I'm grateful justice has been done . . . I would like to say I shall never forget these people who are around me," Pat said, referring to the prosecutors and FBI agents. "They did everything possible to bring my husband back. They have been kind, they have been thorough, they have been thoughtful." She stepped away from the podium without taking any questions. Mike Chertoff stepped forward.

After a few introductory remarks, Chertoff said, "There was

no bargain and there was no mercy because this defendant fully deserves everything the federal government can throw at him." When asked about Seale's remorse, Chertoff called it "eleventh-hour contrition," pointing out that the time for contrition would have been when the Seales discovered that Reso was dead, instead of continuing to "aggressively pursue" their plan to collect the ransom.

Murphy spoke next. He first complimented Pat. "This woman is a tower of strength. She has been an inspiration to all of us." He then addressed the state's case. "Arthur Seale's admissions to U.S. District Judge Garrett Brown Jr. are clearly admissible at the upcoming state trial . . . It makes our case nothing but stronger." Murphy vowed that he would not offer Seale a plea bargain, just as Chertoff had not. "His options will be to plead guilty to our charges and face his sentence or go to trial."

A week later, Art Seale made his decision. He would plead guilty in state court. Seale's attorney, Joseph O'Neill, explained the reasoning: "Once I got those assurances [that the death penalty was eliminated as a possible sentence], I told Arthur, 'Now's the time to exhibit your remorse, admit what you've admitted from the beginning, and be prepared to pay the consequences.'"

Murphy would have sought the death penalty if he could have, but there simply was no evidence that the Seales had intended to kill Sid Reso. Though their efforts to care for Reso had been primitive and neglectful, and though some believed Art Seale never intended to release Reso alive, the Seales supposedly had bandaged Reso's wounds and given him some water and a little fresh air. They'd also purchased him a gray sweat suit to wear when they released him, they claimed, though no sweat suit was ever located. And Jackie had told prosecutors that she and Art Seale always wore masks, sunglasses, and gloves when inside the storage unit and always spoke in disguised voices to protect their identities, which supported their claims that they intended to release Reso.

So at 1:30, at the Superior Court of New Jersey before Judge Reginald Stanton in Morristown, Seale once again sat at the defendant's table with attorneys O'Neill and Keller. Seated across the room sat the prosecution team, Murphy, Chertoff, First Assistant Prosecutor Charles Waldron, and Assistant Prosecutor Joseph Connor Jr. The judge reviewed the plea documents and the kidnapping and felony murder charges with Seale. The charges of conspiracy, extortion, aggravated assault, and use of a deadly weapon were dismissed because they merged into the more serious charges or were duplicated in federal court.

"Bill, would you get the Bible?" the judge asked, calling on a bailiff to administer the oath to Seale. Similar to his statements in federal court, Seale admitted to all the crimes charged against him by the state of New Jersey. The judge concluded by asking Seale if he had any questions.

"Your Honor, I just would like to tell the court that I'm truly sorry for everything that happened, and I'd like to say anything that I can to let Mrs. Reso know that I'm truly sorry, that we never had any intent to harm her husband in any way."

After the plea hearing, O'Neill told reporters, "He wants to write Mrs. Reso a letter to express his remorse to her."

Seale's civil attorney, Rudy Westmoreland, said his client might tell more of the story on an upcoming television program. "He wants the world to know that he is not a monster, that he is a real person with feelings for what happened and whom it affected, particularly Mrs. Reso."

Perhaps if Art Seale had really wanted to prove to Pat Reso that he was sincere in his remorse, he would have simply sat in his cell and quit talking about himself and his despicable crime. That was not to be.

* * *

When a reporter arrived the following Saturday to interview Pat for *The Star-Ledger*, the widow was busy picking up and cleaning her home. She'd recently received a contract from buyers to purchase the house where she and Sid had lived for the last six years. She'd already signed the contract and the deed for a real estate closing to take place on November 19. She didn't plan to attend. She was preparing to move to Texas that August. When the interview took place that Saturday, Pat had only days remaining before she left Jonathan Smith Road and New Jersey for good.

"I felt a twinge of anger when he spoke about Sid dying in his arms," Pat said to the reporter. "I feel that was an out-and-out lie."

The reporter brought up that Seale and his attorneys, both in and out of court, had tried to paint the picture of a man full of remorse over Sid Reso's kidnapping and death.

"I don't believe it," Pat said. "If he was so remorseful, then when Sid died, why didn't he put an end to it? Instead, he proceeded with the whole awful scheme . . . He may not have planned for Sid to die," she continued, "but it didn't seem to make that much difference. If he really cared, at any point in time, he would not have done what he did. He would not have continued with the charade and put us through the anguish that he did."

Pat paused. It was the first time an interviewer had seen her vexed. She'd always been serene during her interviews.

"I believe him to be an evil person, a sick person," Pat said. "He's changed my whole life. He's changed my children's lives. And it's only just beginning. We're just coming out of shock and are now beginning to pay the price for what he has done. No, I don't think he is remorseful."

When asked about Seale's attempts to appear on television to tell his side of the story, Pat said, "As long as [Jackie Seale] gets to say what she has to say, the truth—and hopefully it *is* the truth—as long as the truth is known, then I'll be satisfied."

The reporter discussed assertions made by Jackie Seale's attorney that she had been a battered wife who had been manipulated by her husband into committing the crime. Pat said she didn't buy it. "I hold her equally responsible. A person always has free choice and I think anytime she could have backed out."

Pat was asked if she would read a letter that Art Seale said he planned to write her. She told the reporter that, yes, she would read it "just out of curiosity," though she believed any apology would be insincere.

Art Seale did write a letter. He wrote several. The first he sent to Judges Brown and Stanton. It rambled on for eighteen pages, single-spaced, "to give my version of the crimes" and to make certain that "the Courts, Mrs. Reso, and my wife might understand." Of course, he'd "found Christ," a prison cliché, and was reading to disabled inmates, taking Bible correspondence courses, and, in his words, had become "a model prisoner" who wanted to teach and become involved in church. He also told Mrs. Reso, "There has been a great deal of press and publicity that has portrayed me as a horrible monster. I want you to know that much of that has been untrue. I am searching, both spiritually and through psychiatry and psychology, for the cause that would allow an otherwise totally loving couple to do what we have done."

It just so happened that Art Seale wrote the letter twelve days *prior* to his sentencing by both judges, as though they'd never received self-serving correspondence from a criminal defendant seeking a lighter sentence. On the other hand, Pat had always lived a life guided by her Christian faith and had done much to abide by its tenets. She had relied on that faith throughout the terrible ordeal and continued to do so, particularly when exercising tremendous restraint while speaking about the Seales.

"Even though I don't disagree with the death penalty, I think there's more punishment involved with a person of his type of ego to have all control taken out of his hands. Life in prison is enough because even if that's not enough here, he has to meet his maker along the way. It's in God's hands. Control is what seems to drive him, even more than greed," she continued. "If he really wanted the $18.5 million, the ultimate thing would have been to take good care of Sid. To arrive with a box gave a clue that that was far down on his list."

As examples of his lust for control, Pat pointed toward the angry demands in his numerous ransom letters and his demand that she make televised appeals for her husband's safe return after he was already dead.

A psychiatrist who examined Seale noted, "Being inhumane to Mr. Reso may have been an expression of underlying resentment and hostility" toward Exxon due to issues that arose during his employment there. Though Exxon said Seale had been terminated as part of a corporate restructuring, some believed his termination had more to do with his job performance.

"I think he had a vendetta against Exxon . . . and authority in general," Pat Reso said. "He could have had the money straight out in the beginning if he played it right. But he got lost in his plan . . . Even his decision to plead guilty was a means of taking away the chance [the federal and state prosecutors had] to lay it all out [in court] and show what he was."

Once the interview ended and Pat returned to tidying up her house, she did so as she fought back the anger that she said was "just beginning to surface." She and her children were having a tough time handling the anger and grief. Her remaining living son had taken leave from work to recover, and they were undergoing counseling to help them cope with the terrible ordeal.

"I dreadfully miss Sid. It's lonely," Pat had told the reporter. "I resent deeply what this man has done to our lives. He has changed our lives completely, forever, and I resent it."

Pat would have even more to resent. Art Seale and his

representatives were considering offers for book, movie, and television deals that would commence a public campaign attempting to demonstrate that he was "not a monster." Seale had just accepted an offer from a network and its celebrated interviewer who couldn't wait to give Art Seale that vile opportunity — on prime time television.

Chapter 16

The vultures were circling. A man and his wife had stuck Sid Reso in a box, tortured him, and let him die slowly while giving his tearful wife and children constant hope that her husband and their father would soon be returning home long after he was dead. Yet, the lawyers, agents, television producers, and anyone else looking for a buck or fifteen minutes of fame formed a line for an opportunity to speak to Art Seale's representatives. *Dateline, Primetime Live, 20/20, Inside Edition, Hard Copy, 48 Hours,* and others jockeyed for an exclusive interview.

"I made a comment that Arthur wanted to tell his story and it was like the killer bees," Westmoreland told a reporter for *USA Today.* "I went in there trying to sell my client's story. When I was done, I didn't know who was selling who."

Seale's agent at Sterling Lord even contacted Special Agent-in-Charge Gary Penrith multiple times asking for the FBI's cooperation with a potential book and movie deal. The literary agent wanted "the FBI's side of the story for the sake of journalistic objectivity and accuracy . . . and what I have in mind . . . certainly makes the FBI look terrific." The Bureau wasn't interested.

Those at *60 Minutes* also considered Art Seale's story, but said they smelled a rat. Steve Kroft, a correspondent with *60 Minutes,* told *USA Today,* "It's the most egregious example of how criminals peddle their stories to the media. They wanted money," Kroft said. According to Kroft, Seale's literary agent wanted $25,000. As part of the deal, Kroft said Seale's agent and Westmoreland demanded that *60 Minutes* could not mention the coffin-like box or how the Seales had buried Reso's body in a shallow grave in the Pine Barrens. "It struck me as being like an advertising agency bidding on [the Seale] account."

The Morris County Prosecutor's Office smelled several rats.

Assistant Prosecutor Joseph Connor filed a motion with Superior Court Judge Reginald Stanton to place a freeze on all present and future assets of Art and Jackie Seale. With their sentencing coming up soon, Art Seale faced up to $1.75 million of fines in federal court and another $2 million of fines in state court, along with other penalties payable to the New Jersey Violent Crimes Compensation Board. Jackie Seale faced a total of $600,000 of fines. In the civil tort case for wrongful death filed by the Resos, the Seales also faced a potential judgment of millions in compensatory and punitive damages payable to the Reso family. Though the Seales had no assets at the time, if they made any money from telling their stories, the courts wanted the money paid into the court first, which would then determine its lawful distribution, much like an escrow agent.

"The only thing he has is his story," Seale's attorney, Joseph O'Neill, said to the judge.

"I don't begrudge Mr. Seale being able to sell his story," Judge Stanton replied. "He's certainly free to go ahead and make a deal, but he is a man who has pleaded guilty to charges with a clear potential for substantial fines. He can create assets, but he can't dispose of them without leave of the court."

Murphy was pleased. "As I understand Your Honor's ruling," Murphy said, "there's a dramatic difference between the Son of Sam case and Your Honor's suggested disposition of this matter."

"That's correct," said the judge. "My ruling doesn't interfere with their right to free speech. It interferes with their right to disperse their assets."

The court's decision corked the flow of money to the Seales for a time. And without a sensational trial and with the constant influx of other news stories, perhaps Art Seale's quest for sympathy would grow tiresome and stale. But that didn't stop Seale from trying. O'Neill told reporters that television producer Aaron Spelling and two authors were considering Seale's story. Some even suggested that perhaps Seale had pleaded guilty to keep the facts, as he wished them to be told, out of a public trial so he could reveal them in a book or a movie instead.

* * *

On Tuesday, November 3, 1992, Bill Clinton won an electoral landslide against an incumbent president, 370 electoral votes to President Bush's 168, with Ross Perot allocated none, even though he'd received almost twenty million popular votes. Since 1900, only three elected presidents have lost reelection, and George H.W. Bush had become the fourth. Though third party candidate Ross Perot may have had a lot to do with that, the sting of losing must have felt like a kick in the gut to President Bush, causing him untold emotional pain and perhaps even physical nausea.

Seale learned just how the lame duck president felt when federal marshals removed Seale from Passaic County Jail to the maximum-security section of the Metropolitan Corrections Center in Manhattan, reserved for the most dangerous prisoners or those who needed protection from other inmates. U.S. Marshal Arthur Bornisky told reporters, "He was moved because . . . I think it's pretty unusual that somebody hurts his testicles alone in his cell. That causes me some anxiety."

According to Passaic County Sheriff Edwin "Eddie" Englehardt, who had a reputation for running a tough jail, a guard just happened to find Seale unconscious on his cell floor. Somehow, the sheriff pondered, Seale had managed to rupture his testicles while alone in his cell and passed out in the floor from the intense pain. He explained that Seale had fallen off his bunk and landed on a bed post. The sheriff had just described perhaps the only case of self-inflicted testicular rupture ever recorded in the annals of medical and psychiatric history. But workers at a New Jersey watchdog agency, the Office of Inmate Advocacy, said the Passaic County Jail appeared to them to be the state's most brutal prison. Whatever happened, Seale was rushed to nearby Barnert Hospital under heavy guard where he was admitted for overnight observation and tests. The tests showed no permanent damage and the pain quickly subsided. That was fortunate because Seale had to be sharp for his first television interview later that same day.

"He's been in there for the last hour talking to her about his childhood," Sheriff Englehardt said sarcastically.

The program was recorded in the jail later that day, October 21. After editing, Seale's television debut would air in three weeks.

* * *

Art Seale's sentencing was scheduled for November 30 in both the federal and state courts. The U.S. Attorney's Office had prepared a twenty-five page "Sentencing Memorandum" that laid out Seale's crimes and the office's recommendations for sentencing. It was not something the Seale family desired to have bound in Moroccan leather.

First, clinical psychologist, Dr. James Wulach, evaluated Seale's ability to stand trial. Wulach's report stated:

"While the kidnapping plot reflected a reckless, exploitative, and grandiose aspect of Mr. Seale's personality, he was never psychotic, and the careful planning over a period of time militates against defenses such as insanity or provocation. Regarding competency to stand trial, Mr. Seale clearly understands the charges against him and is able to assist counsel in his defense."

With no question concerning Seale's sanity, the sentencing memorandum detailed the horrific conditions Art Seale had imposed on Sid Reso inside the storage unit. It then stated:

"That these conditions would kill Mr. Reso would hardly surprise anyone except one with chilling indifference to the welfare of a fellow human being. Arthur Seale's conduct was uniquely heinous, cruel, brutal, and degrading to Mr. Reso and to the dignity of the human race as a whole. It was the kind of extreme conduct that unhesitatingly calls for . . . the maximum sentence . . . to run consecutively for a total of ninety-five years' imprisonment and a fine due immediately in accordance with the court's findings of the likely gain derived by the defendant from his crime."

Art Seale may have been enjoying his criminal celebrity status and all the attention it generated from the media, including his upcoming television debut, but federal and state prosecutors had no doubt that soon the final curtain would fall on Seale's vile performance.

* * *

Sheriff Englehardt and guards at the Passaic County Jail were spit and polished in their freshly-pressed black uniforms and crisp hats atop trimmed hair and shaven faces. Acting warden Gerardo Torres also looked sharp in his suit and tie. It was a big day—Barbara Walters and her crew were in the big house!

Westmoreland said Seale decided on *20/20* and Barbara Walters because she agreed to an hour-long segment whereas *60 Minutes* would only give Seale its usual thirteen-minute segment. "I wanted to get enough time so that Arthur's story could be told in depth, not just in sound bites," the lawyer said. He admitted that they had "tried to get them not to talk about the box because it is such a highly inflammatory subject." Westmoreland said that his client "wants the public to hear about Arthur Seale, the person, and then make a judgment on what he is like without merely accepting the law enforcement view that he is an animal and a horrible man."

Lucy Kraus, a spokesperson for 20/20, said they did not pay Seale or permit him to review any of the questions. "They may have asked for any number of things," Kraus told reporters, "but we did not accede to anything."

The camera and sound crews set up inside a light blue-paneled room in the jail with a solitary wooden table and one chair on each side so that Walters and Seale could sit directly across from each other during the interview. On the table sat two cups of water or coffee and a note pad for Walters. Seale was dressed in his orange jumpsuit. He'd removed and folded his eyeglasses and placed them on the table. He was nervous. Walters wore a beige and brown striped business suit with matching skirt and brown blouse.

During the entire interview, two officers in black uniforms sat on opposite sides of the room beneath an orange border with black lettering that read: "SECURITY – CUSTODY – CONTROL." Not to be left out, Westmoreland and O'Neill made non-speaking cameos at the beginning of the program. They watched the interview from an adjacent room.

Seale likely told all the inmates who'd listen that he was going to be on prime time television that evening. It was a good thing for him that the heavyweight boxing match between Riddick Bowe and Evander Holyfield was televised only on HBO Pay-Per-View that same night; otherwise, Seale would have had a tough time convincing fellow inmates to tune in to Barbara Walters.

Pat would be watching from her home in Houston with friends. Just one more indignity at the hands of Art Seale and those who'd made the opportunity possible.

So, on Friday night, at 10:00 p.m. Eastern Time on ABC—it was show time.

"Good evening. I'm Barbara Walters. Hugh Downs is away tonight and this is 20/20."

An announcer with a suspense-filled, rhythmic voice opened the special one-hour presentation with the usual, "From ABC News, around the world and into your home . . . Tonight, the crime that shocked the country . . . A Barbara Walters exclusive — behind bars with a confessed kidnapper, Arthur Seale." The program was called, "No Way Out," presumably a double entendre about the Seales's financial troubles and Sid Reso's confinement in a box.

As part of the introductory buildup consisting of teaser questions and photos of the crime scene, a camera shot of FBI Assistant Special Agent-in-Charge Jere Doyle filled the screen. He stated, "Arthur Seale is one of the most sadistic, manipulative, cold-blooded individuals that I've ever had the misfortune to investigate."

After the first commercial break, Barbara Walters began the interview by asking Seale what he had to say to people who thought he was a "monster?" Seale's arms rested on the table with his hands clasped. He wasn't handcuffed.

Seale answered in a genteel, casual voice, as if sitting in confession. "I would like them to understand that we were normal people driven to absolute desperation, that there was no avenue that we felt we could turn."

When asked to describe himself, Seale spoke intimately to his new friend. "Well, Barbara, my whole life, I've been a hard-working, moral, decent individual and we really epitomized most of the American ethic." He said that, despite their middle-class living, he and his wife "began to think that there must be more to life."

As he'd done during his pleas in federal and state courts, he made sure TV listeners knew that his wife "was a full and willing participant" and they were "full and equal partners." When asked if he built the box, Seale replied that "Jackie and I built the box."

The program would break off from the interview at key

moments with shots of the storage unit, the grave, and photos of Sid and Pat Reso, with a voiceover by Walters. Strategically placed commercial breaks also created suspense so viewers would stay tuned.

As the interview continued, Seale made statements that were inconsistent with the evidence and with Jackie Seale's admissions. He told Walters that he and his wife took care of Sid Reso "at least three times a day." Secure Storage's records revealed that they only visited twice each day for the first three days and then only once on the fourth day. Sid Reso was dead on the morning of the fifth day. Seale insisted they had allowed Reso to sit up, stand up, and even walk around inside the box each day, which Jackie Seale had said didn't happen. He also said they talked to him.

Incredibly, Seale also claimed that he didn't have any idea that Reso wasn't being fed. "I was not aware of the fact, truthfully, that he did not eat at all." He said it was his wife's responsibility to take care of Reso. It was an interesting statement considering he was present each time his wife went inside the storage locker, according to the FBI report. And of course, he told the same story of Sid Reso dying in his arms that fateful Sunday morning.

"We heard him speaking through the box . . . I opened the box. I saw him. He appeared to be paler . . . I pulled him up and sat him up at the edge of the box and I was holding him from behind. Jackie came over and gave him some water . . . He shuddered and he died. I was holding him and he died. I . . . fell apart . . . I tried doing the external heart massage from behind. He shuddered and it was like a liquid noise and he was dead . . . . When he died, I continued to hold him in my arms for several minutes . . ."

When confronted with the fact that Jackie Seale said it didn't happen that way, Art Seale told Walters simply, "I can't explain that." He then looked at the camera, "Jackie—that's not true."

Seale also denied knowing that Sid Reso had a heart condition until after he was dead even though the newspapers had carried that story from the first day of Reso's disappearance. Jackie Seale also had admitted they'd been aware of the heart condition. Moreover, Seale told Walters he'd planned on giving most of the ransom money to charity. She found that to be incredulous.

Then an almost comical scene began. Walters brought up that Jackie Seale's defense was that "she was abused and manipulated by you, that you were the driving force and she was merely a follower."

"Has she said that?" Art Seale asked as if cut to the core. "I have not seen that. I had not been aware of that. Jackie has a unique ability to view things in her own way. Jackie was never abused and never manipulated. Did she really say that? . . . It's not true. She knows that's not true."

Again, it had been in all the newspapers for weeks and his lawyers were well aware of it.

"Are you remorseful, Mr. Seale?" Walters asked.

"Barbara, there hasn't been a day since this incident that I haven't cried over Sidney Reso. There hasn't been a day that I haven't prayed for him."

With that statement, Seale's segment was finished. Before going to commercial break, however, Walters provided a final teaser: "Next, in one of the most haunting interviews we've ever presented, Mrs. Sidney Reso responds to what Arthur Seale has just said."

Pat Reso had agreed two weeks earlier after Walters recorded her segment with Seale to watch the program on tape and then to be interviewed by Walters. It was not something Pat was thrilled to do, but she felt that Seale and ABC had given her little choice. She couldn't let Sid's murderer simply say whatever he wanted on national television. This wasn't about Arthur Seale's image. This was about him brutally killing Sid. So she caught a flight from Houston to New York to be interviewed on October 27.

The interview took place in a very nice hotel suite in

Manhattan, complete with an armoire, bookcase, and side tables with brass lamps that created a sophisticated backdrop. Wearing a coral-colored dress, Pat sat on a lavender camelback sofa facing Barbara Walters, who sat directly across from her in a green upholstered wooden chair.

"Do you remember your husband's last words to you?" Walters asked with an exaggerated tone of sympathy.

"Oh, it was always, 'I love you,'" Pat replied serenely. "It was a ritual in the morning—breakfast together and then I always fixed the hankie . . . I always wanted to see him look really well. I fixed his hankie and fixed his tie a little bit and said I'll see you tonight. I love you, and he said I love you, too."

"What kind of man was he?" Walters asked.

"Sid was the most gentle, kind, loving husband and father—his wonderful smile, his positive outlook. He was a very special person."

Walters asked Pat several questions about the morning Pat discovered Sid's car in the drive, Pat's diary, how she'd maintained hope during the ordeal, and whether she thought Sid's faith had comforted him during his captivity.

"Oh, certainly . . . because I think the greatest torture for Sid was not the physical so much, but wondering how *we* were."

Pat answered all of Walter's questions in a steady and composed voice. She would later admit that her calm demeanor was actually "numbness" not courage. "I went into a mode of, I guess, just total shock," she said months later. It would take several months, she said, for "reality to begin to sit in."

Pat told Walters that she did not believe Art Seale's story that Sid died in Seale's arms. She said she believed Jackie Seale's story to prosecutors instead. But she viewed them equally culpable. "I think that they are extremely evil people to truly believe that a person could endure that many days with very little air and no food and no comfort emotionally, no hope."

"Do you forgive Arthur Seale?"

Pat said she did accept Seale's apology and forgave him. "I have no alternative. It serves no purpose for me not to forgive him. The law has done its job, and justice will do what it should, and he is in the hands of God, not in my hands. And she, as well." Pat also expressed "great pity" for the Seale children and the elder parents. She then read a poem she'd received in the mail from a stranger that had brought her comfort.

That's how the interview ended—with a poem read by Sid Reso's widow. Walters couldn't have choreographed it any better. Walters noted that neither Jackie Seale nor her attorneys responded to requests for an interview. And then she closed with, "Time now to go to Washington where Ted Koppel is preparing tonight's *Nightline*. Ted?"

The next day, an infuriated Chertoff told reporters, "Arthur Seale purposely lied in a pathetic attempt to win some measure of sympathy for himself . . . A little part of me wishes we could put him in a box." Chertoff added that he hoped there is a "more perfect divine justice" awaiting Seale. "The crime is the epitome of depraved indifference and cruelty . . . Uniquely heinous, cruel, brutal and degrading." He reiterated that Seale had forced Sid Reso to remain for days in a narrow wooden box, bound, gagged, blindfolded, wounded, and bleeding inside a stifling corrugated metal and concrete storage locker in Washington Township. "[Mr. Reso] had nothing to keep him company, but the slow passage of time and his own fears."

Regardless of how Pat and the prosecutors may have felt, it had been "sweeps month" when Nielsen TV Ratings conducted its research through "paper diaries" mailed out to millions of U.S. households to determine what people at home were watching. Obviously, ratings for the *20/20* interview soared; over 20 million viewers. Not only that, the following year, Barbara Walters was awarded a "News & Documentary Emmy for Outstanding Interview" for the Seale/Reso program. She smiled broadly as she accepted the shiny gold-plated award during a black-tie dinner and ceremony at the landmark Plaza Hotel in Manhattan.

Pat, on the other hand, simply had won the right to be left alone. Thankfully, there'd be no more ratings and Emmy-seeking interviewers and no book or movie deals. The story would soon die. All the lawyers, agents, interviewers, and networks moved on to the next story of murder and mayhem. Pat also was moving on in Houston with "a lot of work with a doctor," but she'd be back in New Jersey on November 30. She and her children had one last thing to do.

Chapter 17

The day of reckoning had come. Tuesday, November 30, 1992. Seven months and one day since the kidnapping. Two days after Thanksgiving weekend, the first without Sid.

Art Seale entered the Superior Court of New Jersey in the same manner he had numerous times since his arrest—handcuffed, shackled, and flanked by federal marshals.

The weather was mild outside the courthouse, around fifty-one degrees with a slight drizzle that had just stopped, but it would be a stormy day for Seale inside the courtroom. He would be sentenced in both the federal and state courts where he'd hear from Chertoff, Murphy, the Reso children, and both judges, none of whom would have anything good to say to or about him. Only his lawyers, Keller and O'Neill, would, but they were being paid to do so.

All seats in the state courtroom were filled and the walls around the gallery were lined by the last spectators able to gain admittance. Chief among the observers were Pat and her four children, Pat's daughter-in-law, and Sid Reso's two brothers. They occupied the two front rows, along with friends and federal marshals.

If Morris County Prosecutor Mike Murphy needed any motivation, which he didn't, all he had to do was look over at the faces of the Reso family.

"In the history of the twentieth century," Murphy said before New Jersey Superior Court Judge Stanton, "I would submit to the court that we have not seen imprisonment of so cruel a nature as we have seen in this case . . . From the moment of the abduction when Sidney Reso was shot and locked inside that box, and had his eyes and his mouth taped, he never enjoyed even for those four or five days, which were the rest of his life, the comfort of any other human companionship . . . This crime was cruel, it was heinous, it was outrageous, and in light of the special facts and circumstances of this case, it cries out for a maximum penalty."

Seale sat and listened in his blue suit and gray tie with his ankles shackled. Reporters observed the defendant closely. If he looked down, leaned to speak in the ear of an attorney, grimaced, or smiled, the reporters noted it. They hoped to spot tears that could pour across their headlines.

Murphy addressed at length defense attorney O'Neill's argument for leniency for Seale, which basically was that this "was a single act totally out of character . . . a first offense by a hardworking guy."

"In this case, Judge, the single abhorrent act, the single out of character act," began Murphy, "includes the planning of the offense, detailed research, trips to the courthouse to research deed records, trips down to the library to find out who the primary stockholders and corporate officers in Exxon International were . . . the purchase of plywood and the fastening of hasps and the intricate cross-weave that was placed inside that box, and then the actual abduction carried out with a loaded weapon."

Murphy pointed out that if Seale had not intended to harm Sid Reso as he claimed, then why did he load the pistols they carried with them to the kidnapping?

"This defendant . . . and this, very frankly, Judge, is extremely offensive to me . . . tries to create for this court and for the public a Pieta scene of Sidney Reso gently slipping away in his arms. What really happened, Judge . . . is they carved up the box, loaded it onto a Jeep, burned it, and threw the ashes into a river while the corpse of Sidney Reso lay wrapped in plastic in that storage area. And then they went out and . . . enjoyed a family dinner."

Murphy stared at Seale as he continued his attack about the disposal of the box and Sid Reso's body.

"And then that night, I can't think of anything that's more shocking, they went out and attempted to grab $18.5 million with a corpse in the storage area . . . And then the following day drove to the most barren area . . . the New Jersey Pine Barrens, where they dug a shallow grave there, and placed Sidney Reso face down with nothing but his undershorts and his wedding ring. The only marker near the grave was an abandoned and rusted appliance . . . And the threat they made for Pat Reso to go on national TV and beg for her husband's life when he was already dead and buried in the Pine Barrens. Right up to the night of June 18th when they were arrested trying to grab the money again, Your Honor, they were busy doing this single abhorrent, out-of-character act."

Seale's attorney O'Neill listened and scribbled some notes, but really, what could he argue? He'd cast his client's crime as a single, out-of-character act, and Murphy had ripped that argument into shreds.

"Your Honor, if there has ever been a case that absolutely cries out for a maximum sentence, and a consecutive sentence, it is this specific case . . . He deserves no concession, no mercy, he deserves the surest and swiftest and most severe punishment available to this court. Thank you."

Murphy stepped away from the podium and approached the Reso family. He leaned down and whispered for a few seconds before speaking aloud again. "Judge, if I may introduce two of the daughters of Patricia and the late Sidney Reso. They would like to say a few words to the court."

"I'll be glad to hear you," the judge said. "Would you come on up, please?"

Two of the three daughters in attendance walked up to the podium. The twenty-eight-year-old youngest daughter had graduated from law school fewer than six months earlier, sadly without her father in attendance. In addition, the three daughters and their mother had each celebrated a birthday during the last four months without Sid present.

"Thank you, Your Honor," the youngest began. "Your Honor

. . . Mr. Seale committed deeds that are so evil that I cannot even comprehend how he could have done this . . . When my father was taken . . . our worst nightmares and questions were whether he was being allowed to clean up; we wondered whether he was being allowed to brush his teeth or wash his face; we wondered whether he was given magazines or books to read; and whether he was being kept alone or was being kept with other people. Never could we have imagined the true horror of his circumstances . . ."

Standing perfectly erect at the podium, the young Reso, wearing her hair in a ponytail, was poised, articulate, and determined. She continued as the judge looked at her kindly yet intently. The gallery remained silent, except for an occasional sigh or sniffle.

"Never could we have imagined that his captors, the Seales, could have been so inhumane. Only truly evil people could do such a thing. This man, Mr. Seale, not only took my father's life, but he tormented us for more than a month, leading us to believe that my father was alive when they knew that they had already killed him, that he was dead. We waited desperately, hungrily for any news of my father's well-being . . . And yet, they were playing with us and with our hopes, and they were truly cruel in doing so."

The young woman paused and cleared her throat. She'd been a little nervous when she first began speaking, but now all of her thoughts and emotions focused solely on what the Seales had done to her father and to them.

"Mr. Seale has claimed that he was driven to this crime because he was desperate, that he had no choice. But, Your Honor, like most of us here today, myself included, Mr. Seale does not know what true desperation is. To state that he is desperate in today's world is an insult to people we have out on our streets who . . . have no home, have no family to take them in, and have nothing to eat. Desperate people do not commit acts that he committed.

Evil people commit those acts."

"Mr. Seale, in his own words, was looking for a one-time reward. He thought he deserved instantaneously that which my father worked for his whole life. Because of Mr. Seale's lust for money, because of his evil, he took from me the person that I admired most in the world, the person that I respected . . . And all of Mr. Seale's apologies and tears will never change that. And so, myself and my family look to you to deliver justice. Thank you, Your Honor."

"Thank you, Miss Reso," Judge Stanton said tenderly as she stepped aside so that her older sister could speak.

"I have little to add to what my sister has already said, Your Honor," she began, "but I feel I must stand up and give voice to my own anger, outrage, and grief. I speak to bear witness against Arthur Seale . . . 'By their fruits, you shall know them.' The fruits of my father's life were goodness, generosity, kindness, respect, and success . . . The fruits of Arthur Seale's life are greed, arrogance, grandiosity, and violence . . . Such evil is immensely difficult to understand. I and my family will be struggling with its legacy for the rest of our lives . . . I look to this court to pass the most severe sentence allowed under the law on Arthur Seale. Thank you."

Seale's state defense attorney O'Neill then stood to defend his client; a most unenviable time and place to make such an attempt. The Reso daughters had been so compelling with their words that O'Neill may have felt simply like packing up his briefcase and heading for the nearest pub. But he had a job to do.

"Now, we know that Mr. Seale had a prior good record here," O'Neill said. "He's never been convicted of anything. We know that he has done some good things in his life. We know now that he has done some good things while even in jail. He has begun his rehabilitation . . . What I would ask the court is to give Arthur Seale some reason to be, some reason to continue with his life as he must live it in jail . . . And not that he claims to deserve anything. He would like the opportunity to give something back, recognizing he has taken something very dear away from society and from the Reso family."

The judge listened, thanked the attorney, and then asked, "Mr. Seale, would you like to say anything?"

"Just very briefly, Your Honor," Seale said as he rose to speak. He had the attention of everyone in the courtroom.

"I acknowledge everything that the prosecutor and Mr. Reso's daughters said about Mr. Reso. I did not know the man. Everything that I've learned about him, he was a wonderful individual. I acknowledge terrible things that we did . . . I know God forgives me . . . but I wish that I could go back and erase the things we did, and I also wish I could explain to you why we did them. I can't . . . I still seek that understanding. I've asked Mr. O'Neill to see if he could arrange for continued psychological and psychiatric evaluations so that I can begin to deal with some of these things."

"I was devastated the minute Mr. Reso died. He did die in my arms, Your Honor . . ."

The Resos scoffed with sighs from the front pews and shook their heads.

"I felt worse about the fact that he died in my arms because if I had gotten there fifteen minutes earlier perhaps there was something I could have done. That's something I have to live with, Your Honor. That's all."

"Very well," sixty-year-old bespectacled Judge Stanton said. The judge paused as he scanned some papers. A former U.S. Army lieutenant, Rhodes Scholar, and graduate of New York University School of Law, the judge was intelligent and could be sympathetic or harsh behind the bench, depending on what the circumstances required. Everyone watched him as he flipped pages. The courtroom became still. This was what they'd waited for, for months — the sentence.

"Mr. Seale, for the crime of kidnapping Sidney Reso, I sentence you to the custody of the Commissioner of Corrections for the period of thirty years . . . I impose upon you a fine in the amount of $100,000 . . . For the murder of Sidney Reso, I sentence you to be committed to the custody of the Commissioner of Corrections for the remainder of your natural life. I impose upon you a fine in the amount of $100,000 . . . And I make these sentences consecutive to the sentences which were imposed earlier today by Judge Garrett E. Brown in the United States District Court for the District of New Jersey." The judge had intended to impose two fines of $1 million each, but due to a clerical error, $100,000 was imposed for each offense. It didn't matter because the fines were dropped on appeal a year later.

Whispers and rustling in the gallery created a rare clamor, but a hush swept the room when Judge Stanton looked out at the spectators, "I want absolute silence."

"Let me explain to you why I am imposing these sentences upon you," the judge said in a firm voice, returning his gaze upon Seale. "You have indicated that you have some sorrow, that you have some hope for the future that you would like to be rehabilitated, and that you would like forgiveness. I hope that you do get forgiveness from the Reso family. I hope you do get forgiveness from God. God is in the forgiving business. But I am a judge."

Then Judge Stanton said what many may have wished they could have said.

"Your problem, Mr. Seale, is that you are a greedy, self-centered, undisciplined man. You decided to satisfy your economic needs by committing the crime of kidnapping Sidney Reso, a man of great achievement and simple decency who had never done the slightest wrong to you . . . The cruel circumstances in which Mr. Reso was treated during his captivity caused his death. After Mr. Reso died, you continued to attempt to collect payment of ransom by means which can only be described as calculated torture of Mrs. Reso and of the Reso children."

"The cruel taking of an innocent and noble human life calls for the imposition of stern punishment in order to affirm our most basic social values: protecting and prohibiting violent acts against human beings. The safety of the human community requires that you be in prison for the remainder of your life. I regard it as imperative that you shall never, ever again under any circumstances be at liberty in our society."

The Reso family surely felt a sense of justice—legal justice— as the judge's words constructed a legal box and tossed Seale inside it for the rest of his life. Some, like Pat, wept quietly.

"The sentences which have been imposed today are to be carried out forthwith. The officers shall deliver you to the custody of the United States Marshals Service so that you shall begin to serve the federal sentences imposed upon you this morning. The state sentences which I have today imposed shall act as a detainer, and if you are ever released from federal prison, you must then begin to serve these sentences. That will be the disposition of the case." Stanton banged his gavel.

Everyone stood as the judge stepped down from the bench and exited into his chambers. Federal marshals immediately removed Seale from the courtroom as those inside watched. The Reso family embraced one another. The courtroom broke out into chatter, tears, hugs, and pats on the back. The Resos also embraced and thanked Prosecutor Murphy and the assistant prosecutors, and U.S. Attorney Chertoff, who'd sat at the prosecution table during the state sentencing, though didn't speak.

Chertoff had spoken that morning at Seale's sentencing in federal court in Trenton, New Jersey, before Judge Brown. His piercing words insisted that Seale deserved the maximum punishment allowable under federal law for what he called "one of the most infamous crimes in living history." Chertoff emphasized, "If there is a case in which we are confronting evil, this is the case, Your Honor . . . They didn't even stop to bury the dead."

With the judge's permission, Sid Reso's thirty-one-year-old son approached the podium to speak, just as two of his sisters would do that afternoon before Judge Stanton in state court. He resembled his father and had taken his father's murder especially hard. He became emotional more than once during his plea for the judge to impose the maximum sentence.

The judge was moved. Once the Reso's son returned to his seat beside his family, who consoled him, the judge got down to business.

"There is no apology or excuse that can expunge this evil," the judge began, speaking directly to Art Seale. "What you have done is thoroughly evil. Your actions were . . . cold-blooded and calculated. To the same extent you seek mercy, you will be given the same you gave your innocent victim—none."

Judge Brown continued his seething rebuke before eventually imposing a ninety-five-year prison term, the maximum sentence allowed under federal law for seven counts of extortion, conspiracy, using the mails to transmit ransom demands, and interstate travel in aid of extortion. He also imposed a fine of $250,000 per count, for a total fine of $1.75 million (later reversed on appeal in 1994 to $75,000 total).

"Although the law will not stoop to your callous level," the judge concluded, again speaking directly to Seale with a stern, drawn face, "you will die in captivity like your victim . . . You *will* be fed and medically treated, and you *will not* be bound, gagged, shot, or locked in a coffin."

The judge then asked the federal marshals to remove Seale from his sight.

For Art Seale, it was over. The federal and state sentences imposed against him totaled life plus 125 years. Federal prison will be his home until he is escorted out in a coffin-like box. He can take solace, however, that he did achieve one of the goals of his kidnapping scheme—he'd removed himself and his wife from his parents' home, for good.

* * *

Two months later, on January 25, 1993, it was Jackie Seale's turn to be sentenced. She sat in federal court with short brown hair. Her shoulder-length blond hair that once draped her tanned face had long faded away. Her attorney, Sallyanne Floria, stood before U.S. District Court Judge Garrett Brown, the same judge who'd sentenced Art Seale in November. Jackie's attorney continued to blame Art Seale for forcing her client to participate in the kidnapping and murder of Sid Reso. According to Floria, her client was a "kind kidnapper" involved in the "caretaking" of the hostage. Jackie portrayed herself in open court as a victim saying in a quivering voice, among other things, "I never considered the mental and sexual aspects of abuse."

A reporter, Kathleen O'Brien, with *The Record* had written cynically about Jackie Seale's defense prior to sentencing: "This had better be good. This had better involve such things as guns held to her head, frequent trips to the emergency room, tearful midnight calls to the police, and holes in the plaster board. Stuff like that. Anything less should be laughed out of court."

Judge Brown may not have laughed Jackie Seale or her attorney out of court, but he wasn't at all swayed by the battered-wife argument: "The crime was in no way forced upon you," the judge said to Jackie. "You chose this conduct and you planned it . . . You were a fully culpable, fully functioning, and essential member of the conspiracy."

Jackie Seale then read a nine-page letter in open court to Judge Brown. It was the most she'd said since her plea agreement months earlier. Her usual court discourse was simply: "Yes, Your Honor," and "No, Your Honor." But if there ever was a time to be loquacious, this was that time. Though the federal judge was expected to abide by the terms of the plea agreement, Floria may have believed a few words of remorse and deflection certainly couldn't hurt her client, just in case. Tears filled Jackie's eyes as she read her letter.

"Both physical violence and a need for wealth are contrary to everything I stand for . . . How do I express the remorse I feel? Where do I go from here? Obviously to prison. But jail will not cause me to be an honest and decent person. The fact is, I have always been that . . . To say the words, 'I'm sorry,' is surely not enough. Mr. Reso cannot be replaced and the Reso family can never be the same. My family can never be the same. At the time of my arrest, I was physically, mentally, and emotionally exhausted. I have tried to do everything possible to show my remorse by immediately coming forward and telling the truth . . . I had to tell this story."

Though Jackie Seale claimed immediate repentance, her remorse and cooperation had come fifty-three days after Sid Reso's death and a week after a very favorable plea deal. As columnist, Kathleen O'Brien wrote: "By golly, as soon as those handcuffs snapped on Irene Seale's wrists, she felt compassion well up from every pore."

"I was compelled to lead authorities to Mr. Reso's body and thereby give the Reso family closure to their terrible ordeal. By coming forward, I went against my husband. I felt that I was betraying a man I loved and had been married to for almost twenty-six years. Not only was I betraying him, but for the first time in recent history I was not doing what Art told me to do. This was an extremely difficult thing for me to do, but I followed through with my decision because this was the right and only action to take for both the Reso family and my children and mother."

U.S. Attorney Chertoff, who would later say, "This was one of the worst crimes I ever prosecuted," was not moved. "To suggest that Mrs. Seale was not a full participant in the crime is absurd," the federal prosecutor countered. "To claim that she could not foresee the harm to Mr. Reso from the manner of his captivity, and to apply the word 'victim' to one of the two people who carried out this atrocity . . . disparages the scope of the crime and denigrates the humanity of the real victims."

Chertoff also mocked the defense counsel's description of Jackie Seale as a kind caretaker during the kidnapping. He described Sid Reso's terrible ordeal entombed with mouth and eyes taped shut in the coffin-like box with no food or medical care, little air or water, and then asked the judge, "This is caretaking?"

A former employee at the Hilton Head furniture store briefly owned by the Seales provided reporters some insight into why Jackie Seale may have followed along with her husband, other than because she was a battered wife: "Jackie worshipped him. She would never dispute anything he said. She wasn't that smart. Art was the person with all the ideas."

Jackie's reasons for committing the crime didn't matter at this point because Judge Brown felt constrained to impose the federal sentence recommended by prosecutors in the plea agreement: twenty years to run concurrently, not consecutively, with the twenty-year sentence imposed by Judge Stanton in state court later that day, plus a fine of $500,000 (reduced on appeal in 1994 to $30,000). The judge added, "Unlike your unfortunate victim, you will not be tied and gagged. You will not be beaten, shot, and locked in a coffin."

When Judge Stanton imposed the twenty-year concurrent sentence and a $100,000 fine recommended by the prosecutors later that same day in state court, he too was not pleased to accommodate the plea agreement.

"I'll tell you frankly, Mrs. Seale," Stanton said during the state sentencing, "it frustrates me very much to have to impose a sentence as light as the sentence which I am now imposing for the crimes which you have committed . . . You are getting away with murder. You are not being prosecuted for the murder of Sidney Reso and you are not getting the maximum penalty that could be imposed for kidnapping . . . You will probably serve eighteen to twenty years in a federal prison and you will get out when you are still a relatively young woman . . . It is not fair to Mr. Reso and the public . . . When compared with what happened to Mr. Reso you are getting off lightly . . . In my judgment, the sentence should be more."

Incredibly, later that year, Jackie Seale's attorney appealed her client's twenty-year sentence that had been part of the plea deal, requesting that it be reduced. It wasn't. However the fine was dropped on appeal in order to defer to the monetary damages obtained in the Reso's successful wrongful death civil case that year.

* * *

The efforts of prosecutors and law enforcement were greatly appreciated by the Reso family.

"Pat Reso always had the utmost confidence in those working the investigation," Agent Gail Chapman later recalled. "She always appreciated what we were doing."

As Morris County Prosecutor Murphy told reporters following Art Seale's sentencing: "I spoke to Pat Reso from her new home in Texas. She has expressed great satisfaction . . . with the results of this case."

But those results had not provided any closure for the Reso family.

"Not yet," Pat told a reporter. "I think it will take a little bit of time to assimilate what has happened. It's all the same feeling; it's like an ongoing movie and it keeps playing and playing . . . Reality has not yet hit . . . When they talked in the courtroom about the murder of Sidney J. Reso, it was just words that I heard, but it wasn't Sid. It still isn't Sid. It's a really strange thing to try to explain."

"There have been . . . moments of reality that I truly am alone," she continued. "That there is no Sid. That I'm not part of a couple anymore,"

"Essentially, my life is like taking a barrel and emptying it out . . . I'm starting from scratch. I have to find my personhood . . . I'm really looking forward to just putting this behind and starting new. And I really hope that my kids can do this, too. I think they, in a sense, have experienced more reality about this than I have so far. It's been very hard on them."

A judgment from the wrongful death suit filed against the Seales would be awarded to the Reso family in October 1994, though it is extremely doubtful any portion of it will ever be collected. Still, the judgment is in place should the Seales ever collect money from a book, movie, or any other source, which so far they have not. The total judgment for compensatory and punitive damages, plus interest, exceeded $22.5 million. One of Seale's attorneys, Westmoreland, said the judgment was "just a piece of paper that means nothing." It would seem to mean much more than that—an additional symbol of culpability, if nothing else.

But Pat felt no satisfaction. "I don't know how one is satisfied with something like this."

* * *

The kidnapping and murder of Sidney J. Reso, president of Exxon International and loving husband and father, was a horrible and senseless crime that ruined one family and crippled another. As Special Agent-in-Charge Penrith said then, and it's even more true today, kidnappings for ransom simply do not work in the United States. Penrith's professional insight was echoed by former FBI special agent, Jim Fisher, when he said: "Kidnapping is really committed by losers or very desperate people . . . The success of the crime is very low because you have to eventually make an appearance to get the loot."

Jackie Seale entered federal prison in Lexington, Kentucky, but did most of her time in Danbury, Connecticut. She was released on November 20, 2009, fewer than seventeen years after her sentencing, at the age of sixty-three; she has completed her supervised five-year probation. Her shoulder-length blond hair has long been replaced with a short gray cut. She is seventy-four years old, remarried, and now lives in a small town in Illinois, where she still jogs along neighborhood streets — past numerous driveways with newspapers.

Arthur Seale is still incarcerated. He has been moved from prison to prison: Leavenworth, Kansas; Oak Park Heights, Minnesota; Bismarck, North Dakota; Victorville, California; McCreary, Kentucky; Edgefield, South Carolina; and Fairton, New Jersey. With life plus 125 years in prison, Seale has had time to earn a bachelor's degree in psychology from Metropolitan State University in St. Paul, a master's degree in psychology from Antioch College in Ohio, and a doctorate in psychological counseling from Minneapolis-based Capella University, all online correspondence courses. Some have not appreciated that "Dr. Seale" has been allowed to earn all those degrees. Seale's exasperated response has been reported as, "What would people have me do in here? Hang by my thumbs?"

Many might reply: "Yes."

At the age of seventy-four, he is currently being held at FMC Devens in Ayers, Massachusetts. According to his prison records, he is due to be released from federal prison on March 24, 2075. He will be 129 years old when he gets out; just in time to begin serving his life sentence, plus thirty years, in state prison.

In an interview with *The Christian Science Monitor* in 2003, Art Seale said he had twenty-four hours of visitation each month that no one ever used. "I wish for a different ending," Seale said at the end of the interview, "but I can't write it." He said in another interview that same year with the *Bismarck Tribune* that the last time he spoke with Jackie Seale was the day they were arrested.

Art and Jackie Seale's two children are now in their forties, about the same ages that their parents were when they committed this terrible crime. They live in different states, but communicate with their mother and each other.

Republican Michael Chertoff was replaced as U.S. Attorney after the election of Democrat Bill Clinton as president. Chertoff was later nominated by President George W. Bush to a seat on the United States Court of Appeals for the Third Circuit in 2003, and two years later served as the second U.S. Secretary of Homeland Security (where he co-authored the USA PATRIOT Act). He subsequently formed a security and risk management advisory firm.

W. Michael Murphy Jr. is the stepson of former Democratic governor Richard Hughes of New Jersey. Murphy ran for the Democratic nomination for governor of New Jersey in 1997, but was unsuccessful. He is now the managing partner of a lobbying and consulting firm in New Jersey.

Gary Penrith retired from the FBI in October 1992, shortly after the resolution of the Reso kidnapping case.

Sid Reso's mother, Josephine Agnes Reso, died in New Orleans three years after Sid Reso's death at the age of eighty-seven. Reso's father, James Anthony Reso, had died years earlier in 1967. According to their death certificates, Sid Reso and his father both lived to be exactly fifty-seven years, one hundred and thirty-six days.

Incredibly, Pat Reso experienced even more sadness. After losing one son in 1987 and her husband in 1992, she lost her other son in 2000 at the age of thirty-nine and then a son-in-law in 2001 at the age of thirty-eight.

Eventually, Pat did become that new I and experienced much joy with her daughters, grandchildren, and second husband, William Freitag. She also was awarded an honorary degree by LSU, Sid's alma mater. Pat died in Houston, Texas, in August

2011, at the age of seventy-seven and was interred beside Sid's grave at Lake Lawn Metairie Cemetery in New Orleans.

The sweethearts who met at the high school dance when they were just seventeen, and married to raise five wonderful children, were reunited once again.

About the Author

PHILIP JETT is a former corporate attorney now living in Nashville, Tennessee. He has represented corporations, hospitals, CEOs, celebrities from the music, television, and sports industries, and other noteworthy clients. He attended New York University School of Law, and following his legal career, began ghost-writing for business clients. His first nonfiction book, *The Death of an Heir*, was published in 2017 by St. Martin's Press, an imprint of Macmillan Publishers Ltd. He has two adult sons and often volunteers for children's causes.

Please consider reading the author's debut book, *The Death of an Heir: Adolph Coors III and the Murder That Rocked an American Brewing Dynasty*, published by St. Martin's Press. Listed as one of the best true crime stories by *The New York Times* in 2017, it is a must read: In 1960, the CEO and Chairman of the Board of the Coors Brewing Company in Golden, Colorado, was kidnapped. The largest manhunt in U.S. history since the kidnapping of the Lindbergh's baby swept across the continent without any success. A grief stricken wife and four young children waited for word as the weeks passed. Everyone wondered: where is the heir of the Colorado beer empire and his abductors? *The Death of an Heir* will unveil the mystery.

"The rich are human, too. That's the message to take from . . . Philip Jett's compassionate appraisal of the tragedy that shattered the family of Adolph (Ad) Herman Joseph Coors III."
The New York Times

"The author puts his legal experience to good use with behind-the-scenes insights into investigative legwork while crafting a suspenseful true-crime narrative that reads like an edge-of-the-seat detective story."
Booklist

"'The Death of an Heir'" is an excellent account of a 57-year-old tragedy . . ."
The Denver Post

"Jett's amazing research and captivating narrative tell a remarkable Coors family story, occasionally whispered about during my time at Coors. An incredible and tragic story, brilliantly told."
Ralph Hargrow, former Chief Global People Officer, Molson Coors Brewing Company, Denver, Colorado

Author's Note

What a horrible crime. When Sidney Reso's mother bore him, and while he was young, and later throughout his exemplary life, none could have imagined that he would die alone, with his eyes and mouth taped, hands cuffed, and legs strapped down with rope, lying inside a wooden box in his own waste, inside Secure Storage unit 619, in the small rural community of Hackettstown, New Jersey.

The entire kidnapping scheme was senseless and cruel. I feel pity not only for the Reso family, but also for the Seale children. What a terrible burden to bear.

* * *

This is a work of nonfiction. I have stayed true to the facts uncovered during my exhaustive research while using literary techniques that I believe make the story more interesting. From time to time, I deduced scenes and dialogue from the materials I gathered to convey circumstances to the reader where details are unavailable. Despite some occasional liberties, the overall story reflects the information obtained by me from those materials and from individuals willing to speak with me. I have not created any characters or changed any names. I did not wish to disclose the names of some Seale and Szarko family members or reveal their locations, including the current name and location of Jackie Seale, nor did I reveal the names of the Reso children. And though I have more than three hundred photographs, including a few that are shocking, I selected only twelve photos that I felt illustrated the principal facts of the book.

Most of my extensive research centered on transcripts and records from courts, national and state archives, the Federal Bureau of Investigation, and the Morris County Prosecutor's

Office; from contemporary accounts in newspapers and magazines and archival photos; and from many other sources that I list in the Bibliography section. I also interviewed many retired FBI agents, detectives, attorneys, and Exxon employees. I am very appreciative of the individuals and agencies that responded; the story is richer because of them. I did reach out to friends and family of Sid and Pat Reso, but none responded, which is totally understandable. The same was true of the Seale family and those who had represented the Seales. After some correspondence with Art Seale from prison, he decided to decline an interview with me.

* * *

The five most notorious kidnappings in U.S. history based on celebrity and expenditure of law enforcement resources are in my opinion:

1. Charles Lindbergh Jr. (a baby)
2. Patty Hearst
3. Sidney Reso
4. Adolph Coors III
5. Frank Sinatra Jr.

Only Hearst and Sinatra survived and none of the kidnappings were successful, other than perhaps Hearst, which was not purely for money like the others. If there ever has been a crime in the United States that doesn't pay, it's kidnapping. With all the technology, cameras, surveillance, and improved methods of crime detection, kidnapping for ransom is virtually impossible in the United States. For the sakes of the Resos, Seales, and Szarkos, I wish Art Seale had understood that simple fact in 1992.

* * *

My sincere hope is that you derived as much from reading this book as I had in researching and writing it. If you have a few moments, please feel free to add your review of the book to your favorite online site for feedback. Also, if you would like to connect with other books and articles that I have coming in the near future, please visit my website for news on upcoming works, recent blog posts, and to sign up for my newsletter: *http:// www.philipjett.com*. Sincerely, Philip Jett

Bibliography

American Justice, "Kidnapped," Season 4, Episode 2, Arts & Entertainment (Jan 04, 1995).

Arthur Dixon Seale v. United States of America, 2005 U.S. Dist (Dec. 12, 2005).

Autopsy report and certificate of death, Sidney Joseph Reso, signed June 29, 1992. New Jersey State Department of Health.

"Crime of Greed." Time, Vol. 140 No. 24, December 13, 1992.

FBI Criminal Pursuit, "Dangerous Obsessions," Season 1, Episode 2, Investigation Discovery (March 11, 2011).

FBI investigation file received pursuant to FOIA requests filed March 2017.

Files and photographs donated by Gary A. Penrith, former special agent-in-charge of the FBI field office in Newark, New Jersey.

Files and photographs loaned by Gail Chapman, former special agent in the FBI field office in Newark, New Jersey.

Files and photographs loaned by John Walker, former special agent in the GMRA, New Jersey.

Harman, Dana. "Crime & forgiveness." The Christian Science Monitor, October 29, 2003.

Jerri Williams Podcast, "Ed Petersen – Exxon Oil Executive Kidnapping, Sidney Reso," Episode 106 (March 2018).

Sidney J. Reso Estate files No. F5-8959. Morris County Surrogate's Court, State of New Jersey.

"The Birth of Modern Day Criminal Profiling," Psychology Today, May 26, 2015.

The New York Times. Archival clippings.

The Perfect Murder, "Vanishing Act," Season 2, Episode 2, Investigation Discovery (07/08/2015).

The Philadelphia Inquirer. Archival clippings.

The Record (Hackensack, NJ). Archival clippings.

The Star-Ledger. Archival clippings.

The Times (Trenton, NJ). Archival clippings.

Treen, Joe. "Hoping Against Hope." *People*, July 6, 1992.

Unatin, Don. "The Exxon Exec's 5 Days of Hell," *Official Detective*, February 1993, 7-9, 12, 14, 16–18, 22.

United States of America v. Arthur D. Seale and Irene J. Seale, 20 F.2d 1279 (3rd Cir. 1993).

Unusual Suspects, "Missing Executive," Season 1, Episode 8, Investigation Discovery (Aug 2, 2010).

Video disc, ABC News, *20/20: No Way Out* (11/13/1992).

Video disc, CBS Archives, *48 Hours: Kidnapped* (Sept. 16, 1992).

Video, NBC, *Unsolved Mysteries*, Season 4, Episode 31 (May 13, 1992).

Wall Street Journal. Archival clippings.

Woodward, Kenneth L. "Death in a Storage Locker." Newsweek, July 12, 1992.

* I have posted scans of the original ransom notes and additional photographs on my website, www.philipjett.com.

CHRONOS
BOOKS

HISTORY

Chronos Books is an historical non-fiction imprint. Chronos publishes real history for real people; bringing to life people, places and events in an imaginative, easy-to-digest and accessible way - histories that pass on their stories to a generation of new readers.
If you have enjoyed this book, why not tell other readers by posting a review on your preferred book site.

Recent bestsellers from Chronos Books are:

Lady Katherine Knollys
The Unacknowledged Daughter of King Henry VIII
Sarah-Beth Watkins
A comprehensive account of Katherine Knollys' questionable paternity, her previously unexplored life in the Tudor court and her intriguing relationship with Elizabeth I.
Paperback: 978-1-78279-585-8 ebook: 978-1-78279-584-1

Cromwell was Framed
Ireland 1649
Tom Reilly
Revealed: The definitive research that proves the Irish nation owes Oliver Cromwell a huge posthumous apology for wrongly convicting him of civilian atrocities in 1649.
Paperback: 978-1-78279-516-2 ebook: 978-1-78279-515-5

Why The CIA Killed JFK and Malcolm X
The Secret Drug Trade in Laos
John Koerner
A new groundbreaking work presenting evidence that the CIA silenced JFK to protect its secret drug trade in Laos.
Paperback: 978-1-78279-701-2 ebook: 978-1-78279-700-5

The Disappearing Ninth Legion
A Popular History
Mark Olly
The Disappearing Ninth Legion examines hard evidence for the foundation, development, mysterious disappearance, or possible continuation of Rome's lost Legion.
Paperback: 978-1-84694-559-5 ebook: 978-1-84694-931-9

Beaten But Not Defeated

Siegfried Moos - A German anti-Nazi who settled in Britain
Merilyn Moos
Siegi Moos, an anti-Nazi and active member of the German
Communist Party, escaped Germany in 1933 and, exiled in
Britain, sought another route to the transformation
of capitalism.
Paperback: 978-1-78279-677-0 ebook: 978-1-78279-676-3

A Schoolboy's Wartime Letters

An evacuee's life in WWII — A Personal Memoir
Geoffrey Iley
A boy writes home during WWII, revealing his own fascinating
story, full of zest for life, information and humour.
Paperback: 978-1-78279-504-9 ebook: 978-1-78279-503-2

The Life & Times of the Real Robyn Hoode

Mark Olly
A journey of discovery. The chronicles of the genuine historical
character, Robyn Hoode, and how he became one of England's
greatest legends.
Paperback: 978-1-78535-059-7 ebook: 978-1-78535-060-3

Readers of ebooks can buy or view any of these bestsellers by clicking on the live link in the title. Most titles are published in paperback and as an ebook. Paperbacks are available in traditional bookshops. Both print and ebook formats are available online.

Find more titles and sign up to our readers' newsletter at
http://www.johnhuntpublishing.com/history-home

Follow us on Facebook at
https://www.facebook.com/ChronosBooks

and Twitter at https://twitter.com/ChronosBooks